The Origins of
Human Competence

The Origins of Human Competence

The Final Report of the Harvard Preschool Project

Burton L. White
Barbara T. Kaban
Jane S. Attanucci
Center for Parent Education

Lexington Books
D.C. Heath and Company
Lexington, Massachusetts
Toronto

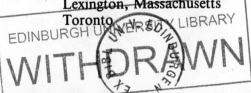

Library of Congress Cataloging in Publication Data

White, Burton L. 1929-
   The origins of human competence.

   Bibliography: p.
   1. Ability in children. 2. Achievement motivation in children. 3. Birth
order. 4. Parent and child. 5. Harvard University. Harvard Preschool
Project. I. Kaban, Barbara T., joint author. II. Attanucci, Jane S., joint
author. III. Title.
BF723.A25W47   155.4'13   77-81793
ISBN 0-669-01943-7

Published simultaneously in Canada

Printed in the United States of America

International Standard Book Number: 0-669-01943-7

Library of Congress Catalog Card Number: 77-81793

Contents

List of Figures and Exhibits

List of Tables

Preface and Acknowledgments

This book is the last of three volumes presenting the research, methodology, and conclusions of the Preschool Project. The two earlier studies were published as *Experience and Environment: Major Influences on the Development of the Young Child* (Prentice-Hall, 1973, 1978). They will be referred to throughout this final report as *Experience and Environment*, Volume 1 and Volume 2.

Volume 1 was written by two research groups who had been studying the same subjects. One group was directed by Burton L. White, the other by Jean Carew Watts. Each group reported its work in separate chapters of that volume. Shortly after the publication of Volume 1, the two groups discontinued coordinated research. The second and third reports are solely the responsibility of the group directed by White.

We wish to extend our gratitude to the many individuals who have participated in the research of the Preschool Project during its 13 years: Jacqueline Allaman, Nancy Apfel, Frances Aversa, Ellen Cardone Banks, Martha Bronson, Barbara Rich Bushell, Martha Carroll, Kitty Riley Clark, Andrew Cohn, Cherry Collins, Elizabeth Constable, Virginia Demos, Anna DiPietrantonio, Marjorie Elias, Jane Feldman, John Frederickson, John Guidubaldi, Miriam Gofseyeff, Christine Halfar, Geraldine Kearse, E.R. LaCrosse, Jr., Patrick C. Lee, Marcus Lieberman, Sandra Lin, Frances Litman, Maxine Manjos, Thomas Marx, Grace McMann, Mary Meader Mokler, Daniel M. Ogilvie, Meredith S. Pandolfi, Diane Schodlatz, Bernice Shapiro, Sylvia Skolnick Staub, Ingrid Stocking, Susan S. Stodolsky, Jolinda Taylor, Eugenia Ware, Eleanor Wasserman, Paul Weene, A. Elise Weinrich, Ruth Wolman, Louise Woodhead, and Melvin Zolot.

Particular gratitude is owed to Theodore Sizer, Gerald Lesser, and Paul Ylvisaker of the Harvard Graduate School of Education and to Edith Grotberg of the Office of Economic Opportunity and Barbara Finberg of the Carnegie Corporation of New York, all of whom were willing to take risks for this project. Special thanks must go to Miriam Fiedler of the Maternal Infant Health Project and to Albert Cohen, director of the pediatric control group.

Long and faithful service on the project has been performed by Mary Comita, as administrative assistant and in the preparation of all manuscripts.

In addition, this study has been made possible by the cooperation of several hundred families and many school personnel from nearby public and private institutions.

The research and development reported herein was performed in part pursuant to contract OE 5-10-39 with the United States Office of Education, under the provisions of the Cooperative Research Program as a project of the Harvard University Center for Research and Development on Educational Differences, the Carnegie Corporation of New York, and the Office of Economic

Opportunity, Head Start Division, and the U.S. Office of Child Development Grant No. OCD-CB-193, 1972-1974. The statements made and views expressed are solely the responsibility of the authors.

Part I
Introduction and
Background

1

History of the Preschool Project

Origins

The Preschool Project began in 1965. It was made possible by a marked increase in interest in the development of children during the preschool years. This interest manifested itself in many ways during the mid-1960s. One manifestation was the inclusion of a focus on early education within the new Research and Development Center at the Harvard Graduate School of Education. The center was funded by the Office of Education at approximately $1 million a year, for a 5-year period. The school at that time had very few faculty whose research interests included early educational topics, even broadly defined. As a result, the Preschool Project was created as a new venture within the Laboratory of Human Development.

The first year was also the first year for Project Head Start, which signaled a remarkable and unprecedented national assault on underachievement in education by children from the nation's low-income families. At the time, the greatest efforts were centered on the possibility of preventing school failures through programs for children 4 and 5 years of age. These programs were usually labeled "compensatory education programs for the disadvantaged."

The pace of activity in generating experimental procedures was quite intense during the late 1960s. We had a comparatively free hand to choose the type of approach to problems of early education that made sense to us. Any approach that seemed promising would have been entertained by both the school and the funding agency.

Our interest in early development was already a long-standing one, going back to the early 1950s. Its origins were very much influenced by the work of Abraham Maslow on what he called "self-actualized" people. Maslow's work also affected the shape of our proposed research. We were not only interested in educational achievement, but more accurately speaking in the development of *all* major coping abilities of young children. We were interested also in *optimizing* development, helping children to develop as much of their potential as possible, rather than in the prevention or treatment of deficiencies. Finally, our interest was not confined to children of low-income families or any other subgroup of the population. We had a broader outlook on the issues of early human development than was popular at the time.

We were also aware of the special opportunities for research at a powerful university such as Harvard. We knew that we could afford to be more

3

unconventional than we might be at other institutions. Even the most outlandish suggestion from Harvard has a chance of being endorsed and supported simply because it is from Harvard. In general, proposals coming from such an institution can afford to be a bit bolder or carry with them a higher price tag or a longer projected life. With these ideas in mind, we proposed a novel approach to the study of early education. We suggested that we would like to attack the basic problem of how to structure experiences during the first 6 years of a child's life so as to help each child make the most of whatever potential he brought into the world. Our interest from the very beginning was in children from *all* socioeconomic levels of the society, but we excluded study of children with substantial handicaps due to serious physical or emotional pathology.

The Research Strategy

The Preschool Project has been in existence for 13 years as of this writing. During that time we have followed what seemed to us to be a rather straightforward plan. Our purpose has been to determine how to structure experiences during the first 6 years of life so as to assist each child to maximize the potential he is born with. We talked initially about maximizing the educability of children. Soon thereafter we dropped the term *educability* in favor of the term *competence*. The steps in our long-range plan were:

Determine what is meant by the concept of a well-developed or competent 6-year-old.

Plot the course of development of competence during the first 6 years of life.

Identify any time period during those first 6 years that appears to be particularly important for the development of competence.

Create measurement techniques to enable us to monitor the development of competence during such periods.

Perform a natural experiment with families who are likely to do an outstandingly good job rearing their children and with families likely to do less well than average. Monitor, in detail, the childrearing practices of each of the families.

Using data on the actual competence levels achieved by the children, generate hypotheses about effective childrearing practices.

Convert those hypotheses into a feasible training program suitable for families.

Test the validity of the hypotheses experimentally by having families with apparently average childrearing capacities put those ideas into practice with their children.

Use the results of the experiment to refine the hypotheses about effective childrearing practices.

Retest the modified hypotheses, etc.

Progress prior to this Report

There were several products of the first years of research on the project. We produced a definition of competence in 3- to 6-year-old children. We created assessment techniques for monitoring the development of abilities (some of which were more useful than others). We learned much on a subjective level about how families rear their young children. We gathered a good deal of useful information about the evolving interests of children during the first years of life. The most challenging goal of the natural longitudinal study was to generate ideas about causal relations among childrearing practices, learning experiences of children, and the achievement of abilities.

Standard scientific procedure dictates that ideas about causal processes should be put to experimental tests whenever possible. The question for our project was: "To what extent can you utilize standard scientific methodology when your focus is the lives of young children and their parents?" Since what we were hoping to do involved recommending childrearing practices to young families, we felt that the prospects for some form of experimental test were reasonable. As was the case with our earlier research on children under 6 months of age (White et al. 1964; White 1967, 1971), nothing that we were going to suggest to parents was likely to be construed as potentially harmful to infants and toddlers. On the contrary, we felt that the childrearing practices and consequential experiences for children that were regularly associated with good development were likely to prove enjoyable and beneficial to all involved.

We were then confronted with a problem of an appropriate experimental design. Here we took our lead from David Weikart's interesting work in the comparative effectiveness of compensatory education programs for 3- to 5-year-old children (Weikart 1969). Obviously, special controls would have to be instituted. For example, it had already been well established, or at least the signs were reasonably clear, that merely testing children repeatedly during the first 3 years of life led to better achievement scores regardless of whether they were involved in any educational program or not.

We began to explore the possibilities of financial support for such a comparative experimental study. A program officer from the Federal Office of

Child Development, Ms. Esther Kresh, pointed out to us that the work we had done had never included training families. She remarked that observational research was quite different in character from work involved in instituting an experimental approach to raising children through families. It soon became clear that Ms. Kresh's observation was sound. We then spent 2 years in pilot work.

2 The Pilot Program

In the longitudinal study that preceded this phase of the work, forty families had been observed as they reared their children in the second and third years of the children's lives (*Experience and Environment*, Volumes 1 and 2). Half these children were observed for 2 full years beginning on or about their first birthday. The other half were first observed on their second birthday and were followed for another year. In addition to comprehensive assessments at or about the third birthday, children were retested on or about their fifth birthday.

We gathered a large amount of information on these forty children.[1] We had data on typical everyday experiences along with information about the behavior of other people as it related to the stream of experience. In most cases the other people were the mothers of these children, but on occasion the fathers, housekeepers, other siblings, and peers would be involved. We also gathered data on the course of acquisition of various competencies of these children. Not only did we collect quantitative data in substantial amounts on these forty children, but the core staff of the project also gained a good deal of informal information about all aspects of the children's lives. It is hard to come away from a study in which each home was visited every other week, twenty-six times a year, for one or two years without an intimate understanding of the family style and the childrearing practices that are involved.

Generating Hypotheses about Effective Childrearing Practices

From our data on the everyday experiences of children, we concluded that a close social relationship, particularly during the few months that followed their first birthday, was a conspicuous feature in the lives of children who developed best. The suggestion was that the parent who for any reason spent very little time in free and easy social interchange with the 1-year-old child was not as likely to provide a rich educational experience as the one who made himself or herself regularly accessible to the baby. By "regularly accessible" we do not mean all day long. Several of the mothers of babies who were developing very well had part-time jobs or for other reasons spent a good deal of time out of the home. There are two notions suggested by such a statement. One is that a rich social experience can be provided by someone other than the child's parents. In a few instances there were very skillful substitutes available. Second, it would appear that a parent or parents do not have to spend their entire day providing a rich social life for the young child in order to provide enough of such experience.[2]

Looking at individual social experiences, we repeatedly have found that a task called *procuring the service of another* seems to be involved with good development. Here we are referring to situations in which a child wants something or wants something done that the child cannot do for himself. He asks someone else for help in order to achieve a desired goal. In other words, the adult *acted as a resource* or a tool for the child. This sort of behavior on the part of the young child can get out of hand. We have come to believe that there can be too much of this type of experience in a child's life. For the time being, suffice it to say that the child who is not attended to regularly by an older person or who is seen as a burden to be dealt with as quickly and as briefly as possible would appear to be less well off from a basic educational standpoint than the child who is freely offered assistance by sympathetic older people. More subtle, but probably just as important, is the notion that an adult who is giving such assistance to the young child is an adult who is interested in what the young child is interested in. This may seem obvious, but we have found in subsequent programs that some adults, for one reason or another, are not inclined to be genuinely interested in an infant's focus of the moment. This lack of interest often precludes their acting as an effective resource for the child.

The second major social task that warrants discussion is *attempts to gain attention*. This category reflects the natural gregariousness of the 12-month-old child. Once again, a child cannot have large amounts of such experience if, by and large, he is not near an adult fairly often during the day. Nor would he have a fair amount of such experience if he were repeatedly rebuffed in his attempts at achieving social contacts. More subtly, a child who is hovered over by an adult has less of a need to develop attention-seeking skills.

Both these social experiences suggested a style of living which appeared to have substantial importance with respect to effective early education.

In nonsocial experiences (those in which the child is not trying to create an effect on another person) we found the interesting and somewhat perplexing category of *gaining information through vision* or of *steady staring* highly significant from a statistical point of view. We have learned, from the work of Phyllis Dohlinow, that young infrahuman primates also engage in a great deal of staring behavior. *Steady staring*, as we define it, is focused attention in contrast to desultory scanning. This simple behavior apparently has an important role to play in the process of development. Obviously, if you do not dwell for long on a scene, you are going to get less out of it than if you examine it carefully. Beyond this simple statement, we did not feel that we could safely speculate about the special significance of the behavior. It is conceivable that the behavior of the parent has something to do with the frequency of steady-staring activity. It is possible that the tendency of the parent to instruct the child, to talk about things seen, to draw the child's attention, if you will, to one or another interesting aspect of the environment, affects the frequency of steady-staring behavior.

The next important nonsocial experience (according to our research) was *listening to live language directed to the child.* We make distinctions among the different kinds of listening-to-language experiences that children have. A child can be concentrating on the language that two nearby people are addressing to each other. Such a task would be coded as *live language overheard.* He may be listening to a record machine or a radio, in which case we would code the activity as *mechanical language.* In the case of a child looking at and listening to, say, "Sesame Street" on television, we code the experience as *language from "Sesame Street."* The category *live language directed to the child* is the one most strongly associated with good development.

What does that mean? First of all, no television program, no matter how excellent, can custom build its output to a child's interest of the moment. In contrast, any adult responding to a child's overtures can, in a perfectly natural way, usually identify the child's interest of the moment (during this period of life) and talk about it to the child. This kind of event was repeated many times every day in the lives of our well-developing subjects. It appeared that *live language on the topic the child is actually thinking about at the moment* probably plays a key role in the achievement of language facility, social skills, and higher mental abilities. In other words, we believed that this particular experience is especially germane to good development. You may say, where is the surprise in that? After all, we have always known that adults should talk to children; and indeed, there is no basic surprise in the finding. We hope that by describing, with some precision, how and when this language experience is delivered, we can add to the general appreciation of the importance of talking to children. Not all speech to children is equally effective. For example, speaking to children while trying to redirect their attention seemed to be less useful than identifying a child's interest of the moment and interesting him in talk about *that* interest. That distinction may seem like a modest one, but it has several practical consequences.

We found that in some homes, especially those of the children doing the least well, restriction of their locomotor efforts was a routine practice; that is, playpens or other restrictive devices were used for the bulk of the day. If a playpen was not used, then long naps, morning and afternoon, frequently were used. A child would be put into his crib for a nap shortly after breakfast and kept there whether he was awake or asleep for 2 or 3 hours. The same thing would be repeated after lunch. Continually we found that children rather quickly became bored under such circumstances. They also became habituated in a matter of a few weeks. Ordinarily there would be toys available in the playpen or crib, sometimes quite a few, but it was a very rare child who managed to find enough to keep himself interested. Such children spent as many as 3 or more hours a day *passing time,* in a state of boredom and unable to alter their circumstances. Regular confinement to either a small room, a crib, a jumpseat, or a playpen was consistently associated with comparatively poor development. On the other hand, relative freedom from these restrictive experiences was a routine feature in the lives of 1-year-old children developing very well. In retrospect, this should not come as much of a surprise. The child who is restricted in such a manner simply cannot satisfy his curiosity in any persistent way, nor can he readily practice newly emerging motor skills. The child who was not restricted, in our experience, found it relatively easy to become involved in many kinds of sustained activities, both social and nonsocial. Furthermore, it was the child who had high *pass-time* experience at 12 to 15 months of age who had enormous nontask experiences at 18 to 21 months of age. What seemed to happen was that restriction was used at 12 to 15 months of age to avoid the work, the physical danger, the breakage, and the other unpleasant consequences of free locomobility of the 12-month-old. The resultant inability to satisfy and build upon one's curiosity seemed to lead to a generally less interested child some 6 months later. This less interested child at 18 months then understood enough language and was steady enough on his feet that he no longer needed to be restricted to the playpen so often. However, he no longer had quite the same zest for exploration that other children have when that zest for exploration is nourished by the opportunity to explore during the earlier age range.

We found that children who at 12 to 15 months of age spent an above-average amount of time practicing large muscle skills, especially those having to do with pulling to stand, cruising, and climbing onto and off of objects, were not, on balance, developing as well as others. Whether this reflected simple maturational lag, or genetically determined individual differences, or the consequences of having been kept in a playpen to the point where the normal achievement of gross motor skills had been delayed, or whether the lack of regular human interaction had somehow resulted in the placement of more emphasis on motor development, were all matters for speculation.

The other nonsocial task that was negatively correlated with good development was *procuring objects.* Again, we found ourselves in a situation in which we really had no lines of analysis and interpretation that seemed clear. All 12- to 15-month-old children have more difficulty getting to things that they want and actually grasping them than adults or older children. Yet, in the case of children not developing very well, we found that the sheer amount of time spent trying to procure objects was greater than with children developing well.

What did that mean? Perhaps opportunities to procure the assistance of adults or older children were less available, and therefore these children had to depend on their own resources more exclusively. Or perhaps the relatively low level of social interaction available to these children predisposed them toward a greater investment in physical reality.

Discussion and Conclusions

What follows next is an attempt not only to fairly accurately present the quantitative results we obtained with respect to the relationship of experiences to the development of competence, but also to add our subjective, consensually agreed-upon judgments about styles of childrearing as they relate to the numerical data. Repeatedly in longitudinal work we find that we learn considerably more than what is contained in the quantitative data. Certainly it was not possible to anticipate all the things that could be profitably measured prior to the execution of this study.

It seems to us, from these years of natural longitudinal experimentation, that effective childrearers essentially perform three major functions in a manner that distinguishes them from other childrearers. These three functions are:

Designing the child's world

Consulting for the child

Disciplining or controlling the child

In a design function, the effective childrearer makes the living area as safe as possible for the naive newly crawling or walking child and then provides maximum access to that living area. These actions lead naturally to the satisfaction of and further development of the child's curiosity and the opportunity to learn much more about the world at large. They also provide the child with the opportunity to enter into natural, useful relationships with people. The childrearer not only provides maximum access to the living area, but in addition, makes kitchen cabinets attractive and available and, in general, pays special attention to the safety and interest qualities of the kitchen area, since the child will spend more time there than in any other room for the next year or so. The childrearer also keeps a few materials in reserve for those times when the child becomes a bit bored. These materials do not have to be special toys; they can be empty ice cream containers filled with a variety of 2- to 3-inch objects with assorted shapes. Some might be plastic measuring cups or empty thread spools. Infants and toddlers are particularly interested in collections of small objects. Anything that is small and has an irregular shape or interesting markings becomes a suitable object for exploration. Other good items to keep in reserve are collections of plastic jars with covers and containers that can be used by the child to practice fine motor skills.

An effective childrearer functions as the child's consultant when he or she needs comforting or assistance, or when the child would simply like to share an exciting discovery. For example, one common consequence of an infant's explorations is a degree of minor frustration. A door may be stuck shut or two items that the child has been putting together and taking apart may refuse to come apart on the fortieth attempt. In instances such as these, the child may move toward the primary caretaker to get help with whatever it is that frustrates him. If someone is around when such a situation occurs, he or she can take advantage of this special opportunity for teaching. In our study, when a child was developing well, there was often someone close by, and *that person was someone who was particularly interested in the child.* On other occasions we saw instances in which someone was around but was not readily available nor terribly interested. In some instances we saw that while the mother was unavailable, the person left in the house was assigned the task of keeping the house clean as well as making sure that the baby was safe, fed, and not in any trouble. Under such circumstances, the common tendency of the child to share enthusiasm or get assistance was often not responded to. In the case of the more fortunate child, someone was there and interested, and that someone usually responded very quickly to the overture. The quick response usually was followed by the provision of whatever it was that the child was seeking. At times, adding a touch of realism to the life of this very young child, the adult would say, "I'm busy now. You are going to have to wait for a moment." This seemed to us to be a symptom of the kind of evenhanded treatment that young children got in homes in which they were developing well. In contrast, in some homes adults dropped everything the moment that the child wanted any kind of attention, almost regardless of what they were doing.

The next step in the apparently effective childrearing pattern involved the attempt by the adult to identify what the child was interested in at the moment. The attempt was almost always successful since children between 1 and 2 years of age do not seem to be terribly devious or complicated. One cannot be certain that the identification was always accurate, but usually the succeeding behaviors revealed its accuracy. Once the interest of the child was accurately identified, the adult had what would seem to be the ideal teaching situation—a motivated student was present and the adult knew what it was the student was focusing on. The adult then responded with what was needed, generally with words at or above the child's level of understanding, and incorporated a related idea, such as "Oh yes, you squeezed your little finger," "You remember Daddy banged his elbow this morning," or "Look at my finger, see the boo-boo I have." At times, more realistic teaching was possible. If, for example, the child wanted his stuffed rabbit to eat some food, the mother would take the opportunity to explain that while they could make-believe that the rabbit would eat food, the rabbit simply would not swallow, and so on. Once the child showed a lessened interest in the interchange, he was allowed to return to whatever he was doing or wanted to do. The entire episode rarely took more than 20 or 30 seconds, although at times there were much longer interchanges. Our impression was that no more than 10 percent of a child's waking time was spent in direct interactions of all kinds with the parent.[3] But you can include quite a number of 20-second interchanges in the hour or so that represents 10 percent of a 1-year-old child's waking time.

These brief episodes, precipitated much more often by the child than by the adult, seemed to us to be the core teaching situations involved in good development. None of the children in our natural experimental study had undergone any kind of regular teaching sessions beyond an occasional, brief, adult-initiated teaching session focusing on a magazine or small book. There were no protracted experiences of adults insisting on teaching reading readiness skills or anything of that sort.

The third core function we saw performed particularly well by effective childrearers consisted of setting limits or disciplining the child. We found that effective childrearers were nearly always firm and consistent with their children, while simultaneously showing deep love for the child and respect for his interests. Different types of control seemed necessary at different stages of infancy and toddlerhood, and a minority of childrearers had happened upon procedures that worked. Children less than a year of age (or so) can usually be controlled by distraction. Out of sight (for more than a few moments) is usually out of mind. Children from 1 to 1½ years of age require distraction and physical removal from circumstances at times or, on the other hand, removal of the object from the child's vicinity. Children from 18 months on require distraction, physical distance, and firm verbal restrictions.

In sum, then, our early work seemed to indicate that the three functions of designing the child's world, consulting for the child, and disciplining or controlling the child were the core of effective childrearing. They therefore formed the nucleus of our training program.

The Training Program

The experience of the natural longitudinal experimental study, along with previously established information on early growth and development, led our staff to focus the parent training program on that period in life between 6 and 8 months of age and the second birthday. We became convinced, from all that we had learned, that children generally manage to get to the crawling stage reasonably intact (from an educational point of view), but that few managed to get the most, educationally, out of the balance of infancy and toddlerhood. We therefore felt that the first priority of any course of research oriented toward the maintenance of optimal development in the early years was to prevent the falling off of development in the 8-to-36-month period.

We had come to believe that there were four educational foundations that were at risk between 8 and 24 months of age:

1. Language development
2. Curiosity development
3. Social skills and attachment development
4. Development of the roots of intelligence

Our experimental treatment-training program was therefore designed to
(1) make parents more aware of the course of development of these four
educational foundation processes, (2) help them emulate the childrearing practices of apparently successful parents, and (3) help them avoid childrearing
practices of apparently unsuccessful parents. Further shaping of the experimental treatment came from the actual experiences we had in attempting to work
with a small group of families as their children grew from 5 to 17 months of age.

Through the mechanism of regular staff discussions of the experiences of
working with parents on their childrearing practices, we believe we strengthened
our experimental treatment. For example, we knew that there would be a good
deal of verbal interchange between staff and families throughout the pilot period
and the training program in general. Therefore, we decided we would relieve the
stress that might be caused by long-term verbal interchange by using a few
well-chosen movies. We screened quite a number before we selected some for
trial, but we could not know in advance how effective the various movies would
be. Final judgment on films was the kind of practical problem which could be
resolved only by trial and error.

Similarly, the optimal frequency of visits to homes was something that we
found difficult to anticipate in advance. We learned how to space the visits
through experience. Numerous other related kinds of learnings were met and
coped with through the actual piloting of the project. Some of the more
interesting aspects will be discussed later.

A Special Problem Selecting Families

We wanted to work with about a dozen families in the pilot program. We
assumed that not every family we began to work with would turn out
satisfactorily for the purposes of our research. We were concerned, for example,
that if a young couple was not getting along well, the family discord might
interfere with the utilization of our ideas about childrearing. We also were
concerned with the possibility of families being unreliable. For example, from
our previous work with families we knew that there were some who failed to
keep appointments. For these reasons we started with a few extra families
($N = 16$) and reduced the number to twelve between the fifth and eighth months
of their children's lives. Subsequently, one additional family dropped out
because of health reasons.

We chose families in a rather special way. We did not want to work with
families who were likely to do such a good job with their children that there was
not much room for improvement, nor did we want to work with families in
which conditions were such that our ideas about effective practices would not be
given a fair chance. So we aimed for families with average childrearing abilities,
although it was clear that we had no very reliable yardstick to measure such

abilities in each family. Our criteria for selection and eligibility will be found in chapter 4; characteristics of the families in the study are indicated in table 2-1. The program we created concentrates on the age range of 5 to 17 months (see *Experience and Environment*, Volume 2, pp. 176-182).

From Schedules I and II, outlined in figures 2-1 and 2-2, you can see that we treated the 5- to 8-month period separately from the 8- to 17-month period. We reasoned that the 5- to 8-month period is a relatively easy one for most families and could be used as a time to prepare them for what was going to happen when the child began to crawl. We used two kinds of activities to introduce the training program to families during this time period. We had group visits at the university featuring discussions and films, and we had follow-up home visits for private discussions and to get to know the individual circumstances in the home. Descriptions of what went on in each of the group and home visits are presented in appendix D of *Experience and Environment*, Volume 2, as part of the description of the training program.

Once the baby turned 8 months of age we intensified our support. The frequency of home visits was increased to approximately every other week. Simultaneously, the frequency of group get-togethers was reduced. In addition, we began to monitor closely the processes of development.

We were particularly interested in the stream of experiences of these children, and the timing of such data collection is represented in Schedule II by the symbol T. We were also interested in the behavior of the mothers and especially the degree to which it corresponded to the behaviors we were advocating. The frequency with which we sampled those behaviors is represented by the placement of the letter M. We collected data on the details of the child's social life (S), and we were assessing the growth of competence periodically throughout the time period (B, L, C_1, C_2, and S). As the child approached 2 years of age, we initiated our first outcome assessments, which can be seen in Schedule III (see figure 2-3).

After each of the home visits, a relatively brief report of what transpired was produced by the particular home visitor. We routinely held staff meetings to discuss our views on how things were going in each of the family situations. The home-visit reports were very important elements in these discussions. Samples of home-visit reports are presented with the training program material in appendix D of Volume 2.

Evaluation of the Pilot Study

Was the Program Acceptable to Families?

At the outset of the study, we had no particularly strong hold over these families. We did pay them for participation at the rate of $5 for a half day, and

Table 2-1
Subject Characteristics, Pilot Study (N = 11)

Subject I.D.	Sex	Bayley Test Score at 5 mos.	Hollings-head Redlich Code	Mother's Education	Father's Education	Mother's Occupation	Father's Occupation	Mother's Ethnic Background	Father's Ethnic Background	Number of Children in Household
46	F	135	IV	High sch. graduate	High sch. graduate	Housewife	Laborer	Irish	Irish	3
47	M	106	III	High sch. and voc. trng.	High sch. and part. col.	Housewife	First line mgmt. tel. co.	Canadian	Irish	2
48	F	123	II	High sch. and part. col.	M.A. in divinity	Housewife	Minister	Scotch-Dutch	Anglo-Saxon	2
49	M	100	III	High sch. graduate	High sch. graduate	Housewife	Plumber	Irish	Irish	2
50	F	117	III	High sch. and part. col.	High sch. and apprentice work	Housewife	Foreman, pipefit. constr.	Irish	Irish	2
51	F	101	IV	High sch. and courses	High sch. and courses	Housewife	MBTA operator	Anglo-Saxon	Canadian	2
52	F	94	III	High sch. graduate	High sch. and part. col.	Housewife	Roofer	Anglo-Saxon	Anglo-Saxon	3
53	M	94	III	High sch. and part. col.	B.A.	Housewife	Video tech.	Anglo-Saxon	Irish	2
54	M	84	IV	High sch.	High sch.	Housewife	Photo-engraver	Anglo-Saxon	Canadian	3

| 55 | M | 102 | III | High sch. and part. col. | High sch. | Housewife | MBTA foreman | Irish | Irish | 2 |
| 56 | F | 102 | III | High sch. | High sch. and apprentice work | Housewife | Electrician | Irish | Irish | 2 |

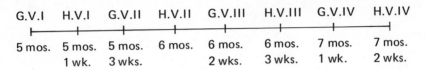

Chronological Age of Child (5 to 8 months)

Key: G.V. = group visit; H.V. = home visit.

Figure 2-1. Schedule I.

certainly none of these families were so well off that the money was not welcomed. However, we asked them for a good deal of cooperation over a protracted period of time. All in all, we were interacting with them for some 19 or 20 months, and we were visiting their homes on the average of two times a month throughout that period. If the program was not deemed useful, or if the people attempting to execute it were not welcome in the home, the degree of participation in the study would probably have reflected such difficulties. Following the early departure of the one family in which there was a health problem, the other eleven families participated faithfully. In total, we scheduled

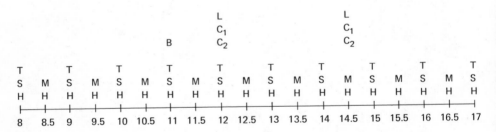

Chronological Age of Child (8 to 17 months)

Key: T = Collection of task data
      S = Collection of social competence data
      M = Collection of maternal behavior data
      H = Home visit
      B = Bayley Scales of Infant Development
      L = Preschool Project Test of Receptive Language Ability
      C_1 = Preschool Project Test of Sensing Dissonance
      C_2 = Preschool Project Test of Abstract Abilities

Figure 2-2. Schedule II.

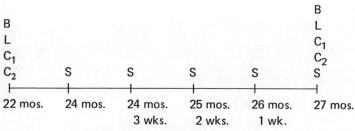

Chronological Age of Child (months and weeks)

Key: S = Collection of social competence data
     B = Bayley Scales of Infant Development
     L = Preschool Project Test of Receptive Language Ability
     C_1 = Preschool Project Test of Sensing Dissonance
     C_2 = Preschool Project Test of Abstract Abilities

Figure 2-3. Schedule III.

approximately 500 home visits with the eleven families. Of those, 495 appointments were kept. Attendance at group visits held at the university was significantly lower (51 attending out of 66 scheduled). While this particular sample is small and somewhat homogeneous, the result seemed rather important.

Did the Program Have Any Effect on Childrearing Practices?

One of the special capacities of research of this sort is that it can go beyond the description of the training procedures to a closer examination of the actual processes involved in the child's development. We sampled the behavior of the mothers involved in the study to see the degree to which they actually emulated the childrearing practices that we believed most desirable and the degree to which they avoided nonbeneficial childrearing practices. In addition to this look at the extent to which the training "took," we sampled the stream of experiences each child underwent using our task instrument. Such "process monitoring" of data is not commonly gathered in most evaluations of educational programs.

Adult Responses to Children's Overtures

Table 2-2 presents summary data on the behavior of the caretakers in this study. It was based on 30-minute continuous observations spaced one month apart and numbering anywhere from a minimum of five to a maximum of ten observations

Table 2-2
Adult Behavior in Response to a Child-Initiated Interaction

Category	Range	Median
Frequency of S's overtures to A[a]	1-13	5.0
Frequency of overtures responded to by A[a]	1-13	4.5
Total duration of responses[a]	40-463 s	105.0 s
X duration of response time[a]	13-40 s	26.0 s
Timing and Direction of A's Response:[a]		
a. Immediate	67-100%	82.0%
b. Delayed	0-20	0.0
c. Ignored	0-33	0.0
d. Rejected	0	0.0
A's Perception of S's Needs:[a]		
a. Accurate	81-100	100.0
b. Partial	0-50	0.0
c. None	0	0.0
Level of Difficulty of A's Words:[a]		
a. Appropriate	0-100	67.0
b. Too complex	0	0.0
c. Too simple	0-50	10.0
d. Babytalk	0	0.0
e. None	0-25	0.0
A's Satisfaction of S's Needs:[a]		
a. Yes	20-100	82.0
b. Partial	0-20	0.0
c. No	0-60	7.0

A = Adult.

S = Child.

Note: The data in this table summarize observations on ten S's during the ages from 8 to 17 months. The number of 30-minute observations on each S range from 5 to 10, with a median of 8 or 9 observations.

[a]Mean per 30-minute observation.

per family, with the modal number between eight and nine. The age of the child during these observations was between 8½ and 16½ months of age, corresponding to the intensive family support phase of our project. Data from one of our eleven families are not included. Because of illness and various other uncontrollable factors, we managed to accumulate only four 30-minute protocols on that family, and the variability of data of this sort is such that we felt that a minimum of five would be necessary before we could have confidence in the representativeness of the information.

1. *What percentage of the time did adults respond to the overtures made by the children?* In nearly every instance, overtures made by a child to an adult were responded to. The response rate never fell below 75 percent. The lowest figure was for the one family on which our staff agreed, as a whole, that we had failed in our attempts to significantly influence the childrearing practices of the adult involved.

2. *How much total time did these adults spend in responding to overtures from the children?* Exclusive of routine caretaking (which will be discussed later), we found the central tendency in our ten family situations to be 106 seconds out of the 30 minutes, or slightly under 2 minutes.

3. *What was the average duration of each individual response to a child's overture?* The average response to a child's overture lasted slightly less than ½ minute.

4. *How quickly was the child responded to?* Here it is clear, for the most part, that the response on the part of the adult was immediate. By immediate we mean no later than 3 seconds after the child initiated an overture. The median value for immediate responses was 86 percent, showing that although responses were not always immediate, delayed responses or ignored overtures were very rare for the group as a whole.

5. *How accurately did the adult perceive the subject's need?* The subject's need was almost always perceived accurately.

6. *To what extent was language used, and when it was used, was it at a level of difficulty which was neither overly complex nor overly simple for the child?* The responses of 72 percent were at the appropriate level, and 9 percent consisted of language that was too simple for the child.

7. *To what extent did the adult meet the child's need?* Complete satisfaction seemed to us to occur slightly over 80 percent of the time. Occasionally, there was only partial satisfaction, and slightly more often there was definite failure to satisfy the young child.

Adult-Initiated Interactions

Table 2-3 contains information about the interactions between caretaker and child that were initiated by the adult. The central tendency was five of such interactions per 30 minutes, which corresponds closely to the central tendency for child-initiated interchanges. The total duration of time spent in such activities averaged 65 seconds, or a bit more than 1 minute per half hour. The average duration of the interchanges was some 16 seconds (considerably shorter than the duration of responses to overtures by the child). The ratio of purposes of stimulating versus control of the child favored stimulating the child (60 to 40 percent).

The final piece of information about maternal behavior is less secure because we did not always make note of it. It concerns the *total* amount of interaction time, including routine caretaking, such as diapering the baby, wiping the child's face, and feeding the child. As far as we can tell, the time spent in such activities was less than 1 minute, but with a rather wide range, in one instance moving up to 19 out of the total 30 minutes. Of *all* time spent in adult-child interactions, an average of 105 seconds was spent responding to a child's overtures, 65 seconds in adult-initiated interchanges, and no time in

Table 2-3
Adult Behavior When Initiating Interaction with a Child

Category	Range	Median
Frequency of A-initiated interactions[a]	3-9	4.0
Total duration of interactions[a]	55-215 s	65.0 s
X duration per interaction	13-30 s	16.0 s
A's Purpose[a]		
a. To stimulate	40-86%	60.0%
b. To control	14-60	40.0

A = Adult.

S = Child.

Note: The data in this table summarize observations on eleven S's during the ages from 8 to 17 months. The number of 30-minute observations on each S range from 5 to 10, with a median of 8 observations.

[a]Mean per 30-minute observation.

routine caretaking. Total interaction time was 170 seconds, or just under 3 minutes for the 30-minute observation span, or approximately 9.5 percent of the time.

These data seem to indicate that by and large the adults in the program (in nearly every instance the mothers of the children) came close to what we asked of them with respect to interchanges with their children. The overall percentage of time involved in interchanges appeared slightly greater than what we had previously experienced in our natural observational data, where no attempt was made to influence the behavior of the parents. This difference was understandable. The data featured rather wide variability in some instances. For example, in the number of overtures to the mother, we found a range of from four to thirteen for a 30-minute observation session. In addition, with regard to the tendency to stimulate a child or to control him, we found rather broad ranges, with one mother stimulating her child 40 percent of the time in such interactions and another stimulating her child 86 percent of the time. Conversely, the range with respect to controlling episodes by the mother went from a low of 14 percent to a high of 60 percent, these figures being the reciprocal of the figures on stimulation. The only place where one might have hoped for significantly better performance by the pilot families was in the area of the difficulty level of the words used by the parents. The central tendency of 72 percent (appropriate behavior) with a range of from 50 to 100 percent stands out as a less impressive performance than other aspects of these data.

Our conclusion was that we did, indeed, manage an effect on the behavior of the mothers, and in the direction that we desired. There was no way of being certain of this because we did not have comparable data from a control group during this phase of our research. Such data will be examined when we deal with the results of the comparative study.

Did the Program Have Any Effect on the
Experiences of the Children?

The data we gathered with our task instrument provided a quantitative picture of the actual experiences of children. By themselves these data could not tell us about *changes* in experience brought about by our training efforts, but fortunately we had comparable data for children whom we had studied in the past. The children studied earlier fell into two special categories. We had data on the experiences of two groups who looked similar in achievement levels at 12 months of age but who were at 3 years of age either outstandingly well developed or much less well developed. The extent to which the tasks of children in the pilot training program resembled the experiences of children developing well or those developing less well should therefore be instructive. One caveat, however: none of the instruments we used are perfect. First there is the question of their reliability, which in some instances was rather low. Then there is the question of the power of the instruments, whether they really capture what it is about the behaviors of mothers or the particular experiences of children that is important. With these warnings in mind, let us take a look at the task data presented in table 2-4.

The data in table 2-4 are for nine of the eleven pilot subjects. In one case, because of illness in the family, we were unable to gather adequate data. In another case, we have deleted the data on the experiences of one child in the frank acknowledgment that our program failed with his family. The data were gathered on five occasions during the 12- to 15-month age range. Data on the experiences of the five highest and five lowest achievers in our preceding study are used to provide some sort of standard against which to judge the data from the pilot subjects.

The most desirable outcome of the pilot study would have been a striking similarity between the typical experiences of our pilot study children and those of our extraordinarily well-developed children. Such was not the outcome. On balance, it appeared that the patterns of experience of the pilot study children more closely resembled those of the well-developing children than those who developed poorly, but there were some exceptions to this statement. The most hopeful signs were in the case of *nontask behavior, fine motor mastery experiences*, and *live language directed to the subject.*

Nontask experiences are those in which a child does not seem to be doing much of anything. We score desultory scanning or aimless wandering as nontask behavior. In table 2-4, well-developing children had the least amount of such experience (9.3 percent). The pilot subjects had 12.9 percent, and the children who subsequently developed rather poorly had by far the greatest amount of such experience at this time in their lives (18.2 percent).

Turning to the area of mastery experiences, we found that unfortunately the breakdown between fine and gross motor mastery tasks was available only for the pilot subjects. At the time we were gathering these data on the other two

Table 2-4
All Tasks Comparative Data

Social Tasks	Pilot Group N = 9	Advanced Group N = 5[a]	Delayed Group N = 5[a]
To please	1	0.3	0
To cooperate	2.5	2.1	2.0
To gain approval	0	0	0
To procure a service	1.3	1.4	0.7
To gain attention	1.4	2.9	1.4
To maintain social contact	2.4	1.7	1.6
To avoid unpleasant circumstances	0	0	0
To annoy	0	0	0
To direct	0	0	0
To assert self	1.2	0.3	0.8
Nonsocial Tasks			
To eat	7.5	4.1	6.2
To gain information (visual)	12.2	21.4	11.0
To gain information (visual and auditory)	5.5	5.8	3.2
Nontask	12.9	9.3	18.2
To pass time	4.4	0.8	4.1
To find something to do	0	0	0
To prepare for activity	0.5	1.5	1.3
To construct a product	0	0	0
To choose	0	0	0
To procure an object	4.4	2.3	4.0
Gross motor activity	0.7	0	0
To gain pleasure	2.1	0.6	0.7
To imitate	0.7	0.1	0.2
To pretend	0	0	0
To ease discomfort	2.3	0.5	1.7
To explore	15.2	14.9	12.5
Mastery, total[b]	11.8	11.4	15.3
Fine motor mastery	6.8	—	—
Gross motor mastery	3.1	—	—
Language, live, direct	2.9	5.8	2.1
Other	0.9	0	0.4

Note: The data on the pilot advanced and delayed groups summarize three to five 30-minute observations on each S during the 12- to 15-month age range.

[a]Thirty-nine S's were ranked according to their achievement levels at 3 years. The data presented in this table represent the scores for the five most advanced and the five most delayed subjects.

[b]At the time the data were recorded for the advanced and the delayed groups, observers did not discriminate between gross and fine motor mastery. Consequently, only total mastery scores are available for these two groups.

groups, we had not routinely been making the distinction between fine and gross motor mastery experiences. We had, however, noticed from the outset and repeatedly throughout our research that a high frequency of fine motor mastery experiences was a regular accompaniment to very good development. The fact that fine motor mastery tasks are very common in our pilot group was therefore a probable good sign.

Moving to the third area, we found that well-developing children had by far the greatest amount of live language directed toward them in this age range (5.8 percent). However, the pilot group had 2.9 percent, and our less-well-developing children had 2.1 percent. These results were perhaps the most disappointing of the study.

Another aspect of the task data was particularly worrisome. You will note that the well-developing children had negligible amounts of pass-time experience at this point in their lives.[4] The children developing less well and the pilot group (4.1 percent) looked very much alike in this regard. Why this happened we really do not know, but we would have been much happier had we seen much less pass-time experience in the lives of our pilot sample.

The only other aspect of these data that we believe merits attention is in the gain information (visual) category. *Gain information (visual)* means steady-staring activity. There was a great deal of it in the daily lives of our well-developing children (21.4 percent), and slightly more than half as much in both our less-well-developing children and our pilot group. Again, we cannot tell the reasons, but we would have preferred to see more of such behavior in our pilot group.

In summary, then, while certain key differences in the stream of experience favored the pilot group, a few important differences went against that group. By and large we did not produce a pattern of experiences in the pilot children that closely resembled that of the children developing unusually well in our previous study.

*Did the Program Have Any Effect on
the Children's Development?*

In order to make some judgments about the effectiveness of our program (in the light of the fact that we did not have a contemporaneous control group), the scores on the various measures for the pilot group were compared to national norms whenever possible or the performance of groups that we had previously worked with.

General Development. *The Bayley Mental Index Performance.* As you can see from table 2-5, we had four Bayley Mental Index scores for each of our eleven pilot subjects, starting when they were 5 months of age and ending when they were 26 months of age. The next to the last column (22 + 26) represents the average for the 22- and 26-month scores combined. At 5 months of age the group looked unremarkable, with a central tendency of 102. At 11 months of age they looked, at first glance, to be slightly advanced, but when you look at the scores for children from the previous study, a different interpretation comes to mind. The score of 106 as a central tendency for the advanced group in the preceding study is not statistically different from the 109 for the pilot group, nor is the 112 for the delayed children in the preceding study significantly

Table 2-5
Comparison Data on the Bayley Scales of Infant Development

Groups	Age at Testing (Months)						
	5	*11*	*12*	*22*	*24*	$\frac{22+26}{\overline{X}}$	*26*
Pilot group							
N	11	11	–	11	–	11	11
Range	84-135	99-117	–	84-145	–	87-131.5	90-127
Group median	102	109	–	109	–	106.5	104
Advanced group[a]							
N	–	–	5	–	5	–	–
Range	–	–	100-134	–	116-143	–	–
Group median	–	–	106	–	132	–	–
Delayed group[a]							
N	–	–	5	–	5	–	–
Range	–	–	103-134	–	66-119	–	–
Group median	–	–	112	–	96	–	–

[a]Thirty-nine S's were ranked according to their achievement levels at 3 years. The data presented in this table represent the scores for the five most advanced and the five most delayed children to the extent that it was available at a particular age range.

different from the score of the pilot group. What these three numbers tend to suggest is that at 11 months of age you cannot predict where children will be when they get to be 3 years of age. At 22 months of age, when the Bayley score is likely to have considerably more predictive power, our pilot group continued to score at 109. At 26 months of age they scored at 104. Their average Bayley score at 2 years of age was 106.5. This figure should then be compared with the figures for the other groups. As you can see, our pilot group clearly cannot compete with the most successful group in the preceding study. What this means will be discussed later. On the other hand, the pilot group does compare favorably with the previously studied children who developed less well. The difference between 106.5 and 96 is very probably a real difference.

Language Development. The same general procedure has been followed in the presentation of data on language development (see table 2-6). At 1 year of age our pilot group looked pretty much like the group who later developed well and perhaps slightly better than the group who later developed less well. At 22 months of age our pilot group had a central tendency score of 24 months in our semiarbitrary developmental scale, whereas at 25 months of age our advanced group scored at 36 months and our slower group scored at 21 months. Although we do not have complete data on our pilot group, the first five pilot subjects that we scored at 26 months of age had a central tendency in their scores of 36 months of age. In each case, the scores represented large gains between 22 and

Table 2-6
Comparison Data on Language Ability

	Age at Testing (Months)				
Groups	12	12½	22	25	26
Pilot group					
Na	11	–	11	–	5
Range	10-16	–	18-36	–	27-48
Group median	14	–	24	–	36
Advanced groupb					
N	–	5	–	5	–
Range	–	10-21	–	36-51	–
Group median	–	14	–	36	–
Delayed groupb					
N	–	5	–	5	–
Range	–	10-16	–	10-40	–
Group median	–	12	–	21	–

aBecause of the cessation of funds for this study, only five of the eleven S's were tested at 26 months.
bThirty-nine S's were ranked according to their achievement levels at 3 years. The data presented in this table represent the scores for the five most advanced and the five most delayed children to the extent that it was available at a particular age range.

26 months of age. In retrospect, it is unfortunate that we did not continue to test all the group until 36 months, but you must remember that research funds were not available and, in addition, we looked upon this study as a learning experience and a trial run only.

Abstract Thinking Ability. Again, using the same format (see table 2-7) we found a small advantage for the pilot group and the advanced group over the slower group at 1 year of age. We found at 22 and 26 months of age considerably higher scores for the pilot group than the slower group (which was encouraging), yet the scores remained lower than for our advanced group.

Sensing Dissonance. We found a pattern that differed from the preceding ones (see table 2-8). Our pilot group looked like our advanced group at 1 year of age, and both looked better than the slower group. At 22 months our pilot group had improved but was nowhere near as impressive as the advanced group. In fact, they looked pretty much like the slower group in this test area, and the picture stayed the same for the five subjects we did test at 26 months of age.

Social Competence. The social competence tests consisted of data gathered through continuous 30-minute observations of children as they went about their ordinary business in their own home. For information about the procedures see our Social Abilities Manual (*Experience and Environment*, Volumes 1 and 2).

Table 2-7
Comparison Data on the Capacity for Abstract Thought

	Age at Testing (Months)				
Groups	12	12½	22	25	26
Pilot group					
N[a]	11	–	11	–	4
Range	8-15.5	–	15.5-20.5	–	20.8-28.5
Group median	15.5	–	20.5	–	22.5
Advanced group[b]					
N	–	5	–	5	–
Range	–	8-15.5	–	20.5-28.5	–
Group median	–	15.5	–	24.5	–
Delayed group[b]					
N	–	5	–	5	–
Range	–	8-15.5	–	16.5-20.5	–
Group median	–	11.0	–	16.5	–

[a]Because of the cessation of funds for this study, only five of the eleven S's were tested at 26 months. One test was declared invalid.

[b]Thirty-nine S's were ranked according to their achievement levels at 3 years. The data presented in this table represent the scores for the five most advanced and the five most delayed children to the extent that it was available at a particular range.

Table 2-8
Comparison Data on the Capacity to Sense Dissonance

	Age at Testing (Months)				
Groups	12	12½	22	25	26
Pilot group					
N[a]	11	–	11	–	5
Range	1-3.5	–	2-7	–	2-8
Group median	2	–	3.5	–	3.5
Advanced group[b]					
N	–	5	–	25	–
Range	–	0-3	–	3.5-7.0	–
Group median	–	2	–	6	–
Delayed group[b]					
N	–	5	–	5	–
Range	–	0-2	–	3.5-7.0	–
Group median	–	0	–	3.5	–

[a]Because of the cessation of funds for this study, only five of the eleven S's were tested at 26 months. One test was declared invalid.

[b]Thirty-nine S's were ranked according to their achievement levels at 3 years. The data presented in this table represent the scores for the five most advanced and the five most delayed children to the extent that it was available at a particular age range.

Since the children in the first 2 years of life had little opportunity to interact with age mates (or indeed anybody other than their own parents), the data we present have to do with interactions with adults who, in most instances, turn out to be the child's own mother (see table 2-3). There are five social abilities reported on:

1.   Getting and holding the attention of an adult in socially acceptable ways.
2.   Using the adult as a resource after first concluding they could not handle the task themselves.
3.   Expressing affection and mild hostility.
4.   Showing pride in achievement.
5.   Engaging in role play.

The data indicated that our pilot group (this time numbering ten subjects because we did not have adequate data on the eleventh) looked a bit more like our advanced group at 12 to 15 months of age than the slower group. We were encouraged by the scores on use of an adult as a resource, where our trained group was even higher than the advanced group, and both groups were considerably above the slower group. At 2 years of age, our pilot group scores were much more like those of the advanced group than like those of the children who developed less well. Pride in conduct and role play abilities were not seen in our pilot group, while there were modest signs of such abilities in both groups in the preceding study.

Discussion

Adding up these results, we felt cautiously optimistic about future experimentation. The Bayley scores and those on the tests of cognitive abilities were somewhat disappointing but hopeful. The scores in the area of language development, particularly those at 26 months, were somewhat promising; and the scores in the area of social development were a bit more promising. The reader should bear in mind that our staff was unanimous in believing that we failed totally in the case of one of our eleven families. We did not believe that the training program worked at all in affecting the family in its childrearing practices. In addition, we believed that the childrearing practices of that family were not naturally oriented toward the ones we were espousing. The child in question developed quite poorly in comparison to the other ten children, and yet we included his achievement data with the entire group. The effect, of course, was to depress the group performance. Furthermore, it is unrealistic to expect to improve the quality of the childrearing practices of high school graduates from the center of our society (in socioeconomic terms) to a level of performance equivalent to the very highest effectiveness we have seen to date in parents. For these reasons, the fact that our children did not always achieve as well as those who did beautifully in the preceding study did not discourage us. In our comparative study, we expected to be somewhat more effective in assisting families in adopting the childrearing practices of apparently effective families. The creation of a pilot program that embodied our best ideas about effective childrearing practices seemed reasonably successful. Of course, time and additional effort would be the ultimate judge of such a statement. We had been forced to recognize that there were certain kinds of impediments to the ideal execution of such a plan. Some parents are considerably more anxious about the child's well-being than others, and our recommendations that the child be allowed to explore involve a degree of real risk. Some parents simply do not listen very well, and others try a bit too hard to please. Nevertheless, we had some reason to be encouraged. We did get remarkable participation on the part of the families. We were inundated with compliments and expressions of gratitude during and after the program ended, and the results, as far as we can tell, were promising.

Notes

1. In addition to the work that the core Preschool Project staff performed in that natural experiment, a simultaneous examination of the lives of these children was conducted under the direction of Jean C. Watts. Her special focus was on environmental factors, especially the role of the primary caretaker. A good deal of interesting information on these same children was therefore generated by Dr. Watts and her staff. In an earlier major report on the results of the longitudinal study (*Experience and Environment*, Volume 1) the data from the two efforts were not fully integrated. Although the same subjects were shared, the research was actually done quite independently in each case. The pilot study did not partake in any substantial degree of the data from Dr. Watts's study. Dr. Watts therefore has no responsibility, formal or otherwise, for any of the research to be discussed.

2. In more recent studies, we have found that total time spent (by parents) in direct contact with 1-year-olds is rarely more than 20 percent of the child's waking hours, or a bit over 2 hours per day. The figure of 20 percent is most likely in the case of first-born children. The figure drops markedly with succeeding children, averaging about 10 percent for second, third, and fourth children.

3. In subsequent studies we have found that mothers spend about twice as much time with their first children.

4. *Passing time* occurs when a child has nothing interesting to do, but he cannot leave the situation. Confinement to a playpen or a car seat, for example, soon becomes pass-time experience most of the time.

Part II
A Comparative
Experiment

3 The Design

The kind of research that we performed in our natural longitudinal experiment produced a good deal of reliable information about the experiences, interests, and abilities of infants and toddlers in their own homes. As for the important question of effective childrearing, however, natural experiments are seriously limited. Ours produced only correlational data with respect to the relationships among experiences and development. When we started this research in 1965, we had made a commitment to the maximum feasible utilization of the scientific method, and therefore we have moved from natural experimentation to true experimentation. Experimenting with young children is a highly problematical endeavor for people with humanistic sensitivity. Indeed, many people flinch when they hear anything about experiments with young children. We feel that educational experimentation in the lives of young children can be done in an ethical way provided that great care is exercised. Furthermore, we know of no other way in which to advance the state of reliable knowledge about how to raise a child. We therefore remain committed to the method.

How, then, does one go about putting to experimental test the hypotheses generated by our natural experiment? Our plan involved one preliminary step and then the design of an experiment. The preliminary step took us 2 years. It consisted of the creation and field trial of a training program which, in scientific terms, is equivalent to the experimental treatment. This is the step we called the pilot study. A major consideration we had to be aware of in designing an experiment on childrearing was the total array of possible important influences on the development of competence in the children we would work with. We knew, for example, that the educational background of families had been repeatedly found to be associated with the level of development of competence. In addition, we were concerned with ancillary or secondary factors which could contribute significantly to developing competence in children. From previous experience and from the experience of others we knew that the kind of attention that we as a professional group from a high prestige university would pay to a family would heighten the family's self-consciousness and interest in the rearing of their young children. J. McVicker Hunt reports that in Earladeen Badger's parent training program this factor of increased attention to the family without any accompanying detailed information about how to raise a child seemed to result in improved test performance for very young children. Our design, therefore, had to control for such sensitization and prestige-type effects which could otherwise be confounded with true experimental effects. Our answer was to arrange for several control groups, one group labeled the pediatric control or PC group, another labeled the monitored control group or C_1, and a third the pretest and posttest group or C_2.

The pediatric control group (PC) was to receive guidance in comparable quantities to that provided by our staff. We hoped (but could not dictate) that the group would be exposed to ideas about childrearing that were substantially different from ours and to a degree comparable to that received by the experimental families. We were fortunate enough to enlist the assistance of a pediatrician with more than 20 years of experience. This gentleman held an appointment at the Harvard Medical School and was highly regarded by both his academic colleagues and the parents in his practice, many of whom had professional backgrounds themselves. He had over the years built up a great deal of experience along with a high degree of frustration with respect to guiding young families in rearing their children. His feeling was that he had never had quite enough time to do the job as well as he would like because of the size of his practice and the pressures of time and economics. We provided him with the same amount of money we were using in our program, and in essence tried to equate his family support resources with ours in every respect, aside from the specificity of the childrearing ideas transmitted in the two training programs.

As a result of the marked increase in research on infant development during the last decade, it has been found (although not published frequently) that repeated testing of children during infancy leads to higher test scores than one would otherwise expect. Infants and toddlers, in other words, seem to become "test savvy." In particular, this topic has been explored by Mark Golden of SUNY-Stony Brook, New York, who has found that a thorough acclimatization period prior to testing a naive infant makes for a very substantial difference in test scores (personal communication). Others have remarked about this phenomenon to us and indeed we seem to see evidence of it in our own data. This factor of the apparent beneficial effects of repeated testing, along with the sensitization of parents to childrearing caused by participation in a research project even if only as a control, had to be controlled for. We employed a control group (C_1) in our design, in which the families received no training but the children were tested on the same schedule as those in the other two groups and data were gathered on their experiences and on the parent's childrearing styles, etc., on precisely the same schedule. A fourth group of children (C_2) was seen only before the study for initial testing and when the study was over for final evaluation. This last group (C_2) as compared with the third group (C_1) was to provide some sense of the impact on achievement scores of repeated testing and the presence of an observer in the home.

We were aware that our design was not flawless. We had limited control over the degree to which the experimental families actually executed what we wanted them to with their children. We had no sure way of knowing precisely how well the families would have done without our help. We were not ideally positioned to select families that really met all the criteria that we created for eligibility. There was no way of seeing to it that the ideas for the experimental group were kept fully from the pediatric group or from the other control groups, etc. But, as in all our previous work, our feeling was that if we were to wait for the perfect research opportunity, we would wait a very long time.

Because we had planned to work closely with families for a fair period of time, we knew that there was a rather modest limit to the numbers of families we could work with. We began with eighteen families in each group and narrowed that number down to fifteen for the ultimate sample. Therefore, the study included sixty families.

The question of when we would work with the children was a rather difficult one. We had noted earlier that the first consistent deviations in the development of competence seemed to occur routinely for many children sometime during the second year of life. Since our hope was to prevent underachievement in children, we wanted to start early enough for such purposes. On the other hand, we were not anxious to invest heavily in the process well before it made much sense. We were quite convinced that during the first 6 or 7 months of life most families managed to get through the task of educating their young children rather well. From our previous work on the development of abilities in the first 6 months of life (White 1971) we were reasonably well acquainted with what went on during that time. In addition, from the results of a whole host of studies on the effects of maternal deprivation in the first few years of life (Bowlby 1951) we knew that a child's first 6 months of life spent in an institution, for example, away from his or her mother and in generally inferior substitute circumstances, usually did not produce lasting harmful effects. We knew from the studies of Bayley (1940) and Honzig et al. (1948) on the longitudinal development of children that scores on infant tests for general development did not seem to predict later achievement terribly well in the first year of life. We knew that children from all parts of the world who did poorly on tests when they were 6, 7, or 8 years of age, on the whole, tended to look perfectly normal well into the second year of life (Brown and Halpern 1971; Schaefer 1968 and 1969).

Therefore, it seemed well established that there were no obvious signs of persistent deficiencies before the middle of the second year of life.[1] Yet others claimed, and continue to claim, that educational development from birth is very often at risk and that people routinely get their children off to a very poor start from the child's first days. Some have claimed that eye contact patterns in the first weeks of life are very important and that parents require guidance in order to establish good social contact with their babies at that time. Others have claimed that certain kinds of perceptual motor stimulation are necessary and not at all assured in the first months of life, etc. When confronted with the fact that these children who supposedly have not had just the right kind of early mother-child interactional pattern test perfectly well throughout the first year of life, such advocates remarked,"Ah, but our tests are very weak. Such children really are in trouble but as yet our measurement techniques are not very sensitive. We dare not assume that there are no difficulties just because we cannot measure them." Such a disagreement will be resolved only as more and more specific evidence on the topic becomes available. We remain much less impressed by the evidence supporting this position than some other people.

Added to this kind of thinking are the following kinds of notions about what happens at 7 months or so in the lives of children which would lead families to do a considerably less effective job of rearing their children. As was pointed out earlier, true language learning begins at 6 to 8 months of life and then moves ahead very rapidly through the next few years. Unlike the acquisition of visually directed reaching skill (which is one of the major achievements of the first 6 months of life), language development is directly dependent on a good deal of input from other human beings. Learning to reach can be done without help from anyone else. In fact, institutionally reared children learn just as well and just as rapidly as those who are reared in the most advantaged of homes.

In addition to language development (which is fundamental to educability and socialization), one must consider the development of curiosity. Curiosity seems to us to be present in great quantities in all but a very few 7- and 8-month-old children, but is often diminished or distorted by the time the child reaches his third birthday. By that we mean that while many children retain a fresh and broad interest in learning right through their second and third years of life, others end up at those ages with considerably less interest or with interests that have been misshapen. The most frequent form of misshaping that we have seen among children is a concentration of curiosity, interest, and exploration on the behavior of the primary caretaker such that by 2 years of age some children no longer "play alone well" but insist on close proximity with the primary caretaker for as many hours of the day as possible.

In addition to curiosity and language there is the process of social differentiation and development in the period between 7 months and 2 years of age. We have been repeatedly fascinated as we have watched the relatively undifferentiated 7-month-old become a complicated social creature by his second birthday. We have noted the social skills that we have identified in very talented 3- to 6-year-olds surfacing with regularity at certain stages during that period. First to appear are an increasing variety of attempts at getting and holding attention, followed by the emergence of the ability to use an adult as a resource, the expression of pride in achievement, the first signs of make-believe or fantasy activities, the expression of interpersonal affection and mild annoyance, and then attempts at leading and following and competing with other people. All these skills surface fairly rapidly under the best of circumstances between 7 and 36 months of age and can lead to a complicated, delightful 3-year-old. On the other hand, the process can easily go sour and produce a

3-year-old who is relatively low on social competencies and/or not terribly pleasant to live with.

Finally, starting at 7 months or so the infant routinely moves away from the first exploration of his own simple hand-eye and body skills on to the beginning of interest in the object world around him. The growth of interest in objects, their motions, their physical characteristics, and in simple cause and effect phenomena has been beautifully detailed by Piaget (1952). How much a child learns as he explores small objects, and how much his intellectual curiosity is stimulated during the process seems to be determined, in large part, by the childrearing practices he is exposed to during the months between 7 and 36.

This view of four fundamental educational processes that seem to be undergoing very rapid development between 7 and 36 months of age and at the same time seem to be at risk underlies our conviction that the time to begin to structure experiences that might help a child develop well should be no later than 7 months.

There are other less theoretical reasons for starting at that point. The difficulties involved in rearing children begin to escalate from 6 or 7 months on as that child begins to be able to crawl about the home. Locomobility markedly increases the likelihood that the child will get hurt or into mischief or damage things in the home or aggravate an older sibling, etc. Children who are just beginning to crawl are quite naive about danger. They are incredibly curious. They use their mouths to explore many things. They are impulsive, clumsy, and forgetful. These characteristics lead to danger to the child and extra work for the parents. A parent who is trying to cope with such stresses is less able to concern herself or himself with the child's educational development. Indeed, one of the most common ways of coping with the onset of locomobility is to confine the child for the better part of the day to prevent the extra work and the danger, etc. Prolonged restriction to playpens and a jumpseat or long naps in the crib morning and afternoon, etc., are often used for these purposes. Simultaneously, from the research we have reported, such practices seem to interfere with the optimal development of abilities in children.

For these reasons we started our program of intervention with the experimental group when the children were 5 months of age. By the time the children were 8 months we entered into more intensive family support that lasted until the children were 18 months of age. By that time the children would have been well into negativism and the parents would have adopted whatever styles of adjustment they deemed suitable.

We could not tell the pediatric control group when they should make their inputs into the families they were guiding. All we asked was that they make their inputs before the child was 2 years of age because by then we assumed that we could get reasonably stable indications of how well the children had done in the study. The design for data collection is presented in figures 3-1, 3-2, and 3-3.

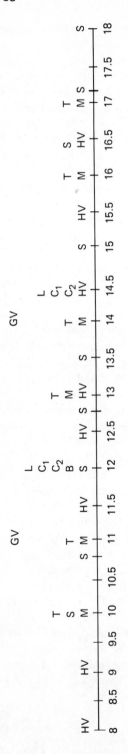

Key: GV = Group visit
      T = Collection of task data
      S = Collection of social competence data
      M = Collection of maternal behavior data
      HV = Home visit
      B = Bayley Scales of Infant Development
      L = Preschool Project Test of Receptive Language Ability
      C₁ = Preschool Project Test of Sensing Dissonance
      C₂ = Preschool Project Test of Abstract Abilities

Figure 3-1. Schedule for Intervention Program and Process Monitoring.

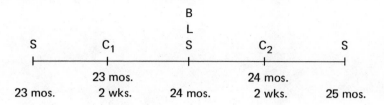

Chronological Age of Child (months and weeks)

Key: S = Preschool Project Test of Social Abilities
       B = Mental Scale, Bayley Test of Infant Development
       L = Preschool Project Test of Language Ability
       C_1 = Preschool Project Test for Sensing Dissonance
       C_2 = Preschool Project Test for Abstract Ability

Figure 3-2. Assessment Schedule I.

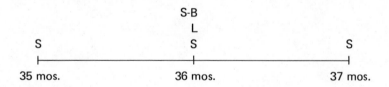

Key: S   = Preschool Project Test of Social Abilities
      S-B = Stanford-Binet Intelligence Test
      L   = Preschool Project Test of Language Ability

Figure 3-3. Assessment Schedule II.

Note

1. Except for children scoring more than one standard deviation below average repeatedly (Passamanick et al. 1956).

4 Subjects

What kinds of subjects were needed for this study? Heber worked with children whose mothers and older siblings were retarded as a result of "sociocultural" factors (Heber et al. 1972). He excluded cases of retardation with a likely physical basis. In the absence of any intervention, these new children would be expected to acquire similarly limited levels of linguistic and intellectual ability. The room for improvement or "experimental impact" was therefore probably maximal. Furthermore, the program involved full-time substitute childrearing by a well-trained staff, thereby heightening the likelihood of a generally good quality of early experience.

The Ira Gordon program (Gordon and Lally 1967), one of the earliest to focus on educational intervention in infancy, also focused on children for whom the prospects for high achievement were poor. The families Gordon worked with were of low income and limited education. Once again the margin for impact of the special training was substantial. Unlike the Heber study, however, the Gordon study was designed to modify and support the parents' childrearing efforts rather than bypass them. In addition, the staff that trained the parents was recruited from welfare ranks. As a result of both factors, the Gordon study was not likely to produce as much of an increase in developing abilities as the Heber study. Indeed, it did not.

We have always been interested in two questions. First, how much of a contribution to developing abilities is made by early experience? And second, how can families do the best possible job of helping their new children make the most of their innate potential? The Heber model would have allowed us to pursue the first question with effectiveness. However, we could not use that model to deal with the second question, family effectiveness. Therefore, we compromised. We decided to work with families with average childrearing capacities. As a result, we could not expect as great an impact on the children we worked with as either Heber or Gordon. On the other hand, we might be able to generalize our results to more of the population than the other studies.

An immediate problem confronted us: How could we tell what the childrearing capacities of a family were? After all, unlike income level, no one had figured out how to rate a family on this dimension. As in our natural experiment, we decided to estimate a family's childrearing capacity from the achievement level of its older children. We designed a set of screening procedures to evaluate the educational level of the older children in eligible families. In addition to the achievement level of the older children, we were interested in other factors that were pertinent to the experiment. We were concerned with anything that might interfere with the implementation of the ideas we wanted to test. We therefore screened for potential language difficulties (was English the family's first language), for competition from other sources of ideas about childrearing, and for the socioeconomic status of the family.

Screening Process

Criteria for Elimination from the Study: Families with More Than One Child

1. If the mother's ethnic background is other than Jewish, Anglo-Saxon, Italian, Irish, or Spanish.
2. If either parent was born someplace other than the United States, Canada, or Puerto Rico (it doesn't matter where the grandparents were born).
3. If the family falls in either Level I or V on the Hollingshead-Redlich Scale.
4. If any language other than English is the primary language spoken in the home.
5. If there are more than three children in the family.
6. If there is any person who has an obvious, strong influence on the mother's childrearing practices (e.g., mother or mother-in-law).
7. If the family does not have a child in the 2 to 5 age range.
8. a.   If Ammons score of older sibling is in 90 to 110 percent range, *include* family in study.
   b.   If Ammons score is in 80 to 90 or 110 to 130 percent range, *test* older sibling with Binet.
   c.   If Binet falls in the 90 to 110 percent range, *include* family in study.
9. If the mother has not completed the eighth grade or has graduated from college with honors or taken any graduate courses.
10. If the infant's Bayley test score is below 90.
11. If the infant is handicapped in any way, either visually or auditorily, or if birth weight was under 5 pounds.

We did not want to restrict our experiment to families with more than one child. It seemed obvious that information about how first-time parents responded to our program was also needed. We therefore decided that eight of the fifteen families in each group would have only one child, others would have two children, and the balance three. Unfortunately, identifying first-time parents of average childrearing ability was even riskier than selecting those whose handiwork could be assessed. Our criteria for screening first-time parents are presented below.

Criteria for Elimination from the Study:
First-Born Children

A. To ensure that ideas will get a fair test, eliminate applicants:

    1. If the mother's ethnic background is other than Jewish, Anglo-Saxon, Italian, Irish, or Spanish.

    2. If either parent was born someplace other than the United States, Canada, or Puerto Rico (it doesn't matter where the grandparents were born).

    3. If the family falls in either Level I or V on the Hollingshead-Redlich Scale.

    4. If any language other than English is the primary language spoken in the home.

    5. If there is any person who has an obvious, strong influence on the mother's childrearing practices (e.g., mother or mother-in-law).

B. To ensure these ideas will have some impact, eliminate applicants:

    6. If the mother has not completed the eighth grade or has attended college (high school graduation is the upper limit on education).

    7. If the mother has any relevant work experience or educational background pertaining to early childhood.

    8. If the mother's intelligence level is above average (to be determined by testing).

C. Infant criteria:

    9. If the infant's Bayley test score is below 90, the family will be eliminated from the study.

    10. If the infant is handicapped in any way, either visually or auditorily, or if birth weight was under 5 pounds, exclude family from study.

Ideally, all four groups of families should have been selected from one simultaneously identified large group. Unfortunately, this was not possible since the director of the pediatric group felt he had to be the medical as well as the educational resource for his families. Therefore, he recruited his group independently. The results were that his group took much longer to recruit and, more important, did not meet our criteria adequately enough to be considered matched. Tables 4-1 and 4-2 indicate the outstanding characteristics of the four groups. As you can see, all groups were well matched except for the pediatric group.

Table 4-1
Distribution of Subjects on Matched Dimensions

	Experimental (N = 14)	Control I (N = 15)	Control II (N = 15)	Medical (N = 15)
Birth order				
1	7	8	8	13
2	5	5	5	2
3	2	2	2	–
Mother's education				
Less than high school	0	0	0	1
High school	8	9	9	4
High school, plus	6	6	6	10
SES				
II	2	2	3	6
III	10	10	8	9
IV	2	3	4	0
Sibling gap				
Median	48 mos.	41 mos.	34 mos.	16 mos.
Sex				
M	7	6	8	10
F	7	9	7	5

Perhaps the most important differences were that thirteen of the fifteen families in the PC had only one child and the verbal abilities of the mothers were considerably higher than those of the other groups. We resigned ourselves to the situation, because by the time all the PC families had been recruited it was too late to do anything else.

The Problem of Self-Selected Samples

A classical problem in intervention research in education is that the families who participate are by virtue of their interest in participating likely to be somewhat atypical. In particular, they appear to be more interested in education and in relating to professionals than other families. This collection of special attributes forms the basis of a common obstacle to proper scientific research known as "self-selection of subjects." There is reason to believe that this factor has contaminated much research, especially that of the last decade. In the work of P. Levenstein, for example, when families were accepted for special training on a first come, first serve basis, the results of training were quite impressive as compared with the results of children from untrained families. This finding was repeated several times and helped establish the Levenstein program as one of the most promising in preschool educational research. It was not until recently, however, that Levenstein began to follow the more traditional practice of random assignment of families to training or control group status. When she

Table 4-2
Distribution of Subjects on Unmatched Dimensions

	Experimental (N = 14)	Control I (N = 15)	Control II (N = 15)	Medical (N = 15)
Mother's Quick Word Test				
Median	67	72	68	85
Range	52-78	51-89	57-85	69-90
Father's education				
Less than high school	1	1	0	0
High school	7	5	8	2
High school, plus	4	6	4	6
College	2	3	2	3
Graduate training	0	0	1	4

did, the impressive effects of training found in previous studies did not reappear (Madden et al. 1976).

Can the confounding effects of self-selected samples be controlled? Random assignment to conditions can equate for self-selection across groups but cannot totally eliminate the effects of self-selection. After all, families that participate in educational research are to some extent not truly representative of *all* families to the extent that some families will *not* participate in such research. All that a research project can do is attempt to minimize the effects of self-selection. To some degree, the rejection rate experienced by a project may be an indication of the degree to which self-selection is a factor. We were comparatively fortunate in this regard. Had we been recruiting families from the lowest levels of the socioeconomic spectrum, we undoubtedly would have been considerably less successful.

Recruitment Process

The details of our recruiting process were as follows.

A. Inspection of birth records, screening out those infants:

1. Which were not born in January, February, March, or April of 1974.
2. Which were not residents of Arlington, Boston (all sections), Cambridge, Chelsea, Everett, Medford, Newton, Somerville, Waltham, or Watertown (areas generally within 20 miles of the university).
3. Which were not of parents born in the United States, Puerto Rico, or Canada.
4. Which were multiple births (twins, etc.).

B.   In the introductory letter, screening out those families:

1.   Which had more than three children.
2.   Which had an older sibling younger than 20 months of age at the infant's birth.
3.   Which had moved out of the selected residential areas.

C.   In the telephone interview, screening out those families:

1.   Which were planning to move out of the area during the time of the study.
2.   Whose cultural background had exceptionally strong influence on the childrearing practices (e.g., Jehovah's Witness).
3.   In which there was some other especially strong influence on the family's childrearing practices (e.g., mother or mother-in-law).
4.   In which English was not the primary language spoken.
5.   Where the mother's education was less than completion of the eighth grade or more than one year past high school.
6.   Where the family was participating in other research.
7.   Where the mother worked such that visits would be difficult to schedule.
8.   Where family health constituted a significant problem.
9.   Where infant health constituted a significant problem.
10. Where the mother had relevant work or educational experience which might conflict with our program.

D.   In the home interview, screening out those families:

1.   Whose SES level was not II, III, or IV on the Hollingshead-Redlich Scale.
2.   Where an older sibling scored too low or too high on the Ammons Language Test.
     a.   If the Ammons score of the older sibling was in the 90 to 110 percent range, we *included* the family in the study.
     b.   If the Ammons score was in the 80 to 90 or 110 to 130 percent range and the older sibling was at least 3 years old, we *tested* with the Stanford-Binet test.
     c.   If the Binet score fell in the 90 to 110 percent range, we *included* the family.
3.   Where the mother's language ability was above or below average, as indicated by the Ammons Quick Word Test.

    a.   For mothers who were not high school graduates, the scores were compared with norms for grades 9 to 12; $X = 60.8$ $(44.9 - 76.7 = 1$ SD$)$.

    b.   For mothers who were high school graduates, the scores were compared with the grade 12 norms; $X = 66.4$ $(51.3 - 81.7 = 1$ SD$)$.

    c.   For mothers who had post-high-school education, the upper limit of the range was extended to 90.

After these four stages of the screening, the infants were tested with the Bayley (Mental) Scale of Infant Development. A score of less than one standard deviation below the mean was used as an additional screening device.

The eligible families were then matched on the dimensions of birth order, mother's education, SES, sibling gap, and sex. They were then randomly assigned to three groups. The experimental group (E) was informed that their commitment would involve home visits every 2 to 3 weeks and group meetings often. The monitored control group (C_1) was informed that home visits would begin when the infant was 8 months old and occur every 2 to 3 weeks until the infant was 27 months old. The pretest and posttest control group (C_2) was told that according to the luck of the draw their involvement would be modest, with home visits when the child was about 2 years of age.

The families were advised that the final selection would reduce each group from eighteen to fifteen families and would be made within 3 months. We reserved those final options in case of unforeseen factors that might have surfaced as we began to work with the families. Indeed, shortly after we made our final sample decisions, a serious illness forced one family to withdraw from the study.

This long selection process produced three reasonably well-matched groups (see table 4-3). Even so, we could not control for *all* important variables. The parents of the children could be matched only imperfectly with regard to childrearing capacities. Further attempts (such as equating for personality characteristics, etc.) seemed to us impractical. In light of the small samples involved and the nature of the research, this was unfortunate and illustrates one of the special difficulties of this type of educational research.

Results of the Recruitment Process

Table 4-4 contains information on the details of our recruitment experience. One important question to ask of any project of this sort is: "What percentage of eligible families declined to participate in the study?" Such information would be of some help in estimating the size of the sample selection impact. Unfortunately, we cannot provide that information. We sent out 1,900 letters

Table 4-3
Demographic Information for Comparative Study

Subject No.	Birth-date	Birth Order[a]	Mother's Education[b]	SES[c]	Sibling Gap[d]	Sex	Mother's Quick Word Test	Father's Education	Father's Occupation
Experimental Group (E), (N = 14)									
1	1-5-74	1	HS	III	—	F	65	HS	Adm. supervisor
2	1-20-74	2	+HS	III	25 mos.	F	70	HS	Service rep.
3	1-28-74	1	HS	III	—	F	67	Partial college	X-ray tech.
4	1-31-74	2	HS	III	51 mos.	M	73	HS	Electronic assembler
5	2-5-74	2	HS	III	30 mos.	F	67	HS	Wallpaper hanger
6	2-7-74	1	+HS	II	—	M	65	College graduate	Teacher
7	2-13-74	3	+HS	III	48 mos. (78 mos.)	F	78	HS	Sales rep.
8	2-26-74	1	+HS	III	—	M	73	Partial college	Mechanic
9	2-27-74	3	HS	III	95 mos. (107 mos.)	M	71	Partial college	Salesman
10	3-14-74	1	HS	IV	—	M	66	Partial HS	Painter
11	3-15-74	1	+HS	III	—	F	60	Partial college	Accountant
12	3-16-74	1	HS	III	—	M	67	HS	Mechanic
13	3-28-74	2	HS	IV	53 mos.	F	52	HS	Truck driver
14	4-10-74	2	+HS	II	47 mos.	M	74	College graduate	Accountant
Observed and Tested on Experimental Schedule Group (C$_1$), N = 15									
15	1-18-74	3	+HS	III	41 mos. (59 mos.)	M	68	College graduate	Insurance appraiser
16	1-24-74	1	+HS	III	—	F	83	Partial HS	Painter
17	1-28-74	2	HS	IV	43 mos.	M	67	HS	Shipper/receiver
18	1-31-74	1	HS	IV	—	F	65	HS	Newspaper handler
19	1-31-74	1	HS	II	—	F	64	College graduate	Fund administrator
20	2-5-74	1	+HS	III	—	F	73	Partial college	Computer programmer
21	2-9-74	2	+HS	III	63 mos.	F	78	Partial college	Steam engineer
22	2-10-74	1	+HS	III	—	M	89	HS	Chemical worker
23	2-14-74	2	HS	III	62 mos.	F	72	Partial college	Electronics technician
24	2-26-74	3	HS	III	32 mos. (48 mos.)	M	76	HS	Phone installer

Subject	Date		Code		Months	Sex	Score	Education	Occupation
25	3-7-74	1	HS	II	–	F	80	College graduate	Insurance supervisor
26	3-15-74	2	+HS	III	25 mos.	M	68	Partial college	Insurance underwriter
27	3-25-74	1	HS	III	–	F	72	Partial college	Elevator mechanic
28	3-29-74	1	HS	III	–	M	56	HS	Mechanic
29	3-31-74	2	HS	IV	30 mos.	F	51	Partial college	Truck driver

Pretest and Posttest Group (C_2), N = 15

Subject	Date		Code		Months	Sex	Score	Education	Occupation
30	1-5-74	1	HS	IV	–	F	68	HS	Shipper
31	1-8-74	1	+HS	II	–	F	61	College graduate	Accountant
32	1-19-74	1	HS	III	–	M	66	HS	Truck driver
33	1-25-74	3	HS	III	43 mos. (80 mos.)	F	62	Partial college	Car salesman
34	2-5-74	2	HS	III	31 mos.	M	57	Partial college	Fireman
35	2-9-74	1	HS	III	–	F	63	HS	Mailman
36	2-13-74	2	HS	III	34 mos.	M	74	Partial college	Student
37	2-19-74	1	+HS	III	–	F	70	HS	Bookkeeper
38	2-27-74	2	HS	III	33 mos.	M	74	Partial college	Engineer aide
39	2-28-74	1	HS	IV	–	M	57	HS	Laborer
40	3-3-74	3	+HS	II	29 mos. (51 mos.)	F	85	Graduate training	Systems analyst
41	3-4-74	1	+HS	II	–	M	70	College graduate	Programmer
42	3-10-74	2	HS	III	52 mos.	M	74	HS	Postal employee
43	3-13-74	1	+HS	IV	–	F	68	HS	Cloth spreader
44	4-13-74	2	+HS	IV	41 mos.	M	84	HS	Unemployed

Medical Group (PC), N = 15

Subject	Date		Code		Months	Sex	Score	Education	Occupation
45	8-17-74	1	+HS	II	–	F	87	+HS	Systems coordinator
46	8-20-74	1	+HS	III	–	F	83	HS	Cabinetmaker
47	8-25-74	1	+HS	II	–	M	69	Graduate training	Guidance counsellor
48	8-30-74	1	+HS	II	–	M	86	College graduate	Probation officer
49	10-4-74	2	+HS	II	21 mos.	M	90	Graduate training	Teacher
50	10-10-74	2	HS	III	12 mos.	F	74	+HS	Mechanic
51	11-9-74	1	HS	III	–	M	80	+HS	Payroll clerk
52	11-18-74	1	+HS	III	–	M	78	College graduate	Accountant
53	11-27-74	1	+HS	III	–	M	75	+HS	Photographer

Table 4-3 continued

Subject No.	Birth-date	Birth-Order[a]	Mother's Education[b]	SES[c]	Sibling Gap[d]	Sex	Mother's Quick Word Test	Father's Education	Father's Occupation
54	11-29-74	1	+HS	II	—	M	85	Graduate training	Student
55	1-8-75	1	-HS	III	—	F	76	+ HS	Foreman
56	1-8-75	1	HS	III	—	M	85	College graduate	Sheetmetal engineer
57	1-23-75	1	HS	III	—	M	88	+HS	Salesman
58	1-28-75	1	HS	III	—	F	86	HS	Post office clerk
59	1-30-75	1	+HS	II	—	M	85	Graduate training	Teacher

[a]Firstborn = 1; second born = 2; third born = 3.

[b]HS = high school; +HS = more than high school; -HS = less than high school.

[c]Hollingshead-Redlich Scale.

[d](x mos.) = gap between oldest (of three) and infant.

Table 4-4
Recruitment Results

Process Stage	Number of Families
I. *Inspection of birth records* (For eligibility concerning residence, birthplace of parents, etc.)	6,713
II. *Introductory letter* (eligible families) (With additional screening functions, see item I)	1,900
Responses	253
Ineligible families and bases for ineligibility	
Number of children (too many)	18
Sibling gap (too narrow)	12
Residence	3
Eligible families remaining	220
III. *Telephone interview*	
Ineligible families and bases for ineligibility	
Planning to move	14
Cultural background	15
Mother's education	58
Other research involvement	1
Mother working full time	7
Family health problems	5
Infant health problems	6
No longer interested	2
Other	15
Eligible families remaining	97
IV. *Home interviews*	
Ineligible families and bases for ineligibility	
Mother's verbal ability (too high or too low)	17
Sibling's verbal ability (too high or too low)	16
Sibling's mental ability (too high or too low)	3
Eligible families remaining	61
V. *The Bayley Mental Index Test* Ineligible families (infant scored too low)	2
Eligible families remaining	59
VI. *Final selection and matching process* Families not retained	14
Families in final enrollment (exclusive of the PC group)	45

Note: One family dropped out of the study some weeks later due to health problems. The final number of families in the E, C_1, and C_2 groups was 44.

during step two of our multistepped recruitment process, but these letters were not simply invitations. They contained eligibility criteria (to save a huge amount of work). As a result, we cannot distinguish between those who were eligible (at that point) but chose *not* to respond and participate versus those who did not respond because they were not eligible according to the requirements listed in

the letter. Throughout the balance of the process, however, nearly all the families we approached seemed anxious to participate.

Other materials involved in the recruitment process and in maintaining contact with the families are contained in exhibits 4-1 through 4-6.

HARVARD UNIVERSITY

GRADUATE SCHOOL OF EDUCATION

Roy E. Larsen Hall, Appian Way
Cambridge, Massachusetts 02138

Spring, 1974

Dear parents:

Congratulations on your new baby. Please excuse us for not writing a personal letter to you; it is just not possible.

We have been studying the development of babies for the past nine years. Our main interest is the experiences that children have in the first few years of life. In order to continue our work we need help from about 60 families. We will visit with some families regularly for about a year, while with others, we will only drop in a few times. The names of families will be kept confidential.

For each visit families will be paid $5. Eligible families will receive from $35 to $200 depending on how often we visit.

Your family may be eligible if:

1. Your income is between $7,000 and $12,000 (approximate).
2. You have a high school education (approximate).
3. You have one, two or three children.
4. English is the main language spoken in your home.
5. Your new baby is in good health.

If you think you may be interested in helping us, please fill out the enclosed form and return it in the envelope we have provided.

If you have any questions, please call the Preschool Project at 495-3530 or 495-3531 and ask for Mrs. Kaban, Mrs. Shapiro or Mrs. Constable.

Yours truly,

Burton L. White, Ph.D.
Director, Preschool Project

Enclosures

Exhibit 4-1. Initial Recruitment Letter

Harvard Preschool Project

Name: _____

Address: _____

_____

Telephone: _____

Names of Children   Birthdates

_____   _____

_____   _____

_____   _____

_____   _____

_____   _____

What would be the best time of day to call you for an appointment?

_____

Exhibit 4-1 continued

Name of S: _____

Birthdate: _____

4-Month Bayley score: _____

Mother's education: _____

Mother's Quick Word Test score: _____

Older sibling's name: _____

Birthdate: _____

Ammons score: _____

    Developmental age _____

    Chronological age _____

    90 to 110 percent range _____

Binet score: _____

Eligible: Yes _____   No _____

If no, state reason: _____

_____

Exhibit 4-2. Eligibility Sheet

Name of child: _____ Interviewer: _____

Birthdate: _____ Date of Interview: _____

Preliminary Interview

Background Information

I would like to ask you some background information. Do not feel obliged

to answer any questions if you want to keep the information private.

1.   Mother's name   _____

2.   Where were you born? _____

3.   When were you born? _____

4.   What is the last grade you completed in school? _____

5.   What education have you had since high school? _____

         What college did you attend? _____

         Did you receive any honors in college? _____

6.   Do you presently work? _____

7.   Did you work before your children were born? _____

8.   Does anyone other than M take care of S on a regular basis? _____

         Who? _____

         When? _____

9.   What is your cultural background?

         Anglo-Saxon_____

         Jewish_____

         Italian_____

         Irish _____

         Spanish _____

         Other_____

Exhibit 4-2 continued

10. Are there any members of your family (e.g., parents or grandparents) who were

    not born in the United States _____

        Where? _____

        Parents _____ Grandparents _____

    At what age did they come to this country?_____

11. Father's name _____

12. Father's address _____

13. Where was your husband born? _____

14. When was your husband born? _____

15. What is your husband's cultural background?

        Anglo-Saxon _____

        Jewish _____

        Italian _____

        Irish _____

        Spanish _____

        Other _____

16. Who in your husband's family was not born in the United States?

        Where? _____

        Parents _____ Grandparents _____

        At what age did they come to this country? _____

17. What is the last grade your husband completed in school? _____

18. What education has he had since high school? _____

        What college did he attend? _____

        Did he receive any honors in college? _____

Exhibit 4-2 continued

19.   What is your husband's occupation? _____

20.   Do you have any plans to move within the next year? _____

                              Where? _____

21.   Do you take a vacation at a specific time each year? _____

             Where? _____

             How long? _____

22.   Does anyone other than your immediate family live with you? _____

             Specify relationship _____

23.   Is any language other than English spoken in the home? _____

             Which? _____

             How frequently? _____

             By whom? _____

24.   What is your primary source of information about child-rearing practices?

             Pediatrician _____

             Dr. Spock _____

             Television _____

             Mother _____

             Mother-in-law _____

             Books _____

             Other _____

25.   Have you or any of your children been involved in a research project before?

             When? _____

             Where? _____

Exhibit 4-2 continued

Medical Information

I would like to ask some general questions about the health of the members

of your family.

1.   Is anyone in the family presently receiving treatment or therapy? _____

        Who? _____

        Why? _____

2.   Has anyone in the family been hospitalized during the past year (excluding

        birth)? _____

        Who? _____

        Why? _____

        How long? _____

3.   Did S or M have any difficulty around the time of birth? _____

_____

4.   What was S's weight at birth? _____

5.   Has S received any special medical treatment since he has come home from

        the hospital? _____

_____

6.   Do you have a specific pediatrician that you use regularly? _____

        Name _____

        Address _____

_____

If the answer is no:

        Is there a clinic that you use regularly for medical care for your children?_____

        Name _____

        Address _____

_____

Exhibit 4-2 continued

HARVARD UNIVERSITY

GRADUATE SCHOOL OF EDUCATION

Roy E. Larsen Hall, Appian Way
Cambridge, Massachusetts 02138

We are enclosing a copy of the schedule of home visits we are planning from the time your baby is 10 months old through 18 months.

You will notice there are two types of visits. First, we will be observing the baby's behavior as it naturally occurs in your home. Secondly, we have planned five games sessions so that we can observe the baby playing with toys and materials that we have selected.

The amount of time a visit will take ranges from 30 to 90 minutes. We schedule these visits at your convenience while your baby is awake.

If you have any questions, please feel free to call Mrs. Kaban, Mrs. Shapiro, or Mrs. Attanucci at 495-3530.

Yours truly,

Burton L. White, Ph.D.
Director, Preschool Project

BK/cl
Enclosure

Exhibit 4-3. Letter to E, C_1, and PC Groups

When the baby is:

Age	Observation
10 months	2 observations of the baby
10 months, 3 weeks	1 observation
11 months	1 observation
12 months	3 games sessions with the baby
12 months	1 observation
12 months, 3 weeks	1 observation
13 months	1 observation
13 months, 2 weeks	1 observation
14 months	1 observation
14 months, 2 weeks	2 games sessions with the baby
16 months	1 observation
16 months, 2 weeks	1 observation
17 months	1 observation
17 months, 1 week	1 observation
18 months	1 observation

Exhibit 4-4. Harvard Preschool Project Schedule of Home Visits

HARVARD UNIVERSITY

GRADUATE SCHOOL OF EDUCATION

Roy E. Larsen Hall, Appian Way
Cambridge, Massachusetts 02138

　　　　We are very grateful for your cooperation with the
Preschool Project during the past year.

　　　　When your child is 23 months old we would like to
begin a number of observations and play sessions which
will involve about two visits per month in the 23-25
month period. A member of our staff, Genie Ware, will
make appointments with you. Make the appointments at
times convenient for you and at times the baby is awake.
We keep records of the visits and will forward a check
for $5 for each observation.

　　　　We hope all is well with you and your baby. If you
have any questions, feel free to call at 495-3530.

　　　　　　　　　　　　　　　Yours truly,

　　　　　　　　　　　　　　　Burton L. White, Ph.D.
　　　　　　　　　　　　　　　Director, Preschool Project

BLW:tk

Exhibit 4-5. Letter to E, C_1, C_2, and PC Groups

HARVARD UNIVERSITY

GRADUATE SCHOOL OF EDUCATION

Roy E. Larsen Hall, Appian Way
Cambridge, Massachusetts 02138

We sincerely appreciate your participation in the
Preschool Project for the past two years. We are
presently planning to follow-up on your child's progress
at three years of age. Would you take a minute to fill
out the enclosed address form so that we can reach you
at that time?

We hope everything is going well with you and look
forward to seeing you again.

Sincerely,

Jane Attanucci

Exhibit 4-6. Second Letter to E, C_1, C_2, and PC Groups

5 Procedures

Experimental Treatment

Having recruited three samples of families, matched for important characteristics, we then faced the task of putting our hypotheses about effective childrearing to an experimental test. This goal required that the families in group E be convinced of the value of our recommendations and then help to act on them with their new children over a period of many months.

We tried to use the experience we gained from the pilot study with the new families. Once again we began to work with the families when their children turned 5 months of age. The first 3 months of contact were oriented toward preparation for the time when the children would begin to crawl and to learn the meaning of words. Group visits at the university were followed by private visits to the home. From 8 through 16 months we emphasized individual home visits considerably more than group visits.

Each home visitor worked with each of the families. After every home visit, a brief report was written and distributed to all home visitors. The home visiting staff met regularly to discuss each family. These discussions and the observational information on new behaviors provided a balanced and detailed picture of each family as the study progressed.

The contents of the training program along with related information, such as which films were used, can be found in the appendixes to *Experience and Environment*, Volume 2. We took pains *not* to overwhelm our families with our teachings. We kept our lesson plans limited in coverage and as free as possible from jargon.

Furthermore, we made it clear from the beginning that we were educational specialists. When other topics came up, we suggested the appropriate professional, medical, welfare, etc., assistance and offered help, if the family needed it, in obtaining such aid.

Data Collection

Monitoring the Process of Development:
Assessing Childrearing Practices

Information on the childrearing practices of the families in groups E and C_1 was gathered by the training staff on a regular basis according to schedule. The information thus obtained helped the training staff determine how well the curriculum was being implemented. To gather this information we used our Adult Assessment Scales.

Sampling the Experiences of Children

The second step in process analysis in this study was the examination of the actual experiences (or tasks) of the children. Once again, the training staff gathered these data on groups E and C_1. The instrument used was the Preschool Project Task Instrument (see *Experience and Environment,* Volume 1). As was the case with data on childrearing practices, the information on the child's patterns of experience was quite useful as feedback for our training efforts.

Monitoring the Development of Competence

All children were tested for general development when they were 4½ months of age. Children in groups E, C_1, and PC were tested several times between then and the time they were 14½ months of age. At 24 months, and again at 36 months, all children were retested. The details of the assessment program are contained in figures 3-2 and 3-3.

6 Findings

Process Analysis: The Behavior of Adults

Intervention studies in the field of early education are not new. Indeed, they have been around for many years (Skeels 1966), and since 1965 their numbers have increased dramatically. Typically, one proposes some sort of modification of the experiences of the children which is expected to either prevent or overcome a deficit in developing abilities. These modifications of experience very often are brought about by teachers dealing directly with children. At other times the impact is less direct; that is, an intervention can be designed to modify the stream of experience of children but not necessarily involve adults in any immediate didactic relationship to them. A case in point is our own early research with infants in which the role of the adult was to modify the physical circumstances around the cribs of young children (White 1971). The consequences of the experiences of children over many months were very substantial, but they did not follow from or include changes in the direct interactions of adults with children.

Over the years, research that monitored closely the actual behaviors of adults implementing curricula *and* the child's continuous stream of experience has rarely been attempted (see Barker 1963; Wright 1960; Schoggen and Schoggen 1971; Caldwell 1968; Clarke-Stewart 1973; and *Experience and Environment*, Volumes 1 and 2 for exceptions). More commonly, when a researcher wanted to evaluate the effects on children of various preschool curricula, for example, the design of the research involved identification of the curriculum, selection of matched groups, random assignment of groups to treatments, and gathering of information on how well the children did after having undergone exposure to each of the curricula for a set period of time. The problem with such evaluation research is that two important steps are left out. These steps are part of what we call *process analysis*.

The first step consists of an examination of how the curriculum manifests itself in the child's environment, that is, implementation. There have been many times in our experience when observations of classrooms and homes which supposedly differed dramatically on paper revealed that the situations were much more similar than assumed. One has to know the degree to which the adults act in a manner that is consistent with the curriculum objectives. The more specific the curriculum, the more analytical the analysis of the adults' behavior must be.

Next, there is the question of the relationships among the behaviors of the adults and the kinds of experiences the children undergo. For example, in our observations in nursery school classrooms, the curriculum at times dictated that there be a storytelling session for the 3- or 4-year-old children. The teacher might very well be reading a story to a group of children. From the schedule and the teacher's behavior an evaluator might assume that the experience of the children during that period of time consisted of listening to a story. But anybody who has ever been in a nursery school for any length of time has learned that the degree of attention paid to teacher-directed activity varies widely from child to child. Though the curriculum may dictate that the period be devoted to storytelling, the reaction of the children might range from rapt attention to the teacher to intermittent attention, horseplay with a neighbor, or daydreaming. For each of these children the experience would be quite different, despite the fact that the stated curriculum and the teacher behavior were for each child identical. The point is simple, but fundamental: if one wants to do substantial research in the area of intervention studies, one has no alternative but to design the research to include process analysis, so that the particular learning events that children are exposed to are dealt with in a reliable and quantitative fashion. Anything short of this approach is less valid scientifically.

To say that process analysis is essential in good educational research is relatively easy. To perform such research is something else again. First of all, it is difficult and expensive. Another deterrent is the well-known observer effect. Anyone who does this kind of research is aware of the fact that an evaluation team in the classroom or in the home, or even a single evaluator in either place, is likely to have a substantial impact on the behavior of the people being observed (especially the adults) and therefore on the entire process. The distortion of reality caused by the observer is something that people have been concerned about for some time, but no one as yet has managed to find a solution to the problem.

It is a rare evaluation design that includes an attempt at process analysis. It is rarer yet to find a design that covers the process as thoroughly as one might. For example, a recent book by Yarrow et al. (1975) describes an attempt at a closer look at the problem of experience and development during human infancy. Their large, high-quality effort included an attempt at sampling the behavior of parents and the experiences of children during infancy. Unfortunately, the design was such that the researchers visited the homes of the subjects only twice during the sixth month of life. The sixth month of life happens to be a relatively inappropriate time to gather such data because it is not representative of infancy for several reasons. This fact notwithstanding, however, the practice of going to a home for only one or two or even three or four data-gathering sessions is, in our opinion, unwise. We have found over a period of almost a decade of observational research in homes that it takes a minimum of four or five visits before parents reduce their efforts to put on a special exhibition for you. To allow a research project access to your home while you go about your ordinary activities turns out to be too difficult for most of the adults we know to assimilate with ease.

One has to add to this set of difficulties the fact that all but the most trivial kinds of data-gathering processes in intervention studies are very difficult and expensive to execute. Unless you are interested solely in the physical movements of a subject, you will run into problems of conceptual design and the reliability of the assessment procedure. A few researchers have grappled with this problem over the years (Clarke-Stewart 1973; Caldwell 1968; Schoggen and Schoggen 1971; Barker 1963; Wright 1960; and *Experience and Environment*, Volumes 1 and 2). None of us has come away unscatched. The richer one makes one's data-gathering procedure conceptually, the further away one gets from acceptable interobserver reliabilities. The fact of the matter is that this is a difficult chore, one for which the field has not, over the years, provided a history of successful activity to build upon.

If one does indeed manage to create a workable adult observation scale, one then runs into the problem of sampling the behavior stream of the child. Many an instrument has been created to tap only those times in the child's life when mother and child (or adult and child) are actively interacting. Unfortunately for science, in the normal home situation such a situation takes place only during a small fraction of the waking hours. By and large our estimates are that direct interaction between mother and child in a wide assortment of home situations ranges from as little as 5 to 10 percent of the day to a typical maximum of about 30 to 40 percent of the day. This leaves the majority of the child's experience, and therefore learning opportunities, untouched by adult-child interaction data-collecting processes. What then?

Our answer is inspired by the work of Barker and Wright, and Kurt Lewin (1951) before them. We systematically sample the continuous stream of experience of the young child. This turns out to be a complicated task, details of which have been dealt with in *Experience and Environment,* Volumes 1 and 2, and, of course, by the followers of Lewin.

There are then several points to make with respect to process analysis:

1. If you do not monitor the behavior of adults and the continuous stream of experience of the children involved, your research has to remain primitive.

2. Monitoring the implementation of a curriculum or a set of childrearing practices by an adult is an extremely difficult and expensive task. It involves sampling the process in question a minimum of four or five times with difficulty to construct and administer observational systems.

3. Monitoring or sampling the stream of experience of young children is even more complicated than data gathering on the performance of adults in that *under natural conditions* infants and toddlers spend four to five times more time each day in activities that do not involve interaction with adults than they do in interacting with them.

Is it any wonder that process analysis is rarely attempted, let alone done well? We have tried over the last 13 years to use process analysis in our research on the role of experience in the development of competence in preschool age children. We have not mastered the problems, but we have made a serious effort over a comparatively long period of time. What follows is a presentation of some of the results of such an approach with respect to our longitudinal experiment.

Monitoring the Behavior of Adults

Adults influence an infant's day-to-day experiences in two ways: by direct participation in events the child is experiencing at the moment (i.e., interacting proximally), and by their control over the child's daily schedule and general life circumstances (i.e., remote influence). Studies of direct interaction between adults and young children have been performed (e.g., Hess and Shipman 1965; Schoggen and Schoggen 1971), but not often, and especially not often outside the laboratory. They are particularly rare in the case of infants and toddlers in their own homes (*Experience and Environment*, Volumes 1 and 2; White et al., 1977; Caldwell 1968; Clarke-Stewart 1973).

As scarce as such studies are, it is quite important to note that they capture only a fraction of the adult influence on a young child's stream of experiences. We have found repeatedly that interactions between young children and their mothers (at home) rarely exceed 30 to 35 percent of the child's waking time. The major portion that remains is spent by the young child in solitary activities such as steady staring, examining small objects, or merely idling. Clearly the nature of such solitary activities is to some degree influenced by decisions made by adults. For example, if an infant's mother decides that her child will be put into a playpen for periods longer than 5 to 10 minutes at a time, the child will be unable to pursue certain activities because of the restrictions on his mobility. We have learned that he will soon usually show signs of boredom. In our observation of data gathering we label such situations *pass-time.* In previous work (*Experience and Environment*, Volume 2) the amount of such activity during the twelfth to fifteenth month was inversely related to achievement levels at 3 years of age.

It seems clear then that one needs to do more than sample interactions between infants and adults to understand the range of influences adults have on young children. We have approached this problem in two ways, neither of which is completely satisfactory. First, we have created two rating scales (*Experience and Environment*, Volume 2). One focuses on those aspects of an adult's childrearing tactics which we believe distinguished effective childrearers in the past. Practices rated include the availability of the mother to the child, the amount of access to the home allowed the child, etc. The second scale focuses on the likely effects of an adult's behavior on the development of the particular competencies we have found to distinguish well-developed 3- to 6-year-olds from other children. We have never placed much stock in rating scales, and perhaps as a result we have neither developed these instruments very well nor have we made much use of the data collected with them. We shall, however, present whatever we believe useful from our ratings information.

The second approach to the problem of assessing the indirect or distal influences of adults on infants is through our task instrument. Ultimately any influence, indirect or direct, must be reflected in the stream of experience. If our instrument is well designed and used, all adult influences, indeed all influences of any kind that have relevance for a child's learning opportunities, should be captured in the process that samples the stream of behavior. This distinction between levels of analysis is but one portion of a larger complex. For example, distal maternal influences, such as playpen use or a decision to seek day care for a child, are in turn influenced by the marital status of the child's parents and the larger milieu within which the family is nested. As one moves further from the child's stream of experience, the research domain shifts from educational psychology to social psychology to sociology, etc. It seems that a complete understanding of how a child develops will ultimately require a multileveled analysis. It also appears that we are some distance away from such a capability. At any rate, it is of some comfort to note that short of venturing beneath the skin in the manner of physiological psychologists, it is the educational psychologist who samples the stream of experience, who studies the actual consequences of all the external influences on the learning opportunities of the young child.

General Information on Child-Adult Interchanges

Table 6-1 presents information gathered with our adult-assessment scale about the quantity and quality of such interactions between mothers and children in our study. As a matter of standard procedure, we begin by combining as much of our data as possible across groups within the study for the purpose of giving the reader some sense of the general phenomena. In previous reports, before looking at differences in patterns of experience (tasks) as a function of levels of competence, for example, we started out by presenting information on patterns of experience on all children at different ages in the course of the study. In table 6-1, therefore, we have combined the data on the children in the experimental group with those of the children in the control group, who were monitored as they grew. The result is data on twenty-eight adult-infant or mother-infant pairs, half of whom were being actively guided by us as to their childrearing procedures and half of whom depended on a variety of other factors not directly influenced by us. A word of caution: Ideally, we should have data from a population that is representative of families at large. Unfortunately, such data do not exist; we offer this combination of information only as the best we have on

Table 6-1
Adult Assessment Scales Data

Behaviors		Ages of Children (months)		
		10-11	13-14	16-17
Interactions Initiated by the Child (All Children), N = 28				
Frequency of overtures				
(30-minute observation)	Median	5.3	6.0	7.5
	Range	2.5-11.0	0.0-12.5	2.0-12.5
Frequency of child purposes				
Procure a service	Median	0.5	1.5	2.0
	Range	0.0-3.0	0.0-7.0	0.0-6.0
Gain attention	Median	2.0	2.5	2.0
	Range	0.0-6.5	0.5-6.0	0.0-7.0
Maintain social contact	Median	0.0	0.8	1.0
	Range	0.0-2.0	0.0-2.5	0.0-5.5
Ease discomfort	Median	0.8	0.3	0.0
	Range	0.0-5.0	0.0-2.0	0.0-2.0
Quality of adults' responses (percent frequency)				
Timing of response				
Immediate (< 3 s)	Median	71.0	90.0	92.8
	Range	16.7-100.0	0.0-100.0	40.0-100.0
Delayed (>5 s)	Median	18.3	6.9	2.0
	Range	0.0-80.0	0.0-66.7	0.0-46.7
No response	Median	0.0	0.0	0.0
	Range	0.0-60.0	0.0-50.0	0.0-15.3
Rejects	Median	0.0	0.0	0.0
	Range	0.0	0.0-20.0	0.0-22.2
Perception of child's need				
Accurately	Median	97.2	100.0	100.0
	Range	20.0-100.0	0.0-100.0	50.0-100.0
Partially	Median	2.8	0.0	0.0
	Range	0.0-33.3	0.0-30.0	0.0-50.0
Not at all	Median	0.0	0.0	0.0
	Range	0.0-60.0	0.0-33.3	0.0-100.0
Level of difficulty of words				
Appropriate	Median	55.0	68.6	69.0
	Range	0.0-100.0	0.0-100.0	0.0-100.0
Too complex	Median	0.0	0.0	0.0
	Range	0.0	0.0	0.0
Too simple	Median	35.4	22.0	25.0
	Range	0.0-100.0	0.0-85.0	0.0-76.9
Babytalk	Median	0.0	0.0	0.0
	Range	0.0-20.0	0.0-25.0	0.0-14.3
None	Median	10.8	5.3	6.4
	Range	0.0-50.0	0.0-50.0	0.0-40.0
Provision of related ideas				
Yes	Median	40.8	64.3	52.9
	Range	11.0-93.3	0.0-100.0	0.0-93.7
No	Median	59.1	33.4	47.0
	Range	6.7-88.9	0.0-100.0	6.2-100.0
Complexity of language				
Complex sentence (>3 s)	Median	0.0	10.2	20.7
	Range	0.0-46.2	0.0-83.3	0.0-68.4
Phrase/sentence (<3 s)	Median	78.0	64.6	48.3
	Range	38.5-100.0	0.0-100.0	15.8-100.0

Table 6-1 continued

Behaviors		Ages of Children (months)		
		10-11	13-14	16-17
One word	Median	0.0	0.0	9.4
	Range	0.0-50.0	0.0-50.0	0.0-54.5
None	Median	10.8	2.6	5.7
	Range	0.0-50.0	0.0-50.0	0.0-28.6
Provision of encouragement, reinforcement, or enthusiasm				
Yes	Median	66.7	86.9	85.6
	Range	20.0-100.0	0.0-100.0	36.8-100.0
No	Median	13.5	0.0	9.7
	Range	0.0-71.4	0.0-50.0	0.0-46.7
Inappropriate	Median	17.0	0.0	2.0
	Range	0.0-80.0	0.0-50.0	0.0-28.6
Teaching realistic limits				
Yes	Median	12.7	9.5	12.1
	Range	0.0-53.3	0.0-50.0	0.0-57.9
No	Median	0.0	0.0	0.0
	Range	0.0-40.0	0.0-36.4	0.0-46.2
Inappropriate	Median	80.5	84.5	85.7
	Range	46.7-100.0	0.0-100.0	23.1-100.0
Satisfaction of child's needs				
Yes	Median	84.5	87.2	87.8
	Range	44.4-100.0	0.0-100.0	50.0-100.0
No	Median	2.8	2.6	0.0
	Range	0.0-30.8	0.0-50.0	0.0-42.9
Partial	Median	3.8	0.0	5.6
	Range	0.0-33.3	0.0-20.0	0.0-26.2
Average duration of adults' responses (seconds)	Median	22.8	45.3	26.6
Time spent by adults responding (percent duration)	Median	6.9	15.3	11.5
	Range	1.5-20.9	0.0-29.3	2.6-35.1

Interactions Initiated by the Adult, N = 28

Frequency of overtures (30-minute observation)				
	Median	6.8	8.5	9.5
	Range	1.0-17.0	1.0-24.0	2.5-17.5
Purpose of the interaction (percent frequency)				
Stimulating child	Median	4.6	6.6	5.9
	Range	0.0-45.3	0.0-28.3	0.0-36.8
Use of positive techniques to control the child	Median	1.0	2.7	2.1
	Range	0.0-24.2	0.0-23.1	0.0-9.3
Use of negative techniques to control the child	Median	0.5	0.7	0.6
	Range	0.0-5.1	0.0-7.2	0.0-4.4
Routine caretaking	Median	0.2	1.1	1.2
	Range	0.0-16.2	0.0-16.7	0.0-12.2
Emotional tone of the interaction (percent frequency)				
Positive	Median	85.0	86.6	84.7
	Range	0.0-100.0	25.0-100.0	4.1-100.0
Negative	Median	2.4	2.4	2.2
	Range	0.0-32.6	0.0-54.2	0.0-30.8
Neutral	Median	4.1	4.1	5.5
	Range	0.0-100.0	0.0-41.7	0.0-92.3

Table 6-1 continued

Behaviors		Ages of Children (months)		
		10-11	13-14	16-17
Average duration of adult-initiated interactions (seconds)	Median	20.1	30.9	22.2
Time spent by adult in adult-initiated interactions (percent duration)	Median Range	8.1 1.0-52.9	15.1 2.5-46.0	11.8 1.8-46.1
Total time spent by adults in interactions with children (percent duration)	Median Range	18.9 3.7-57.9	30.2 2.5-64.4	24.8 9.7-64.6

the subject. Some may feel that this procedure is hardly worth the effort. It is our judgment that it can be of value. We visited children and interacting adults in their own homes at several times throughout the day (between 9 A.M. and 6 P.M. weekdays) for 30 continuous minutes, twice in the 10- to 11-month age range, twice in the 13- to 14-month age range, and twice in the 16- to 17-month age range.[1] We present the data in those three groupings and also across the 11- to 16-month period. To the best of our knowledge, these data are unique, although people have been studying mother-infant interactions in other ways for some time.

Interchanges Initiated by the Child.

Frequency of Children's Overtures. At the beginning of the study when the children were 10 months old, the typical number of overtures for each 30-minute observational session was 5.3. As the children grew we found a steady increase in such behavior to 7.5 six months later. Though the range of such behavior was broad (0 to 12.5), this is somewhat misleading. In fact, nearly all the children made four to six or seven overtures per session. We were quite impressed by the stability of this type of behavior. The increase in overtures as the children entered the second year of life reflects the steady growth in social orientation (primarily toward the primary caretaker) which is a central feature of that period. Interestingly, firstborn children made only slightly more overtures than did later-born children.

Purposes. The apparent purposes children of this age have in mind when they approach an adult are few. They seek attention or help or comforting. At this tender age, they do not yet seek approval, nor do they try to direct the behavior of the adult, nor do they try to deliberately annoy other people. Before their third birthday, however, most children begin to engage in all the aforementioned activities (see Volumes 1 and 2). The most common purpose during this age range is seeking attention, followed by seeking assistance, and then seeking comfort.

The Quality of the Adult's Response to the Child. The most common occurrence was an immediate response (within 3 seconds), especially in the case of a firstborn child. On occasion a response was delayed for a few seconds, and deliberate or inadvertent absence of a response was quite rare.

Consistent with our previous findings, adults seem to nearly always identify the infant's need accurately. Those occasions when they do not identify the need correctly seem to have more to do with inattention than judgment, and such occurrences happen more with second and third rather than first children.

We were rather surprised at how far from the ideal (as induced from earlier observational studies) was the language actually used by these parents. Use of the appropriate difficulty level of words was from 55 percent up to a maximum of 69 percent of the time. The language was judged as too simple by our observers at least one-fifth of the time, and on a fair number of occasions, no language at all was used in responding to the overtures of these young children. Similarly, in the area of the provision of related ideas, we were somewhat surprised to find that this was not done more often, although in about half the instances it was. The data on the complexity of language once again indicate that utterances by adults to children in this age range are by and large quite brief.

As you might expect (especially with observers in the home), the provision of encouragement and enthusiasm in response to an overture by a child was generally high, ranging from 66.7 percent of the interchanges up to better than 85 percent. At times, teaching realistic limits was inappropriate, indeed on four out of five occasions. When it was appropriate, adults nearly always took the opportunity to do so. Finally, we generally found that babies came away pretty well satisfied after their overtures to adults during this age range.

Turning to age trends, we found that as the child got older and more skillful at communicating, the likelihood of an immediate response increased. Perceptions of the child's needs remained accurate throughout the period studied. The level of word difficulty used was relatively constant, although it did rise from its initial lowest levels. The same is true with respect to the provision of related ideas to the child. This makes sense in light of the increased tendencies of children to say meaningful words as they move from their tenth to their seventeenth months. The same trend is also true with respect to the complexity of language. As for the provision of encouragement, we saw consistently high scores after the very first period, and the teaching of realistic limits remains fairly constant across age, as did satisfaction of the needs of the child.

Bear in mind that we looked closely at the actual responses of adults to overtures by children in this study because it was our judgment from our earlier naturalistic work that some of the most important differences in childrearing practices were in a distinctive pattern of response to the overtures of babies. It is for this reason that these data are particularly interesting to us. They also serve to tell us the degree to which our guidelines for childrearing were actually put into practice by the individual parents and the degree to which such practices were employed by our control population, which was not being guided by us at all.

Interchanges Initiated by the Adult.

Frequency of Overtures by Adults. Although in our previous work mothers and infants initiated about the same number of interactions, in this study mothers consistently initiated more contacts than their infants. This difference seems primarily due to the presence in this study of so many families with only one child. This point will be treated at length later, since it turns out to be perhaps *the* dominant factor in this study.

Purposes. Mothers in this study initiated contact with their infants to *stimulate* them about twice as often as to *control* them or to *provide routine care.* The emotional tone of these events was usually warm. On rare occasions (2.8 percent of the time) these mothers appeared angry or stern when initiating a contact with their infants.

Total Interaction Times. The next item of significance concerns the total interaction time as a percentage of the observation period. As you can see, interaction time ranges from a low of 18.9 percent to a high of 30.2 percent. This represents a minimum of about 11 minutes an hour and a maximum of about 18 minutes an hour. In previous reports, we had cited an estimated value of about 6 minutes an hour for the thirty-nine families observed in our natural longitudinal experiment (*Experience and Environment,* Volumes 1 and 2). Fourteen of the families whose data are reported here were being urged to spend a great deal of time interacting with their children. Even more important is the fact that half the families in this study had only one child, whereas in our previous work we nearly always studied families with two or more children.

Total interaction time rose in the middle of this period of observations (during the thirteenth and fourteenth months of the child's life) and then dropped back as the child got a bit older.

The next observation to note is the distribution of interaction time between episodes initiated by the infant and those initiated by the adult. The number of episodes initiated by adults in the study was much greater than the number initiated by the children. Total time spent on each of these events, however, was remarkably even.

The Effects of Sibling Order on
Child-Adult Interchanges

Tables 6-2 and 6-3 present information on child-adult interactions organized according to whether or not the child was a firstborn.

Interchanges Initiated by the Child.

Frequency of the Children's Overtures. Whether a child was a firstborn or later-born infant did not affect the frequency of his overtures to his mother. The variability of behavior was remarkably low.

Purposes. As for the child's purposes, firstborns asked for help more often and needed comforting somewhat less. The latter is probably due to the absence of aggressive older siblings. Attention seeking was about the same regardless of sibling status.

The Quality of the Adult's Responses to the Child. In the case of the firstborn child, the parents consistently responded much more quickly to an overture by the child. In addition, when there was no response to an overture by a child, the child was usually a second or third born rather than a first child. Second, adult perception of the child's needs was more accurate.

Third, the verbal input to the child was dramatically different in the case of the firstborn child. Mothers used higher quality language with firstborn children as compared to later-born children, and this held true across the entire age range.

Even in the area of provision of encouragement, or the reinforcement of enthusiasm, the firstborn child received more than the later-born child. The same is true with respect to the teaching of realistic limits, which was more often done for the firstborn child. The only category of the eight in which the differences were not impressive is the category of satisfaction of subject needs, where by and large all children found their needs being satisfied reasonably well.

Interchanges Initiated by the Adult.

Frequency of Overtures by Adults. Mothers of firstborns in this study initiated more than twice as many interchanges with their infants as did mothers of later-born children (median values 11.2 versus 5.6).

Purposes. Their purposes were generally similar regardless of group affiliation. Stimulating the child was about twice as common as either control or routine care.

Total Interaction Times. Turning to the total interaction time, we found that the central tendency for the firstborn child was nearly 40 percent. In contrast,

Table 6-2
Adult Assessment Scales Data: Sibling Effects

Behaviors		All N = 28	Firstborns N = 15	Later-Borns N = 13
			Groups	
Interactions Initiated by the Child, 11 to 16 Months				
Frequency of overtures (30-minute observation)				
	Median	5.3	5.9	5.7
	Range	3.0-11.5	4.3-11.9	4.0-10.0
Frequency of child purposes				
Procure a service	Median	1.0	1.5	1.0
	Range	0.0-3.5	0.5-3.5	0.0-3.5
Gain attention	Median	2.5	2.5	2.5
	Range	0.5-6.5	0.5-6.5	0.5-5.0
Maintain social contact	Median	0.0	0.0	0.5
	Range	0.0-2.5	0.0-1.5	0.0-2.5
Ease discomfort	Median	0.0	0.0	0.0
	Range	0.0-1.0	0.0-1.0	0.0-1.0
Quality of adults' responses (percent frequency)				
Timing of response				
Immediate (<3 s)	Median	83.3	90.3	76.7
	Range	41.7-100.0	73.7-100.0	41.7-90.0
Delayed (>5 s)	Median	10.2	6.5	15.3
	Range	0.0-33.3	0.0-20.8	5.7-33.3
No response	Median	1.4	0.0	5.3
	Range	0.0-26.1	0.0-15.8	0.0-26.1
Rejects	Median	0.0	0.0	0.0
	Range	0.0-18.5	0.0-11.1	0.0-18.5
Perception of child's need				
Accurately	Median	96.4	100.0	86.4
	Range	71.4-100.0	88.6-100.0	71.4-100.0
Partially	Median	3.5	0.0	6.0
	Range	0.0-23.8	0.0-11.4	0.0-23.8
Not at all	Median	0.0	0.0	0.0
	Range	0.0-11.1	0.0	0.0-11.1
Level of difficulty of words				
Appropriate	Median	57.3	82.6	35.0
	Range	11.8-100.0	18.7-100.0	11.8-88.2
Too complex	Median	0.0	0.0	0.0
	Range	0.0	0.0	0.0
Too simple	Median	25.6	14.3	38.2
	Range	0.0-75.0	0.0-75.0	8.3-75.0
Babytalk	Median	0.0	0.0	0.0
	Range	0.0-14.3	0.0	0.0-14.3
None	Median	6.4	5.3	10.5
	Range	0.0-35.7	0.0-17.0	0.0-35.7
Provision of related ideas				
Yes	Median	53.3	68.6	31.1
	Range	5.9-96.2	27.8-96.2	5.9-94.1
No	Median	46.6	31.4	66.2
	Range	3.8-94.1	3.8-72.2	5.9-94.1

Table 6-2 continued

Behaviors		Groups		
		All N = 28	Firstborns N = 15	Later-Borns N = 13
Complexity of language				
Complex sentence (>3 s)	Median	12.7	22.2	0.0
	Range	0.0-69.6	0.0-69.7	0.0-25.8
Phrase/sentence (<3 s)	Median	59.5	59.1	57.8
	Range	21.7-94.1	21.7-78.3	35.3-94.1
One word	Median	5.8	4.3	9.8
	Range	0.0-47.1	0.0-27.3	0.0-47.1
None	Median	7.0	5.6	11.8
	Range	0.0-35.7	0.0-17.0	0.0-35.7
Provision of encouragement, reinforcement, or enthusiasm				
Yes	Median	83.1	83.3	77.5
	Range	44.3-100.0	57.1-100.0	44.3-100.0
No	Median	6.7	5.6	11.3
	Range	0.0-38.9	0.0-26.5	0.0-38.9
Inappropriate	Median	10.0	11.1	7.4
	Range	0.0-27.8	0.0-23.5	0.0-27.8
Teaching realistic limits				
Yes	Median	12.1	16.7	10.9
	Range	0.0-47.1	0.0-29.4	0.0-33.3
No	Median	1.0	0.0	2.5
	Range	0.0-22.9	0.0-19.2	0.0-22.9
Inappropriate	Median	78.0	77.8	78.1
	Range	47.1-95.8	47.1-95.8	54.3-95.0
Satisfaction of child's needs				
Yes	Median	87.1	87.5	85.8
	Range	60.0-100.0	66.7-100.0	60.0-100.0
No	Median	5.9	5.7	6.0
	Range	0.0-29.4	0.0-29.4	0.0-25.0
Partial	Median	5.7	5.6	6.6
	Range	0.0-15.0	0.0-14.3	0.0-15.0
Average duration of adults' responses (seconds)	Median	34.8	37.3	32.6
	Range	2.2-56.5	20.2-56.5	2.2-53.3
Time spent by adults responding (percent duration)	Median	10.5	14.9	8.9
	Range	3.6-29.6	5.9-22.3	3.6-29.6
Interactions Initiated by the Adult				
Frequency of overtures (30-minute observation)				
	Median	7.5	11.2	5.6
	Range	2.0-23.0	5.8-20.2	3.1-11.2
Purpose of the interaction (percent frequency)				
Stimulating child	Median	5.7	8.9	3.4
	Range	0.0-29.9	2.8-29.9	0.0-10.7
Use of positive techniques to control the child	Median	2.3	3.9	1.3
	Range	0.0-19.7	0.7-19.7	0.0-4.0
Use of negative techniques to control the child	Median	1.0	1.7	6.5
	Range	0.0-4.2	0.0-3.5	0.0-4.2
Routine caretaking	Median	1.7	2.2	1.4
	Range	0.0-11.7	0.4-11.7	0.0-4.6

Table 6-2 continued

		Groups		
Behaviors		All N = 28	Firstborns N = 15	Later-Borns N = 13
Emotional tone of the Interaction (percent frequency)				
Positive	Median	82.7	87.0	72.4
	Range	40.5-99.6	40.5-99.6	42.6-95.8
Negative	Median	3.4	2.7	3.7
	Range	0.0-38.5	0.0-20.0	0.0-38.5
Neutral	Median	8.5	3.2	13.5
	Range	0.0-43.4	0.0-43.4	0.0-25.5
Average duration of adult-initiated interactions (seconds)	Median	30.4	37.1	24.2
	Range	13.1-57.6	25.1-57.6	13.1-43.2
Time spent by adult in adult-initiated interactions (percent duration)	Median	12.9	24.0	6.6
	Range	4.4-46.7	8.5-46.7	4.4-15.1
Total time spent by adults in interactions with children (percent duration)	Median	24.7	39.7	16.4
	Range	9.6-61.9	15.0-61.9	9.6-44.0

for later-born children the central tendency was 16.4 percent. This difference is both large and consistent.

Turning to the subscores, the percentage of time of interaction when the *child initiated* the interaction, we found similar patterns favoring the firstborn child, with a central tendency for firstborns of about 15 percent, and for the other children, 8.9 percent. In the case of maternal initiated interchanges, for firstborns the central tendency was 24.0 percent. In contrast, the other children averaged just 6.6 percent.

Basically, what this set of numbers means is that in the twenty-eight families in these two groups, parents of firstborn children spent more than twice as much time interacting with them as did the parents of the same age children who were second or third born. Furthermore, the greater amount of interaction time was due to the mother's increased initiation of interchanges. Overtures by children to their mothers varied little across groups. This finding did not come as a total surprise to us, nor should it to anyone, but the size of the difference is substantially greater than we expected, and so great as to preclude the combining of any data relatable to this phenomenon across firstborn and later-born children. Later we shall discuss more fully the ramifications of this finding for the host of analyses of intervention studies being performed and reported on currently.

All in all, we find these differences as to whether the child was a firstborn or not to be persistent and of fundamental importance. All our future analyses, and indeed any future analyses of the effects of parent intervention programs, must separate children and families according to this powerful factor.

Table 6-3

Adult Assessment Scales Data: Group Differences—Mann Whitney U Comparisons, Levels of Significance

(two-tailed values)

Behaviors	Firstborns vs. Later-Borns	E_1 vs. $C_{1,1}$	E_2 vs. $C_{1,2}$
Interactions Initiated by the Child, 11 to 16 Months			
Frequency of overtures (30-minute observation)	.42	.91	.52
Quality of adults' responses (percent frequency)			
Timing of response			
Immediate (<3 s)	.004	.01	.15
Perception of child's need			
accurately	.002	.04	.35
Level of difficulty of words			
appropriate	.004	.03	.52
Provision of related ideas			
Yes	.007	.10	.28
Complexity of language			
Complex sentence (> 3s)	.01	.69	1.0
Phrase/sentence (<3 s)	.76	.68	.94
Provision of encouragement, reinforcement or enthusiasm			
Yes	.33	.27	.89
Teaching realistic limits			
Yes	.50	.95	.94
Satisfaction of child's needs			
Yes	.60	.60	.39
Average duration of adults responses (seconds)	.22	1.0	.89
Time spent by adults responding (percent duration)	.23	.49	.72
Interactions Initiated by the Adult			
Frequency of overtures (30-minute observation)	.06	.15	.13
Purpose of the interaction (percent frequency)			
Stimulating child	.001	.64	.15
Use of positive techniques to control the child	.001	.22	.10
Use of negative techniques to control the child	.43	.32	.01
Routine caretaking	.46	.91	.78
Emotional tone of the interaction (percent frequency)			
Positive	.01	.11	.89
Negative	.59	.68	.05
Neutral	.07	.05	.47
Average duration of adult-initiated interactions (seconds)	.002	1.0	.89
Time spent by adult in adult-initiated interactions (percent duration)	.0002	.20	.18
Total time spent by adults in interactions with children (percent duration)	.002	.25	.47

Treatment Effects: Firstborn Children

Table 6-4 contains information for firstborn children about adult-child interactions arranged according to whether the child was a member of the experimental or control group.

Interchanges Initiated by the Child.

The Frequency of the Children's Overtures. Once again we found low variability
in the number of overtures by an infant to its mother. In a 30-minute
observation we usually saw between four and seven approaches by the child
regardless of group affiliation.

Purposes. Control group firstborn children sought attention and assistance more
than experimental group firstborn children.

The Quality of the Adult's Responses to the Child. Table 6-4 indicates that
mothers of firstborn children in the experimental group responded somewhat
differently than mothers in the control group to overtures by their infants. The
differences were in the directions we wanted them to be. Mothers of firstborn
experimental children responded more quickly, perceived their child's purpose
more accurately, used more appropriate language, provided related ideas more
often, encouraged their children more often, and satisfied their needs more often
than did mothers of control group children.

    We concluded that by and large both groups did rather well in comparison
to previously studied parents, with the experimental group having a small but
consistent advantage. The only place in which both groups seemed a bit weak
was in the area of language. Even the treatment group provided less complete
language than we had hoped.

    On the whole we felt that the quality of response by the mothers of
firstborn children in the experimental group was very good. We also were
impressed by the performance of the mothers in the control group.

Interchanges Initiated by the Adults.

Frequency of Overtures by Adults. The mothers of firstborn children in the
experimental group initiated considerably greater numbers of contacts with their
children than did those in the control group (median values 13.5 versus 9.1).
This result reinforces the judgment that the treatment had a substantial impact.

Purposes. Mothers of experimental group firstborn children were slightly more
inclined to initiate teaching interchanges than mothers in the control group.
Since the experimental group mothers also initiated a greater total number of
interchanges, they generally did more proactive teaching than mothers of
firstborn children in the control group.

Table 6-4
Adult Assessment Scales Data: Treatment Effects—Firstborn Children

		Groups	
		Experimental	Monitored Controls
Behaviors		(N = 7)	(N = 8)

Interactions Initiated by the Child, 11 to 16 Months

		Experimental (N = 7)	Monitored Controls (N = 8)
Frequency of overtures (30-minute observation)			
	Median	5.7	6.4
	Range	4.3-11.9	4.5-9.2
Frequency of child purposes			
Procure a service	Median	1.0	2.0
	Range	1.0-3.5	0.5-3.5
Gain attention	Median	1.5	2.5
	Range	0.5-6.5	0.5-4.5
Maintain social contact	Median	0	0.3
	Range	0.0-0.5	0.0-1.5
Ease discomfort	Median	0	0.3
	Range	0.0-1.0	0.0-0.5
Quality of adults' responses (percent frequency)			
Timing of response	Median	96.2	84.9
Immediate (<3 s)	Range	76.2-100.0	73.7-92.6
Delayed (>5 s)	Median	3.8	9.3
	Range	0.0-9.5	5.6-20.8
No response	Median	0.0	1.4
	Range	0.0-14.3	0.0-15.8
Rejects	Median	0.0	0.0
	Range	0.0	0.0-11.1
Perception of child's need			
Accurately	Median	100.0	96.4
	Range	97.9-100.0	88.6-100.0
Partially	Median	0.0	3.5
	Range	0.0-2.1	0.0-11.4
Not at all	Median	0.0	0.0
	Range	0.0	0.0
Level of difficulty of words			
Appropriate	Median	91.3	68.7
	Range	48.9-100.0	18.7-91.4
Too complex	Median	0.0	0.0
	Range	0.0	0.0
Too simple	Median	5.3	24.3
	Range	0.0-34.0	8.6-75.0
Babytalk	Median	0.0	0.0
	Range	0.0	0.0
None	Median	3.8	6.4
	Range	0.0-17.0	0.0-11.4
Provision of related ideas			
Yes	Median	70.6	62.8
	Range	38.3-96.2	27.8-77.1
No	Median	29.4	37.3
	Range	3.8-61.7	22.9-72.2
Complexity of language			
Complex sentence (>3 s)	Median	41.2	16.1
	Range	0.0-69.6	0.0-57.1

Table 6-4 continued

Behaviors		Groups	
		Experimental (N = 7)	Monitored Controls (N = 8)
Phrase/sentence (<3 s)	Median	58.8	66.2
	Range	21.7-78.3	34.3-77.8
One word	Median	0.0	5.9
	Range	0.0-12.8	0.0-27.3
None	Median	3.8	6.4
	Range	0.0-17.0	0.0-11.4
Provision of encouragement, reinforcement or enthusiasm			
Yes	Median	84.2	80.6
	Range	76.5-100.0	57.1-93.7
No	Median	4.3	8.9
	Range	0.0-8.7	0.0-26.5
Inappropriate	Median	10.5	11.1
	Range	0.0-23.5	0.0-20.0
Teaching realistic limits			
Yes	Median	16.7	14.3
	Range	5.6-29.4	0.0-47.1
No	Median	0.0	5.0
	Range	0.0-5.6	0.0-19.2
Inappropriate	Median	82.6	76.4
	Range	70.6-94.4	47.1-95.8
Satisfaction of child's needs			
Yes	Median	88.2	85.4
	Range	70.6-100.0	66.7-96.7
No	Median	4.3	5.9
	Range	0.0-13.0	0.0-14.3
Partial	Median	4.3	5.6
	Range	0.0-13.0	0.0-14.3
Average duration of adults' responses (seconds)	Median	37.3	36.9
	Range	20.2-47.0	24.3-56.5
Time spent by adults responding (percent duration)	Median	11.9	15.6
	Range	5.9-20.3	6.2-22.3
Interactions Initiated by the Adult			
Frequency of overtures (30-minute observation)			
	Median	13.7	9.1
	Range	5.8-20.2	6.2-12.0
Purpose of the interaction (percent frequency)			
Stimulating child	Median	15.9	8.1
	Range	2.8-29.9	4.7-29.2
Use of positive techniques to control the child	Median	5.9	3.4
	Range	2.0-19.7	0.7-12.6
Use of negative techniques to control the child	Median	0.8	1.8
	Range	0.0-2.2	0.1-3.5
Routine caretaking	Median	2.6	1.9
	Range	0.4-11.7	0.6-7.4
Emotional tone of the interaction (percent frequency)			
Positive	Median	93.2	83.3
	Range	80.0-99.6	40.5-99.4

Table 6-4 continued

		Groups	
Behaviors		Experimental *(N = 7)*	Monitored Controls *(N = 8)*
Negative	Median	2.1	3.4
	Range	0.0-20.0	0.0-17.7
Neutral	Median	1.0	9.3
	Range	0.0-13.0	0.3-43.4
Average duration of adult-initiated interactions (seconds)	Median	37.1	37.1
	Range	26.6-53.4	25.1-57.6
Time spent by adult in adult-initiated interactions (percent duration)	Median	28.7	17.0
	Range	8.5-46.7	8.7-35.2
Total time spent by adults in interactions with children (percent duration)	Median	42.4	34.5
	Range	19.1-61.9	15.0-51.6

Total Interaction Times. The next information of interest is the total amount of interaction time as a function of group affiliation. What we found was that the experimental mother-infant pairs spent more time interacting together than did the control pairs across the 11- to 16-month age range. The total median scores were 42.4 percent for the experimental group versus 34.5 percent for the control group. These numbers once again indicate some impact of our training.

The control group adults provided more interaction as a consequence of the child's overtures than did the experimental group (15.6 versus 11.9 percent). This difference was due to greater numbers of overtures by the children. Response length by mothers was about the same across groups.

Treatment Effects: Later-Born Children

Table 6-5 contains information for later-born children about adult-child interactions arranged according to whether the child was a member of the experimental or control group.

Interchanges Initiated by the Child.

The Frequency of the Children's Overtures. Later-born children in the control group initiated slightly more overtures toward adults than their counterparts in the experimental group (median values: C_2, 5.9 versus E_2, 5.0).

Purposes. Later-born children in the control group sought services and attention somewhat more often than those in the experimental group.

Table 6-5
Adult Assessment Scales Data: Treatment Effects—Later-Born Children

		Groups	
Behaviors		Experimental (N = 7)	Monitored Controls (N = 6)
Interactions Initiated by the Child, 11 to 16 Months			
Frequency of overtures (30-minute observation)			
	Median	5.0	5.9
	Range	4.0-8.8	4.5-10.0
Frequency of child purposes			
Procure a service	Median	1.0	1.3
	Range	0.0-2.0	0.0-3.5
Gain attention	Median	2.0	2.8
	Range	0.5-5.0	1.5-3.5
Maintain social contact	Median	0.5	0.5
	Range	0.0-2.0	0.0-2.5
Ease discomfort	Median	0.5	0.0
	Range	0.0-0.5	0.0-0.5
Quality of adults' responses (percent frequency)			
Timing of response			
Immediate (<3 s)	Median	82.9	65.7
	Range	55.6-90.0	41.7-87.1
Delayed (>5 s)	Median	14.8	19.8
	Range	5.7-25.0	9.7-33.3
No response	Median	5.3	13.8
	Range	0.0-11.4	0.0-26.1
Rejects	Median	0.0	0.0
	Range	0.0	0.0-2.7
Perception of child's need			
Accurately	Median	91.7	84.0
	Range	71.4-100.0	80.0-100.0
Partially	Median	6.2	6.8
	Range	0.0-23.8	0.0-20.0
Not at all	Median	0.0	2.8
	Range	0.5-5.9	0.0-11.1
Level of difficulty of words			
Appropriate	Median	40.0	32.6
	Range	14.3-88.2	11.8-66.7
Too complex	Median	0.0	0.0
	Range	0.0	0.0
Too simple	Median	45.0	47.2
	Range	8.3-68.7	21.4-75.0
Babytalk	Median	0.0	0.0
	Range	0.0-5.6	0.0-14.3
None	Median	10.0	14.1
	Range	0.0-25.8	0.0-35.7
Provision of related ideas			
Yes	Median	33.3	29.8
	Range	19.0-94.1	5.9-44.4
No	Median	66.7	70.3
	Range	5.9-75.0	55.6-94.1

Table 6-5 continued

Behaviors		Experimental (N = 7)	Monitored Controls (N = 6)
		Groups	
Complexity of language			
Complex sentence (>3 s)	Median	0.0	5.5
	Range	0.0-25.8	0.0-20.0
Phrase/sentence (<3 s)	Median	55.6	60.0
	Range	38.7-94.1	35.3-85.0
One word	Median	10.0	8.9
	Range	4.3-31.2	0.0-47.1
None	Median	12.5	14.1
	Range	0.0-25.8	0.0-35.7
Provision of encouragement, reinforcement, or enthusiasm			
Yes	Median	80.0	77.5
	Range	44.4-94.1	63.3-100.0
No	Median	10.0	14.2
	Range	0.0-38.9	0.0-36.7
Inappropriate	Median	10.0	2.8
	Range	0.0-16.7	0.0-27.8
Teaching realistic limits			
Yes	Median	11.8	14.2
	Range	0.0-33.3	0.0-22.9
No	Median	5.0	7.1
	Range	0.0-11.8	0.0-22.9
Inappropriate	Median	87.5	77.2
	Range	55.6-95.0	54.3-93.7
Satisfaction of child's needs			
Yes	Median	90.3	84.1
	Range	60.0-100.0	71.0-92.9
No	Median	5.9	8.6
	Range	0.0-25.0	0.0-19.4
Partial	Median	5.6	8.4
	Range	0.0-15.0	5.6-11.1
Average duration of adults' responses (seconds)	Median	32.6	27.6
	Range	2.2-51.6	11.3-53.3
Time spent by adults responding (percent duration)	Median	8.7	10.3
	Range	5.5-17.2	3.6-29.6

Interactions Initiated by the Adult

Frequency of overtures (30-minute observation)			
	Median	5.0	6.9
	Range	3.1-8.8	5.0-11.2
Purpose of the interaction (percent frequency)			
Stimulating child	Median	3.1	4.8
	Range	0.0-5.1	1.2-10.7
Use of positive techniques to control the child	Median	1.9	0.8
	Range	1.0-3.2	0.0-4.0
Use of negative techniques to control the child	Median	0.2	1.6
	Range	0.0-1.2	0.3-4.2
Routine caretaking	Median	1.2	1.5
	Range	0.0-3.9	0.3-4.6

Table 6-5 continued

		Groups	
		Experimental (N = 7)	Monitored Controls (N = 6)
Behaviors			
Emotional tone of the interaction (percent frequency)			
Positive	Median	73.4	73.3
	Range	66.7-95.8	42.6-84.4
Negative	Median	1.1	7.8
	Range	0.0-6.8	1.1-38.5
Neutral	Median	18.7	10.9
	Range	0.0-25.5	6.7-18.9
Average duration of adult-	Median	23.4	24.5
initiated interactions	Range	19.8-43.2	13.1-37.8
(seconds)			
Time spent by adult in adult-	Median	6.6	10.4
initiated interactions	Range	4.4-10.1	6.0-15.1
(percent duration)			
Total time spent by adults in	Median	15.7	20.8
interactions with children	Range	12.6-23.6	9.6-44.0
(percent duration)			

Interchanges Initiated by the Adult.

The Frequency of Overtures by Adults. Mothers of later-born children in the control group initiated more interchanges with their 11- to 16-month-old infants than did mothers in the experimental group (median values: C_2, 6.9 versus E_2, 5.0).

Purposes. The purposes of adult-initiated interchanges were similar in both groups, with teaching (or stimulating) again about twice as common as controlling or caretaking.

Discussion

Clearly the most striking finding in these data on interchanges between twenty-eight mothers and their infants is the effect of the child's ordinal position. Firstborn children receive markedly different input from their mothers than do later-born children. The differences in both quantity and quality are very large. They are so large as to render any analyses of early human development useless unless data are analyzed according to this factor.

From time to time reports have appeared which suggest substantial effects of being a firstborn child (Fox 1977; Caldwell et al. 1970; Leiderman 1973;

Kilbride et al. 1977; Jacobs and Moss 1976). We predict that more such findings will surface as research on the home lives of young children progresses.

It seems clear from these data that most of the mothers in the experimental group did modify their childrearing behavior in directions we were urging, at least with regard to that portion of the day when they were interacting directly with their children. Of course, there were important differences across families. This was true for families in the control group as well. As was the case in our pilot study (White et al. 1974), we felt limited in our capacity to control the major influences in the lives of the infants in the study. First, we could do nothing about the number of children in each home, once a family was admitted to the study. Second, we could only *suggest* parental actions. Third, working with small samples puts the researcher at the mercy of sampling errors.

For the purposes of the research, a few additional points should be stated. As far as direct interaction is concerned, the experimental group with one child only implemented the curriculum well. The other families in the experimental group did not do as well as we had hoped. The control group families with a firstborn child performed better than the experimental group with more than one child but not quite as effectively as the experimental group with firstborn children.

Our small sample was a risk from the beginning, but we knew we could not deal with any more families. Finding huge differences as a function of the number of children in the family prevented us from collapsing our groups. The consequence is that our subsamples are even smaller. Is it better to learn a modest amount about families with one child and others with more than one, or is it better to learn more about either?

Indirect Influences

Earlier we had noted that adults influence their children's learning experiences in indirect as well as direct ways. A considerable number of previous studies concentrated on direct influences involved in adult-child interactions. Since we have found repeatedly that infants and toddlers in virtually every instance spend much more daily time acting alone, it is clear that studies of mother-child interactions are not in themselves representative of a young child's total learning experiences.

From our naturalistic studies we concluded that effective childrearing (of infants and toddlers) includes the following adult practices:

Altering the design of the home to make it as safe as possible for an exploring baby.

Altering the design of the home to make it as interesting as possible for an exploring baby.

Allowing the newly mobile child access to as much of the home as possible, keeping restrictive practices such as playpen use to a minimum.

Scheduling activities during the day that will interest the baby (e.g., walks, shopping trips, playground visits, etc.).

Providing access to materials that are appropriate for the baby's developmental level (e.g., many small diverse objects, utensils for water play, balls, etc.).

Making oneself readily available to the child for several hours each day.

We designed a five-point rating scale for scoring adults on these practices, each of our four home visitors rating each adult after each home visit. We produced six ratings for each adult. Since all our visitors saw most of the families, three or four visitors rated each adult. To be conservative we collapsed our five-point scale to three points: average, clearly better than average, and clearly worse than average. Average performance was to be determined by each observer on the basis of extensive experience with a broad range of families over an average of about 10 years of home visiting. We weighed each of the six dimensions equally, added each adult median score, then ranked the adults.

As a whole, we rated the twenty-eight adults as above average in childrearing practices with indirect influence on children. The range of performance was broad, with five adults receiving perfect scores and only three rated as below average. The ratings agreed in most instances with our subjective judgments, but there were a few exceptions.

Parents of firstborns were once again rated as providing better childrearing than those with two or more children. Parents of children in the experimental group were given much higher ratings than those in the control group. It is to be remembered that these data, unlike the data on the achievement of the children, were gathered by the home visiting staff rather than by blind testers. As such, the possibility of bias must be acknowledged.

We present now a view of four situations, the first where a mother performed closest to our hypothesized ideal, then one who performed farthest from that ideal, then one who seemed average, and then one special case (see table 6-6).

To the extent that these ratings are accurate, we once again found a substantial effect according to the number of children in the family. In these data, however, the apparent effect of being in the training group was about as large. Once again it appears that the mothers in the experimental group were responding to the treatment. Of course, we do not as yet know whether these numerical differences are educationally significant.

Table 6-6
Some Individual Patterns of Childrearing

	A	B	C	D
Number of overtures by the child				
Median/30 mins.	6.5	4.5	6	0
Child's purposes				
Procure a service	6.2	2.4	3.3	0.0
Gain attention	7.8	1.7	3.3	0.0
Maintain social contact	1.5	0.0	0.0	0.0
Ease discomfort	0.6	0.0	1.5	0.0
Adult's response				
Timing and direction				
Immediate	96.2	55.6	75.0	0.0
Delayed	3.8	22.2	20.8	0.0
No response	0.0	22.2	0.0	0.0
Rejects	0.0	0.0	4.2	0.0
Perception of child's needs				
Accurately	100.0	84.6	95.8	0.0
Partly	0.0	7.7	4.2	0.0
Not at all	0.0	7.7	0.0	0.0
Level of words				
Appropriate	96.2	28.6	37.5	0.0
Too complicated	0.0	0.0	0.0	0.0
Too simple	0.0	21.4	54.2	0.0
Babytalk	0.0	14.3	0.0	0.0
None	3.8	35.7	8.3	0.0
Provision of ideas				
Yes	96.2	7.1	41.7	0.0
No	3.8	92.9	58.3	0.0
Complexity of language				
Complex (>3 s)	46.2	14.3	4.5	0.0
Phrase/sentence (<3 s)	50.0	50.0	59.1	0.0
One word	0.0	0.0	27.3	0.0
None	3.8	35.7	9.1	0.0
Provision of Encouragement				
Yes	100.0	100.0	66.7	0.0
No	0.0	0.0	16.7	0.0
Inappropriate	0.0	0.0	16.7	0.0
Teaching realistic limits				
Yes	11.5	0.0	0.0	0.0
No	0.0	14.3	4.2	0.0
Inappropriate	88.5	85.7	95.8	0.0
Satisfaction of subject's needs				
Yes	10.0	92.9	87.5	0.0
No	0.0	0.0	4.2	0.0
Partial	0.0	7.1	8.3	0.0
Total time responding				
Median (%)	16.7	4.2	8.1	0.0
$\bar{X}$ Response length (s)	46.2	16.8	2.4	0.0
Number of interchanges initiated by adult				
Median/30 mins.	12.0	5.0	12.0	0.5

Table 6-6 continued

	A	B	C	D
Adult's purposes				
Stimulate	15.9	4.2	7.3	0.0
Control—positive	5.9	1.4	3.1	0.8
Control—negative	0.0	0.3	3.5	0.0
Routine care	3.5	0.3	2.8	1.7
Emotional tone				
Positive	95.9	84.4	40.5	68.6
Negative	0.3	1.1	16.1	0.0
Neutral	0.0	14.4	43.4	31.4
Total time				
Median (%)	25.7	6.2	16.8	2.4
$\overline{X}$ Episode time (s)	38.6	22.3	25.2	86.4
Total number of interactions				
Median/30 mins.	18.5	10.4	18.0	0.5
Total interactive time				
Median (%)	42.4	9.5	24.9	2.4
Adult's indirect influence (median ratings)				
Materials	1	3	3	3
Safety precautions	1	3	3	3
Child proofing	1	5	3	3
Access to home	1	5	3	3
Adult's availability	1	3	1	3
Daily activities	1	4	3	4
Overall rating	(Tied for first place 3/28)	(28/28)	(Tied at 19.5)	—

Comparing these four patterns of childrearing reveals some expected and some unexpected results. The two children whose mothers were usually available made similar numbers of overtures to them. In the case of child C, the fewer overtures might have been due to the lower availability of mother C. Child D was dropped from our analyses because his very low achievement scores at 12 months of age forced us to alert his family to possibly serious developmental delay. He is included here because his parents' style of childrearing was quite different from that of any of the other forty-three families on whom we gathered data.[2] His usual day consisted of lengthy periods in his playpen in a room with only rare appearances by any other family members. He was of course fed and changed, etc., but he had the least human contact of any of the children during his 10- to 17-month age period. (It should be remembered that we sampled his experiences only between 9 A.M. and 6 P.M. weekdays.)

Mother and Child A. Child A was either seeking a service or attention when she initiated a contact with her mother. She was nearly always responded to immediately. She was never ignored. Her mother nearly always identified her needs accurately and responded with encouragement, with words at or slightly above the child's apparent level of understanding, and with related ideas. Whenever it was appropriate, she also taught realistic limits. The only qualitative feature of her responses that did not meet the desired standard was the complexity of the language. Full sentences were used less than half the time. This performance was, however, among the very best for the group of twenty-eight mothers.

On average, mother A spent a bit more time responding to child A's overtures than we expected (46.2 seconds) and also spent a greater total amount of time than we expected in this kind of behavior (16.7 percent).

Mother A initiated interactions quite often (median value 12 times per 30 minutes). She clearly wanted very much to do a very good job with her child and she very much enjoyed their direct interactions. When she initiated an exchange, it was most often to point out something interesting or to get the child involved in an activity. Even when she set limits or otherwise controlled the child, she usually offered the child an interesting option rather than simply insisting on compliance. As you might predict, the emotional tone of these episodes was usually warm. The average length of these maternal behaviors was 38.6 seconds. Combined with their high frequency, the result was a huge 25.7 percent of time spent in such exchanges. Another result of this high level of maternal proactivity was that the total number of all interchanges between mother A and her child was 18.5 per 30 minutes, and the total duration of such activity was 42.4 percent of the time. We doubt that such a large investment is needed or for that matter possible in most homes.

Mother and Child B. Child B also had the same purposes in mind when he approached his mother, procuring a service and gaining attention. However, he found a less reliable response and often no response at all. Bear in mind that child A was an only child, while child B was a second child. Interestingly, child B's mother usually knew what he wanted (92 percent of the time). Her language directed to the child was very different from that of mother A. It was more often one or two words, baby talk, or totally absent than appropriate to what we see as the child's language learning needs. The other aspects of mother B's language were also far from our hypothesized ideal. Interestingly, mother B was supportive of child B in these encounters, although she rarely taught anything directly. Also interesting is the fact that child B seemed quite happy with his lot after each of these interchanges (satisfaction of S's needs, yes 92.9 percent).

The average length of mother B's responses was only 16.8 seconds, about one-third of those of mother A. Total time spent this way was only 4.2 percent, or less than one-fourth as much as mother A.

Mother B initiated contact with her child about five times per half hour. When she did, however, it was usually to teach the child or in some way simulate his interest. The emotional tone was usually warm, and never harsh.

On average, the length of these actions was brief (22.3 seconds), and in total they occupied only 6.2 percent of the time. Combined with interchanges initiated by the child, the total number of interactions averaged 10.4, and total time 9.5 percent, or just under 6 minutes an hour.

With respect to perception and satisfaction of the child's needs and emotional tone, mother B's behavior resembled that of mother A. In all other respects, however, there were wide differences in maternal interaction style. At least on this basis, we would predict a very different pattern of experience and much better development for child A than for child B.

It should be noted that although mother B received one of our lowest ratings, we believe that her performance was far closer to the national average than to the poorest practices children currently experience. After all, the family of child B participated faithfully in a university-based research project. This fact alone says a good deal about them and makes it quite impossible to generalize about national childrearing practices from their behavior.

Mother and Child C. Child C made about six overtures per 30-minute session to his mother. This number was near the average for all our children. His purposes also were typical, to get help or attention. He sought comforting a bit more than children A and B. His mother's response pattern fell between those of mothers A and B. Mother C was quicker and more regular in her responses than mother B but less so than mother A. The same is true with most of the response categories, with the exception of encouragement and satisfaction of the child's needs, where she had lower scores than both other mothers. Her average response lasted 24.0 seconds, and in total she spent 8.1 percent of the time responding to her child's overtures.

Mother C initiated quite a few interchanges with her child in comparison to mother B. She was one of the more active mothers in this respect. The pattern of her purposes, however, was slightly less didactic than either of the other mothers, and her tone was far more likely to be neutral or negative. She averaged 25.2 seconds for each act and in all spent 16.8 percent of the time in such activity. In all, there were 18 interchanges per session and 24.9 percent of time, or 15 minutes per hour, devoted to direct mother-child interaction.

Mother and Child D. As mentioned briefly earlier, interactions between this pair were quite rare. When they did occur it was nearly always because mother D, on checking her child in his playpen, decided he needed some sort of routine care such as a diaper change. We could not tell the degree, if any, to which child D's very low test scores at 1 year of age (65 on the Bayley Mental Developmental Index) were due to the unusual childrearing practices of the family, but we could not withhold such worrisome information from the child's parents. Shortly after his first birthday, we told child D's mother that we were worried about his rate of development and urged her to explore the situation with a physician and to provide more social contact for the child. Although the child therefore could no longer be a part of the research analysis, we continued to monitor his progress.

Discussion

Although the families in this study were, to some extent, self-selected and, in addition, did not include examples of the neediest families in the country, we found a broad range of childrearing styles. In the next part of this report we will try to relate our data on childrearing practices to the moment-to-moment experiences of the children. For now, we have learned that most of the childrearing in these twenty-eight families was at least of good quality. We have also learned that having only one child to raise is probably the most powerful factor distinguishing the behaviors of the mothers in the study. Furthermore, the data indicate that mothers in the experimental group did modify their childrearing methods to some degree in the directions advocated by the program. There were exceptions. Some mothers in the experimental group seemed less willing or able than others in this regard, while some mothers in the control group, without specific guidance from us, raised their children in a manner much like what we were recommending.

Process Analysis—Tasks: The Actual
Experiences of Children

At times it is clear that teachers and parents do not act toward children in the manner prescribed by a curriculum. In his early work with 3- to 5-year-old children, Weikart demonstrated how to select, train, and supervise staff to see to it that curriculum ideas were actually put into practice (Weikart 1969). Few educational programs for young children have been executed as well. Indeed, filmed presentations of programs with curricula which supposedly vary in important ways are often impossible to tell apart in the absence of labels. More commonly, programs do not have the funds for personnel trained to monitor staff performance.

Yet to know how participation in a special program affects a particular child, the researcher has to go even further. He has to study the actual stream of experience of the children. Very few studies have gathered such information. Barker (1963), Schoggen and Schoggen (1971), Caldwell (1968), Clarke-Stewart (1973), and *Experience and Environment*, Volumes 1 and 2, are among the few that have made efforts in this direction.

We have been sampling the stream of behavior of children for better than a decade. It continues to be difficult, time consuming, and necessary. The full array of tasks children experience during the preschool years has been previously reported in *Experience and Environment*, Volume 1.

Social Tasks: Labels, Definitions, and Examples

1. *To Please:* To attempt to obtain another's good favor by means of a sustained display of affection, or by offering an object to the other person.
2. *To Cooperate:* To comply with another's directive when there is little evidence that the compliance is unwilling, to listen when brief demands are made on one's attention.
3. *To Gain Approval:* To ask (verbally or nonverbally) for favorable comment on a piece of work or on behavior.
4. *To Procure a Service:* To try to obtain aid from another.
5. *To Gain Attention or to Achieve Social Contact:* (a) To join a group, (b) to initiate social contact, (c) to maximize the chance of being noticed.
6. *To Maintain Social Contact:* To be absorbed in ensuring that a social contact continues, or to be interested in the social pleasantry rather than in the content of a conversation or other activity.
7. *To Avoid Unpleasant Circumstances:* To do something for the purpose of evading actual disapproval, possible disapproval, or simply a clash.
8. *To Reject Overtures and Peer Contact, to Avoid Attention:* To refuse to allow a peer to join one's group or become sociable with oneself. Rarely: To act in order to minimize the possibility of being noticed.
9. *To Annoy:* To disturb another, to act in a manner designed to displease or provoke by means of irritating teasing.
10. *To Dominate, to Direct or Lead:* To play the leader role or to demonstrate a process to others or advise others; in short, to direct a specific activity of others.
11. *To Compete, to Gain Status:* To contend for something (e.g., in games involving competition), to make comparisons between own "superior" product (possession, etc.) and other's product (possession, etc.), or to try to elevate one's standing (in one's own eyes or in the eyes of an audience) by appealing to an authority figure.
12. *To Resist Domination, to Assert Self:* To oppose any intrusion on one's personal domain, including both (a) resistance to demands, orders, or any trampling underfoot, and (b) protection of property.
13. *To Enjoy Pets:* Affectionate play with animals.
14. *To Provide Information:* To indicate or communicate, in a public way, one's affects, desires, needs, or specific intelligence.
15. *To Converse:* Any give and take of verbalization when there is mutual interest in the conversation rather than a social or some other overtone or where the communications cannot be heard.

16. *Production of Verbalizations:* The actual production of communication, that is, when a child is engaged in the give and take of exchanging communications and is deficient in language skills and cannot get across what he wants to say.

Nonsocial Tasks: Labels, Definitions, and Examples

1. *To Eat:* To ingest food and drink.
2. *To Relieve Oneself:* To void or to eliminate.
3. *To Dress/Undress Oneself:* Self-explanatory.
4. *To Ease Discomfort:* Purposeful behavior to alleviate physical or psychic discomfort, in contrast to apparently aimless or habitual behavior.
5. *To Restore Order:* To return things to a previously acceptable state but not for the purpose of easing discomfort, pleasing another, or preparing for an activity.
6. *To Choose:* To choose a specific object from an array.
7. *To Procure an Object:* To get something, not as an instrumental task for constructing a product, but as a task per se. If procuring an object in order to use it for constructing a product, or for any purpose, takes longer than 15 seconds, it is coded as focal.
8. *To Construct a Product:* Involves the whole complex of behavior of procuring materials and using the materials (e.g., glue, pencils, piece of puzzle), oriented toward the end product as a consequence of the use of the materials.
9. *To Engage in Large-Muscle Activity:* To engage in large-muscle activity as an end in itself, not as a means of getting attention, being a member of a group, etc. To use gross motor muscles to propel all or some part of the body or to perform other motor activities that require unusual physical effort and coordination. Working hard to do something with the body that is out of the ordinary, for example, bike riding up a hill (after the skill has been mastered).
10. *Nontask Behavior:* To remain in place and not dwell on any specific object (e.g., desultory scanning, sitting with eyes closed, or holding a blank stare), or to wander aimlessly from one location to another.
11. *To Pass Time:* To occupy onself with some alternative task in a situation in which one is captive (i.e., must remain in the field) and where the prescribed activity holds no appeal. To occupy oneself while waiting for a prescribed activity to begin.
12. *To Find Something to Do:* To move around, sampling objects and activities in a purposeful fashion, but not settling on anything specific.
13. *To Prepare for an Activity:* To perform the socially prescribed activities or

sequence of actions that a child carries out almost automatically owing to previous experience and/or practice in order to prepare for something that the child anticipates.

14. *To Explore:* To explore materials, objects, activities, people. To investigate the properties or nature of materials, objects, activities, or people through touch, taste, vision, etc. Experimenting with an object's or material's possibilities by adding to it or taking something away from it as the primary concern rather than for the purpose of constructing a product or because of interest in the process per se (as is evident in *to pretend*).

15. *To Pretend, to Role Play:* To fantasize in any of the following ways: to pretend to be someone or something else; to pretend to be doing something one really is not doing; to pretend an object is something other than it really is; to pretend to be in an imaginary situation.

16. *To Improve a Developing Motor, Intellectual, or Verbal Skill:* To improve a developing motor, intellectual, or verbal skill is typically distinguished by the redundancy of S's behavior (i.e., repeats the same sequence of actions again and again) and by less-than-masterful skill in performing the activity in question.

17. *To Gain Information (Visual):* Sustained visual inquiry directed toward a specific object or person.

18. *To Gain Information (Auditory and Visual):* To attend to language from any source, to gain information through looking and listening when the prime interest is on the context of information being made available.

19. *To Gain Pleasure:* To engage in a task for no other reason than to achieve a state of gaiety, excitement, or amusement.

20. *To Imitate:* The immediate reproduction of the behavior of another person.

21. *To Operate a Mechanism:* To attempt to use or manipulate a mechanism. Operating a mechanism is, by definition, instrumental but becomes focal because it takes 15 seconds or longer to execute.

The number of tasks a child experiences in his first few years is smaller than this full list. For example, 1-year-olds do not construct products or engage in competitive behaviors, whereas 4-year-olds do (at times).

In this study only those experiences that were observed to occur at least 0.1 percent of the time in at least one of our groups will be discussed. On the basis of a 12-hour waking day, 0.1 percent of the time represents about 45 seconds.

Experiences of the Children in the
E and C_1 Groups

Table 6-7 and figure 6-1 presents data on twenty-seven children from their tenth to seventeenth months. They represent all but two of our original twenty-nine experimental and control children (in the monitored control group).

Table 6-7
Task Patterns ($N = 27$)

	Median Percent Duration		
Social Tasks	10 to 11 Months	13 to 14 Months	16 to 17 Months
All social	5.3	8.9	8.3
To cooperate	0.7	1.6	1.1
To procure a service	0.0	0.6	0.8
To gain attention	1.5	1.4	1.0
To maintain social contact	0.8	2.5	0.9
To assert self	0.0	0.1	0.0
Nonsocial Tasks			
To eat	1.2	1.9	2.6
To gain information (visual)	7.8	5.9	5.1
To gain information (visual and auditory)	9.0	12.5	16.2
Live language	4.7	7.0	4.6
Overheard	0.0	0.0	0.0
Mechanical	0.0	0.0	0.0
Nontask	7.5	9.8	5.6
To pass time	1.1	0.0	0.0
To procure object	1.3	1.2	0.8
To gain pleasure	0.0	0.0	0.0
To ease discomfort	0.3	0.0	0.0
To explore	20.0	8.7	4.8
Mastery	5.1	13.3	10.5
Gross motor	1.9	3.1	1.5
Fine motor	1.5	4.5	3.3

The first feature to note is that social experience constitutes a minor percentage of the child's daily life throughout the 10- to 17-month period. We have found this to be the case throughout the first 3 years of life for all groups of children we have studied. This dominance of nonsocial experiences such as small object play and steady looking holds regardless of factors such as family income, parent's educational background, ethnicity, and number of children. This fact must be considered when theories of early development are being constructed. To concentrate on mother-child interactions, for example, is to exclude more than half of an infant's daily experiences from consideration. Yet it is fair to say that studies of infants and toddlers have more often than not focused primarily on mother-child interactions.

Only a small number of social tasks appear in the infant's daily activities. He is asked to comply with simple requests (to cooperate), he seeks help (procure a service) and attention (gain attention and maintain social contact), and he occasionally resists a parental or sibling demand (to assert self).

By contrast he spends more time in steady staring and listening to relevant language (gain information visual and auditory) than in all social tasks combined. To be sure, social experience is involved when a mother describes an object she is looking at with an infant, but we prefer to distinguish tasks in which the child

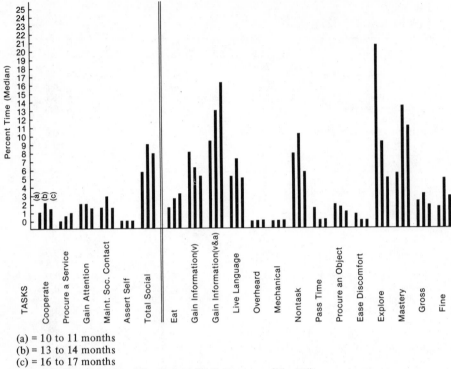

(a) = 10 to 11 months
(b) = 13 to 14 months
(c) = 16 to 17 months

Figure 6-1. Task Patterns ($N = 27$).

seems to be focusing on understanding a verbal and visual input from those in which he is focusing on social interchanges such as seeking assistance or attention.

The children in this study engaged in a good deal of steady staring, unaccompanied by any language. They listened to a good deal of language directed to them from other people, nearly always their mothers. Idling or desultory scanning was very common, as it has been in our previous studies.

Activity involving physical objects is very common during infancy. Small portable objects of all kinds are much more often involved than larger items such as chairs or tables. Infants stare at objects, explore their physical properties with their hands and mouths, or practice simple skills on them. Most of such activity is coded under four categories in our task system: *gain information (visual), gain information (visual and auditory), explore,* and *mastery.* Mastery tasks or experiences are, in turn, subdivisible into gross and fine motor tasks. (Verbal mastery tasks do not ordinarily involve physical objects but focus on practice in expressing words.) Exploratory experiences were very common and more frequent than fine motor mastery tasks (with physical objects). Television viewing of any kind was too infrequent to show up in our summaries, although occasional attention to a set was usually noted, especially to sudden noises featured in commercials.

Age Trends. Over the 7 months involved, remarkable growth is taking place. Babies move from crawling to competent unaided walking. Language ability and interest in language are growing very rapidly. Social awareness, sensitivity, and interest are also progressing with notable speed. If there is a slightly older sibling in the home, the baby is usually learning how to cope with a steadily growing amount of interpersonal hostility. It is because of such an impressive collection of important developments that our research focuses on this particular age range.

With these twenty-seven children there seemed to be an increased tendency to seek help from adults, but no other trends of note in social tasks.

Between-meal eating increases steadily. This makes sense in the light of the emergence of negativism and clinginess during the second year of life. Offering a baby a cookie is a good way of keeping him occupied.

Steady staring drops slightly, whereas staring while listening to language increases substantially. Idling (nontask) behavior rises, then falls, but is always common. Exploring objects is very common at first, then drops markedly during the period. It seems to be supplanted somewhat by mastery (practice) experiences.

Task-Initiation Data. Tables 6-8, 6-9, and 6-10 contain information on the initiation of the children's experiences. In previous work (Volumes 1 and 2), we

Table 6-8
Task-Initiation Data, All Tasks

Group		Self-Initiated	Mother-Initiated
All children	Median	80.4	19.8
(N = 27)	Range	56.4-93.3	1.1-39.8
All firstborns	Median	76.7	20.3
(N = 15)	Range	56.4-88.9	10.5-39.8
All others	Median	79.0	11.0
(N = 12)	Range	70.8-93.3	1.1-27.5
Experimental	Median	84.0	12.5
(N = 13)	Range	64.7-93.3	1.1-39.8
Experimental, firstborns	Median	71.9	29.5
(N = 7)	Range	64.7-88.9	10.5-39.8
Experimental, other	Median	88.2	8.0
(N = 6)	Range	70.8-93.3	1.1-27.5
Control	Median	79.0	17.2
(N = 14)	Range	56.4-85.1	16.0-36.6
Control, firstborns	Median	78.1	17.8
(N = 8)	Range	56.4-85.1	16.0-36.6
Control, other	Median	79.7	13.3
(N = 6)	Range	76.0-84.5	10.9-23.7

Table 6-9
Task-Initiation Data, Social Tasks

Groups		Self-Initiated	Mother-Initiated
All children	Median	75.6	24.4
(N = 27)	Range	20.4-100.0	0.0-79.6
All firstborns	Median	75.6	24.4
(N = 15)	Range	20.4-92.2	7.8-79.6
All others	Median	73.2	20.3
(N = 12)	Range	48.2-100.0	0.0-51.8
Experimental	Median	81.0	22.9
(N = 13)	Range	23.6-100.0	0.0-76.4
Experimental, firstborns	Median	77.1	22.9
(N = 7)	Range	23.6-91.5	8.5-76.4
Experimental, other	Median	84.5	15.5
(N = 6)	Range	58.2-100.0	0.0-41.8
Control	Median	73.5	23.7
(N = 14)	Range	20.4-92.2	7.8-79.6
Control, firstborns	Median	74.8	25.2
(N = 8)	Range	20.4-92.2	7.8-79.6
Control, other	Median	64.3	26.8
(N = 6)	Range	59.3-84.2	15.4-51.8

reported that 12- to 15-month-old children initiate most of their own experiences, especially the nonsocial ones. In this study, the overall pattern was similar, with children initiating about 80 percent of their own experiences and others (almost always their mothers) initiating the balance.

Comparisons with Related Data

All these trends are what we have come to expect from our earlier studies and those of Wenar (1976) and Clarke-Stewart (1973). Comparing these data with previous findings is a comparatively crude process, since the populations involved vary in important ways. To a degree, however, data from this study can be used to judge the replicability of our earlier findings on the everyday experiences of babies in their own homes.

In previous studies we gathered extensive data on the early experiences of fifty other children. Firstborn children are apparently treated quite differently than later-born children. In addition, families in training programs were being urged to modify their children's experiences. Moreover, the experiences of young children shift dramatically as the child passes through the first 3 years of life. For all these reasons, therefore, we cannot simply compare our new data with previous findings. The closest we can come to matched groups is to compare the experiences of the six monitored control group later-born children $(C_{1,2})$ of the current study during the 11- to 16-month period with those of nineteen later-born subjects of our earlier longitudinal study during their 12- to

Table 6-10
Task-Initiation Data, Nonsocial Tasks

Groups		Self-Initiated	Mother-Initiated
All children	Median	84.6	15.0
(N = 27)	Range	47.2-96.6	0.0-52.8
All firstborns	Median	83.4	17.3
(N = 15)	Range	47.2-91.8	8.2-52.8
All others	Median	89.6	8.1
(N = 12)	Range	74.2-96.6	0.0-25.8
Experimental	Median	88.2	8.6
(N = 13)	Range	48.4-96.6	0.0-51.6
Experimental, firstborns	Median	71.6	28.4
(N = 7)	Range	48.4-91.8	8.2-51.6
Experimental, other	Median	93.6	6.5
(N = 6)	Range	91.4-94.6	0.0-8.6
Control	Median	84.0	15.6
(N = 14)	Range	47.2-87.9	6.1-52.8
Control, firstborns	Median	83.2	16.4
(N = 8)	Range	47.2-85.8	14.2-52.8
Control, other	Median	85.4	14.5
(N = 6)	Range	74.2-87.9	6.1-25.8

15-month period (see *Experience and Environment*, Volumes 1 and 2). Table 6-11 contains those data. The families predicted to do well were Hollingshead and Redlich levels I through IV, while those predicted to do less well were Hollingshead and Redlich levels II through V. The families in the current study were from Hollingshead and Redlich levels II, III, and IV (see figure 6-2).

By and large, the quantity and quality of social experiences in the group from the current study are quite similar to those found earlier. Attempts to please another were less frequent in the new study, but such behavior was never observed to be common at this stage of infancy.

There were some substantial differences in nonsocial tasks. The new group ate more between meals, did much less steady staring, but did more staring while listening to language, and in general seemed to have more language experience. Doing nothing much at all (nontask) was much greater with the current group, while procuring objects took less time than in the case of the previous group. Television viewing was again a minor occupation, and small object play was again substantial and qualitatively similar.

In all, in contrast to social experiences, the pattern of nonsocial experiences was different in several potentially important areas. Whether these differences constitute a failure to replicate our earlier findings, normal sampling variations, or the effects of other factors such as increased awareness by parents of the educational significance of infancy we cannot say. It should be noted, however, that unlike the earlier study, parents in the current study knew we were actively guiding the childrearing practices of some of the families.

Table 6-11

Task Patterns, Later-Born Children

Social Tasks	$C_{2,2}$ Children Current Study (N = 6), 11 to 16 Months	Later-Born Children Previous Study (N = 19), 12 to 15 Months
All social	10.2	10.3
To cooperate	2.1	2.8
To procure a service	6.2	1.0
To gain attention	2.0	2.2
To maintain social contact	2.7	2.2
To assert self	0.3	0.5
Nonsocial Tasks		
To eat	7.0	4.4
To gain information (visual)	7.2	16.0
To gain information (visual and auditory)	10.7	6.0
Live language	2.8	1.7
Overheard	3.3	0.8
Mechanical	0.0	0.2
Nontask	21.1	12.2
To pass time	2.4	3.4
To procure object	1.2	3.3
To gain pleasure	0.0	0.0
To ease discomfort	0.8	0.6
To explore	10.2	12.8
Mastery	5.1	8.7
Gross motor	3.1	6.7
Fine motor	2.7	2.4

Sibling Status Effects

The next factor of interest is the influence of sibling status. We know from our data on the behavior of their parents that firstborn children were treated very differently from second- and third-born children. Just how different were their day-to-day experiences? Tables 6-12 and 6-13 and figure 6-3 contain these data.

Sophisticated procedures exist to test whether the overall patterns of experiences in groups differ significantly. We do not have the financial resources to utilize them. In considering differences across individual experiences, the reader should bear in mind the spurious inflation of statistically significant differences that result as a function of the number of comparisons being made. The formula for calculating adjustments in significance level is:

$$P = (1 - a)^n$$

where P is the original significance level, a_1 is the adjusted significance level, and n_1 is the number of comparisons made for the $p = 0.05$ level.

N	1	2	3	4	5	6	7
a_1	0.050	0.025	0.017	0.012	0.010	0.008	0.007

Since our greatest interest is in differences in patterns of experience, we shall focus more on the results of multiple regression analyses to be presented in later sections than on the significance of differences of individual tasks. The significance figures on task differences should be used only as general indicators of trends.

Firstborns experienced fewer social tasks than did later-born children (11.0 versus 13.8 percent, $p = 0.24$). At first, this finding surprised us. We expected the opposite to happen. We had reported previously that social experience as a whole was positively correlated with later achievement. The bulk of the difference seems to be due to much greater amounts of experience by firstborns listening to their mothers talk to them (gain information, auditory and visual, 18.9 versus 8.4 percent, $p = 0.008$).

There were several noteworthy differences among nonsocial experiences.

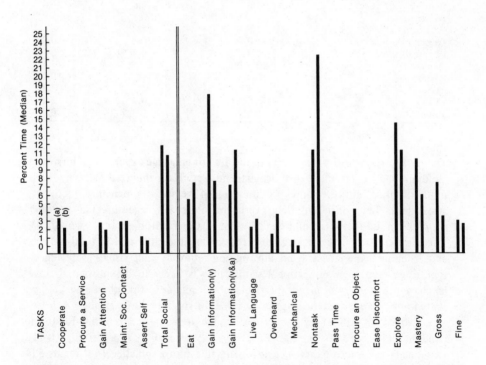

Figure 6-2. Task Patterns: (a) Comparisons Between Children from Previous Study (12 to 15 Months later-born) and (b) Later-Born Monitored Control Children ($C_{1,2}$) in Current Study (11 to 16 months).

Table 6-12
Task Patterns, Sibling Effects (11 to 16 Months)

	Median Percent Duration		
Social Tasks	All E and C (N = 27)	All Firstborns (N = 15)	Later-Borns (N = 12)
All social	11.0	11.0	13.8
To cooperate	2.0	2.2	1.9
To procure a service	1.0	0.7	0.4
To gain attention	2.0	1.4	2.2
To maintain social contact	3.2	2.8	5.3
To assert self	0.0	0.0	0.3
Nonsocial Tasks			
To eat	2.7	2.4	4.4
To gain information (visual)	6.4	6.0	7.2
To gain information (visual and auditory)	11.0	18.9	8.4
Live language	7.1	10.4	4.1
Overheard	0.0	0.0	2.7
Mechanical	0.0	0.0	0.0
Nontask	11.6	9.6	20.0
To pass time	1.6	0.6	1.9
To procure object	1.8	1.8	1.6
To gain pleasure	0.0	0.0	0.0
To ease discomfort	0.4	0.3	0.3
To explore	13.5	12.5	13.4
Mastery	11.0	11.2	10.4
Gross	3.4	3.1	3.7
Fine	5.6	6.0	5.0
To imitate	0.0	0.0	0.0

The most striking differences were in the area of language experiences. Firstborn children had much more live language directed *to them* (usually by their mothers) than did the other children (10.4 versus 4.1 percent, $p = 0.004$, two-tailed). Later-born children overheard more language directed *at other people* than did firstborn children (2.7 versus 0.0 percent, $p = 0.001$, two-tailed). The differences in live language directed toward the child and in total looking and listening experiences (gain information, auditory and visual) were highly significant, and their educational significance is likely to be substantial. Live language directed *to an infant*, particularly if it relates to the infant's concern *at that moment*, appears to be of primary value for good development.

Two other differences were large enough to warrant attention. Firstborn children had less empty (nontask) experience (9.6 versus 20.0 percent, $p = 0.11$, two-tailed) and more experience involving fine motor practice (6.0 versus 5.0 percent, $p = 0.08$, two-tailed). Both differences appear to be advantageous to firstborn children.

Since fewer than twenty types of experience account for most of the

Table 6-13
Sibling Effects on Tasks, Statistical Analysis (Mann Whitney U)

Social Tasks	E vs. C (one-tailed) p Values		Firstborn vs. Others (two-tailed) p Values
All social	E > C	0.26	0.24
To cooperate	E > C	0.13	0.30
To procure a service		0.29	0.34
To gain attention		0.35	0.37
To maintain social contact		0.22	0.15
To assert self		0.28	0.14
Nonsocial Tasks			
To eat		0.18	0.29
To gain information (visual)	C > E	0.11	0.68
To gain information (visual and auditory)		0.29	0.008**
Live	E > C	0.12	0.004**
Overheard		0.26	0.001***
Mechanical		0.35	0.18
Nontask	C > E	0.06	0.11
To pass time	C > E	0.07	0.45
To procure object	E > C	0.009**	0.94
To gain pleasure		0.33	0.19
To ease discomfort		0.61	0.41
To explore		0.47	0.96
Mastery	E > C	0.002**	0.12
Gross motor	E > C	0.04*	0.92
Fine motor	C > E	0.06	0.08

*$p = 0.05$.
**$p = 0.025$.
***$p = 0.001$.

infant's day, even such a modest number of differences between groups in a small-sample study seems noteworthy.

A Note of Importance

We labeled a task *social* if the apparent purpose was to effect a change in the social behavior of either the subject child or the other person. Thus a child's attempts to achieve or maintain contact with another were designated as social tasks. In the same spirit, when a child resisted an encroachment by another person on his property or rights, we labeled the episode *to assert self* and called it social. The key to the classification is the child's *purpose*.

When a child is offered food and he accepts it and concentrates on eating, we label the experience as nonsocial, even though another person may have given him the food or even remain nearby while the child eats. The same procedure

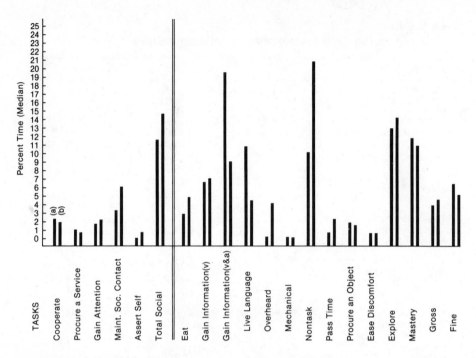

Figure 6-3. Task Patterns: Sibling Effects: (a) Firstborn Children (*N* = 15) versus (b) Later-Born Children (*N* = 12), Age Range 11 to 16 Months.

results in labeling staring behavior as *gaining information through vision* and making believe as a *pretend* task.

Language experiences are at times more complex. If an infant is watching television and listening to language from the set, we call the experience *gaining information through looking and listening* and classify it as nonsocial. What then do we do with a situation in which an infant is being read to by her mother? Is this a social task, or might it be classified otherwise? If the infant seems to be genuinely interested in the content of the story, we label the experience as *gaining information through listening to live language directed to her.* If her attention wanders or if she interrupts her mother and changes the subject or in any other way indicates that she is more interested in the social contact than in the story, we label the task *maintain social contact*, a social task. Clearly then, certain language tasks that we code as nonsocial have social qualities to them. Nevertheless, if the child's purpose seems to be primarily to understand and enjoy the contents of the language, we believe that the event is best coded as nonsocial. The other side of the coin is also true. Events we code as social at times clearly contain language the child attends to, yet that information is neither focused upon nor preserved in our analyses. Cooperate experiences usually are precipitated by a verbal request made by an adult to the infant.

Initiation Data. Mothers of firstborn children initiated nearly twice as many of their children's experiences than did mothers of later-born children (20.3 versus 11.0 percent). The bulk of the differences seemed to be in nonsocial rather than social experience (17.3 versus 8.1 percent).

Treatment Differences

Because birth-order differences have been so substantial in this study, the conventional practice of emphasizing comparisons of the total experimental group with the total control groups will not be pursued in this report. We shall instead concentrate on subgroup analyses, that is, firstborn experimental group children versus firstborn control group children. The consequential reductions in cell sizes are particularly unfortunate in intensive small-group studies such as this. Nevertheless, we have no choice, since combining data from families with one child with data from families with two or more children would obscure rather than clarify the issues.

Treatment Effects: Firstborn Children Only (E_1 versus $C_{1,1}$ Data). Data on the experiences of firstborn children are especially important for practical purposes. In general, we and others have found that first-time parents are more receptive to programs in education for parenthood than those with two or more children. If programs of education for parenthood become more numerous, those for new parents will be more common than any other. Earlier in this chapter we reported that our training efforts were only moderately successful in separating the childrearing practices of the mothers in the training program from those of the mothers who were visited just as often but who received no training. There were some noticeable differences apparently attributable to the training, but the similarities were perhaps more impressive. What then did the chldren in those two primary groups actually experience in their daily lives?

The data in tables 6-14 and 6-15 and figure 6-4 deal with that issue. The most striking differences between groups were as follows: experimental children had more *cooperative, live language, procure an object*, and *gross* and *fine mastery* experiences; control children had more *nontask, pass-time*, and *exploratory* experiences. Bear in mind that these differences should be considered only as trends because of the crude nature of our statistical analyses.

Two questions seem appropriate here. First, did we create substantial differences in the everyday experiences of these children? If so, were they in the directions we intended? A third question of interest is: How did participating in this kind of study affect the experiences of (and development of) the control

Table 6-14
Task Patterns, Treatment Effects: Firstborn Children (11 to 16 Months)

	Median Percent Duration	
Social Tasks	E_1 (N = 7)	$C_{1,1}$ (N = 8)
All social	9.1	11.0
To cooperate	3.1	1.1
To procure a service	0.4	0.4
To gain attention	1.6	1.5
To maintain social contact	1.4	2.1
To assert self	0.0	0.0
Nonsocial Tasks		
To eat	2.2	5.1
To gain information (visual)	6.0	8.6
To gain information	24.3	13.8
(visual and auditory)		
Live	17.2	8.3
Overheard	0.0	0.0
Mechanical	0.8	0.0
Nontask	6.2	13.5
To pass time	0.0	0.7
To procure object	2.5	1.4
To gain pleasure	0.6	0.0
To ease discomfort	0.0	0.6
To explore	7.5	12.1
Mastery	14.2	11.9
Gross motor	2.4	1.4
Fine motor	6.8	6.0

group? Can we learn anything about the phenomenon of "the climbing control group" from these process-analysis data?

Did we create substantial differences between groups of children? Without a directly appropriate statistical analysis we cannot provide a firm answer to this question. On the basis of Mann-Whitney U tests of differences in central tendencies as well as the apparent size of some of the differences in important categories of experience, the answer is a qualified yes. In particular, the differences in the amounts of *live language directed to the child, nontask* episodes, and *procure an object* experiences seem more than incidental. On the other hand, several types of experiences that we hoped to increase or decrease did not seem to differ across the groups, namely, *total social experiences, procure a service, gain attention, gain information through looking (visual), passing time,* and *fine motor mastery.* There are then at least two bases for a qualified answer. First, because of small samples and limited resources, we have no convincing statistical data. Second, several possibly important categories of experiences did not vary directly as a function of group assignment.

Did the children in the experimental group receive more beneficial experiences than those in the control group? In *Experience and Environment,* Volume

Table 6-15
Treatment Effects on Tasks: Firstborn Children, Statistical Analysis
(Mann-Whitney U)

Social Tasks	Prediction	E_1 vs. C_1 (N = 7) (N = 8) p Values
All social	E > C	0.32 C > E
To cooperate	E > C	0.04*E > E
To procure a service	E > C	0.81
To gain attention	E > C	0.52
To maintain social contact	E > C	0.91
To assert self	–	0.45
Nonsocial Tasks		
To eat	C > E	0.45
To gain information (visual)	E > C	0.73
To gain information (visual and auditory)	E > C	0.30
Live	E > C	0.16 E > C
Overheard	–	0.17
Mechanical	–	0.95
Nontask	C > E	0.13 C > E
To pass time	C > E	0.23 C > E
To procure object	C > E	0.04*E > C
To gain pleasure	–	0.60
To ease discomfort	–	0.50
To explore	–	0.10 C > E
Mastery	–	0.06 C > E
Gross motor	C > E	0.09
Fine motor	E > C	0.22

*p = 0.05.

2, analyses suggested that certain experiences were especially significant for educational development during the first years of life. Table 6-16 is derived from the extreme group and multiple regression analyses of the natural experimental study.

In this study, the firstborn children in the experimental group appeared to have had different experiences from those of the control group as follows: in the case of *live language directed to them* and *pass time*, they appeared to have an advantage, especially with respect to language experience. In the case of *procure an object*, the control group children seemed to have had an edge. In the other eight categories the differences were small and evenly balanced. Therefore, although it appears that there were some interesting experiential differences between these primary groups apparently related to our training efforts, the indications are that our attempts to move the children of the experimental group closer than those in the control group to the hypothesized desirable pattern of experiences did not fully succeed. Whatever we were suggesting to the parents in

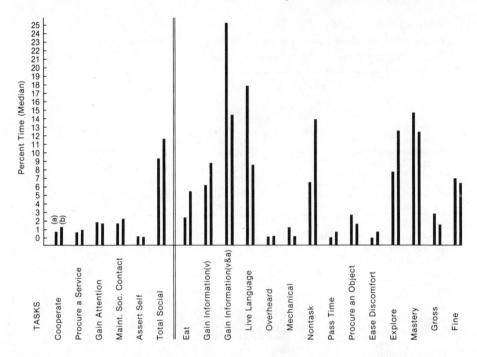

Figure 6-4. Task Patterns: Treatment Effects: (a) Experimental Firstborns (*N* = 7) versus (b) Control Firstborns (*N* = 8), Age Range 11 to 16 Months.

the training group did not lead to the kinds of differences in the experiences of these groups of firstborn children that we sought to achieve.

What does this result mean? Were we unable to modify the childrearing practices of the parents in the experimental group? Did the parents in the monitored control group change their styles too? A look at the patterns of development we previously found associated with differing levels of achievement might shed some light on these issues. The achievement levels of the children in this study will also provide relevant information.

If the firstborn children in this study had experiences similar to those we advocated on the basis of our previous work, they should have done well. They should score well on achievement tests at 2 and 3 years of age.

If the firstborn children in the control group had experiences like those of the children in the experimental group and also similar to those previously associated with high levels of achievement, they too should have shown high levels of ability at 2 and 3 years of age.

How did the experiences of all firstborn children in this study relate to the hypothesized pattern of beneficial experiences? In general, the individual social

Table 6-16
Relation of Tasks at 12 to 15 Months of Age to Level of
Abilities at 3 Years of Age (from the Previous Study)

	Desirable Quantities	
	Higher than Average	Lower than Average
All social	X	
To please	X	
Procure a service	X	
Gain attention	X	
Gain attention (visual)	X	
Live language directed to S	X	
Language overheard by S	X	
Pass time		X
Procure object		X
Prepare for an activity	X	
Gross motor mastery		X

experiences of the firstborn children in this study were midway between those of the strongest and weakest children in the previous study. They did, however, resemble the better developing children with regard to the total quantity of social experience, both of these groups undergoing considerably more than the children developing least well (see figure 6-5).

In the nonsocial realm, the most striking differences are in the area of language experience. Firstborns in the current study had far more focused language experience than the children in the previous study. This finding was offset to some degree by smaller amounts of *steady staring* without associated language by the newer children. In the areas of *nontask, pass-time, procure an object*, and *gross motor mastery* experiences, the firstborn children had amounts of experience more like the well-developing than the less-well-developing children in the previous study. Aside from *eating* and *seeking attention*, where there were modest similarities to the experiences of the less-well-developing children, it seems clear that *all* firstborn children in the current study had experiences during their eleventh to sixteenth months that were likely to lead to healthy educational development. The reader should note that the differences between the experiences of firstborn experimental children and those of firstborn children in the control group seem to give the experimental group children a slight edge.

Our conclusion therefore is that the experimental and control group firstborn children in this study had experiences during the 11- to 16-month period that were more similar than different in regard to educational development and that overall the experiences of both groups should have resulted in better than average levels of development of competence.

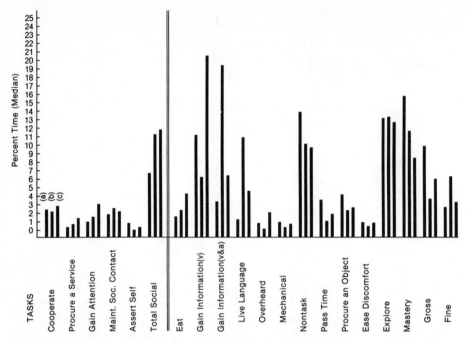

Figure 6-5. Task Patterns: (a) Firstborn Children Current Study (*N* = 15), Age range 11 to 16 Months, versus (b) Patterns for Best-Developing (*N* = 8) and (c) Least-Well-Developing (*N* = 15) Children in Previous Study, Age Range 12 to 15 Months.

Treatment Effects: Later-Born Children (E$_2$ versus C$_2$ Data). Half the families in this study at its outset had more than one child. In each of the three primary groups, five families had two children and two had three children. In the experimental group, we lost one family with two children because of illness. In the monitored control group, we also lost one family with two children because we had to inform the parents that the child was developing very slowly and that special attention was therefore advisable. The result is that the group sizes in the cases of groups E$_2$ and C$_{1,2}$ were reduced to only six children.

Comparisons based on so few families are not likely to be of great value. In retrospect, we should perhaps have designed the study so that more families were involved with less contact with each family. Yet hindsight is usually more accurate than the ability to foresee events.

Tables 6-17 and 6-18 and figure 6-6 contain data on our later-born subjects in the experimental and monitored control (C$_1$) groups.

Did we create substantial experiential differences between the groups? In spite of small group size, it looks as though children in the experimental group had more social experiences than those in the monitored control group (16.5

Table 6-17
Task Patterns, Treatment Effects: Later-Born Children (11 to 16 Months)

	Median Percent Duration	
Social Tasks	E_2 (N = 6)	$C_{1,2}$ (N = 6)
All social	16.5	10.2
To cooperate	1.8	2.1
To procure a service	0.6	0.2
To gain attention	2.1	2.0
To maintain social contact	4.7	2.7
To assert self	0.5	0.3
Nonsocial Tasks		
To eat	3.9	7.0
To gain information (visual)	5.3	7.2
To gain information (visual and auditory)	11.0	10.7
Live	4.9	2.8
Overheard	2.2	3.3
Mechanical	0.0	0.0
Nontask	14.0	21.1
To pass time	0.0	2.4
To procure object	1.9	1.2
To gain pleasure	0.0	0.0
To ease discomfort	0.4	0.8
To explore	17.5	10.2
Mastery	10.3	5.1
Gross motor	1.1	3.1
Fine motor	2.2	2.7

versus 10.2 percent, $p = 0.13$, one-tailed). This difference seems to be attributable to two categories, *maintain social contact* and *procure a service*.

Turning to nonsocial tasks, the largest differences seen were in three categories, *pass-time, explore*, and *mastery* experiences. Children in the experimental group had less *pass-time* and more *explore* and *mastery* experiences than children in the monitored control group.

These differences are not the same as those seen in a comparison of the experiences of the groups of firstborn children in this study. Whether this is due to interaction effects or extraneous factors that surface because of small group size or some other source, we do not know.

Did the children in the experimental group receive more beneficial experiences than those in the control group? Referring once again to the tasks presented in tables 6-17 and 6-18 as especially related to educational development, we find the children in the experimental group differed from the others with respect to total *social experience, procure a service, pass-time*, and *gross motor mastery* experiences. In the case of the first three categories, the children in the experimental group had more appropriate amounts of experience. In the case of the last category, the control group children held an advantage. In the

Table 6-18
Treatment Effects on Tasks: Later-Born Children,
Statistical Analysis (Mann-Whitney U)

Social Tasks	Prediction	E_2 (N = 6) vs. $C_{1,2}$ (N = 6) p Values
All social	E > C	0.13
To cooperate	E > C	0.47
To procure a service	E > C	0.17
To gain attention	E > C	0.69
To maintain social contact	E > C	0.20
To assert self	–	0.87
Nonsocial Tasks		
To eat	C > E	0.63
To gain information (visual)	E > C	0.26
To gain information (visual and auditory)	E > C	0.94
Live	E > C	0.34
Overheard	–	0.81
Mechanical	–	0.53
Nontask	C > E	0.42
To pass time	C > E	0.17
To procure object	C > E	0.26
To gain pleasure	–	0.14
To ease discomfort	–	1.00
To explore	–	0.09
Mastery	–	0.01**
Gross motor	C > E	0.42
Fine motor	E > C	0.33

$**p = 0.025$.

other seven categories, the groups were more alike. As was the case with firstborn children, we seemed to have had a modest beneficial impact on the children in the experimental group.

In the light of previous findings, how appropriate were the experiences of these groups for good educational development? The most striking similarity in social experiences across these groups is that later-born children in the current study had amounts of social experience comparable to the better developing group in our earlier work (see figure 6-7). Much of this resemblance seems to be due to the *maintain social contact* category. In nonsocial tasks, the picture also seems to favor children in the current study with respect to key experiences. In the current study, children experienced desirable quantities of *live language directed to them* as well as *overheard*. They had appropriately limited *pass-time, procure an object*, and *gross motor* experiences.

In all, it appears that the later-born children in the current study had experiences more consistent with good development than with poor develop-

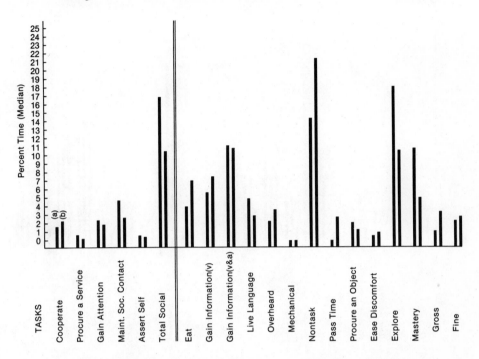

Figure 6-6. Task Patterns: (a) Later-Born Experimental Children $(E_2)(N = 6)$ versus (b) Later-Born Monitored Control Children $(C_{1,2})(N = 6)$, Age Range 11 to 15 Months.

ment. Considering the central importance of language development and the considerably greater amounts of *live language* directed toward firstborns, we might expect higher levels of intellectual and linguistic achievement by the firstborn than by later-born children in this study.

The Development of Competence

Our research has sought to explain how experiences affect the development of abilities in children. We have become convinced that the experiences of the period of life between about 7 months and 3 years are of unique importance. We performed a longitudinal natural experiment (*Experience and Environment*, Volumes 1 and 2) to generate hypotheses about the effects of various early experiences on development and their relation to the childrearing practices of families. This study sought to put those hypotheses to experimental test.

In this study, we tried to persuade average parents (E group) to raise their children during the seventh to twenty-fourth months of life in a manner

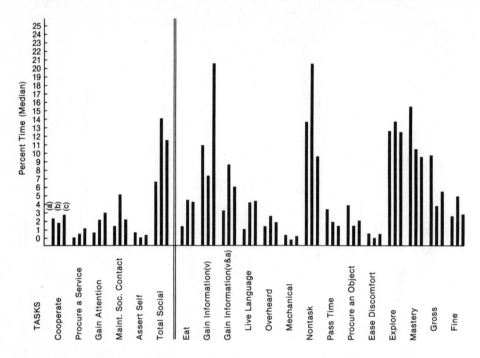

Figure 6-7. Task Patterns: (a) Later-Born Children Study (N = 12), Age Range 11 to 16 Months, versus (b) Patterns for Best-Developing (N = 8) and (c) Least-Well-Developing (N = 5) Children in Previous Study, Age Range 12 to 15 Months.

consistent with practices that seemed to work best with the children in our previous studies. To control for the effects of extraneous factors such as the attention paid the families by university personnel, the sensitization to the possible special importance of childrearing during infancy, and the repeated testing and observing of their children, we worked with three other groups of families. One was treated similarly to the experimental group, except that ideas about childrearing were provided by a pediatric team which emphasized the importance of interpersonal relations and emotional support (PC). Another group (C_1) was observed and tested on the same schedule but received no guidance on childrearing practices. A fourth group of families (C_2) was seen at the beginning of the study but not again until their children reached 2 years of age. The children were tested then and also at 3 years of age.

The purpose of this design was to try to isolate the effects of our hypotheses from other factors likely to affect early human development. We were limited by certain realities. First, any family that participates in a research project has to be considered as a member of a subgroup of the population. Clearly many families, for a number of reasons, *would not*. Some would prefer that their privacy remain intact. Others would no doubt have stresses in their lives that would make participation in a research program seem like too much of a burden. We do not know enough about these and other relevant factors to justify a thorough analysis. We did feel, however, that the design of the study required that we focus on families with average childrearing capacities. Our screening procedures (see chapter 4) seemed to have worked reasonably well in that regard, especially in the case of families with more than one child.[3] In such instances we were able to go beyond assessment of general family characteristics such as SES and the mother's language ability level by sampling the abilities of the next oldest child.

Unlike the majority of recent studies of preschool development, our focus has always been broader than the development of intelligence and language. Our work has included the development of social skills as well.

Our battery of test procedures therefore has been broad. It has included standardized tests of general development such as the Bayley tests of motor and mental development. It has also included tests of language and intelligence, some standardized (the Stanford-Binet and Wechsler tests) and others developed by our own staff (the Preschool Project Language, Abstract Abilities, and Dissonance tests). In the case of the latter instruments, we borrowed liberally from the work of others, namely, C.E. Meyer; J. McV. Hunt and I. Uzgiris; D. MacNeill; U. Bellugi-Klima; and R.B. Ammons and J.C. Holmes. For assessing social skill development, we created a behavior checklist (see *Experience and Environment*, volumes 1 and 2). In earlier work we have combined scores in several ways so as to yield indices of nonsocial competence and of overall (social plus nonsocial) competence. The combinatorial procedures are, of course, somewhat arbitrary given the state of knowledge. Nevertheless, we believed they were useful.

A Significant Loss of Data

The assessments of the competencies of our subjects were all performed by testers who knew nothing about the group membership of the sixty families in the study. The core staff therefore did not have access to achievement data until very recently. Examination of the test scores revealed that one of the testers who gathered much of the data on the development of social competence was using the instrument in a manner that was grossly different from its intended use. That tester's records revealed a scoring of about three times as many individual social acts as scored by previous users of the instrument. In addition, the same tester recorded many instances of a type of social behavior never before reported for the age range involved.

Our records indicated that the tester in question was trained to use the instrument according to our ordinary routines. The interobserver reliability study used to judge the tester's performance produced a very high Pearson product-moment correlation figure ($r = +0.942$). Nevertheless, it was clear that the data collection by this tester could not be considered valid. Unfortunately, as a result of circumstances beyond our control, this tester became the sole collector of social competence data when another tester had to leave the project. We therefore lost all our outcome data on social development.

This loss is obviously quite serious. There is unfortunately nothing we can do about the situation except to report it and comment on why it happened.

No one (including us) has yet developed a refined procedure for assessing the development of social competence in children during the first 3 years of life (Meyerhoff 1977; Walker 1973). We have identified a set of behaviors through extensive field observational work (Volume I) that specifically defines social competence in preschoolers. We deal with interpersonal behaviors exclusively, unlike others who have recently approached this important subject area (Anderson and Messick 1974). In these latter projects, the scope of *social competence* has been expanded to include intelligence, language, motor skills, perceptual abilities, and indeed *all* human abilities.

To conceptualize social competencies adequately, to identify *what* should be measured, is the first step. To assess a child in this area, to determine *how* to measure social competence, is the second. A reliable, easy to administer, brief procedure would be ideal. The typical 20- to 60-minute procedure to assess intelligence or language or general development is based on such requirements. Unfortunately, we have not yet figured out how to induce an infant or toddler to demonstrate his leadership skills, his ability to use an adult as a resource, or his several other social competences in such a manner. Instead, we have observed each child in his own home, 30 minutes at a time, on repeated occasions, recording social behavior as it occurs naturally. From such behavior we derive a score for social competence (Volume I). Though we trained several people to use the procedure, we are not at all satisfied with it. First of all, it is expensive. And second, although our trainers have usually reported high levels of interobserver reliabilities (better than $+0.85$), we believe that those levels are probably inflated by a less than ideal method of calculating reliability. Support for this position comes from the loss of data in this study.

Intellectual Development

Tables 6-19 and 6-20 contain data on intellectual development of children in our experimental (E), monitored control (C_1), and pretest and posttest control (E_2) groups. In an attempt to detect the earliest effects on intellectual growth, we devised our own measure of the growth of abstract thinking ability during infancy (*Experience and Environment*, Volume 1). From the work of Piaget (1952) it seems that there is very limited ability of this sort much before 18 to

Table 6-19
Intellectual Development: Preschool Project Test of Abstract Abilities
(12 to 24 Months) and Stanford-Binet Test (36 Months)

Groups		12 Months	14½ Months	24 Months	36 Months
All	N	27	26	39	43
$(E + C_1 + C_2)$	Range	<1-3	2-4	4-8.5	83-137
	Median	2	2.5	7	113
First born	N	14	15	21	23
	Range	1-3	2-3	4-8	83-137
	Median	2	2	7	118
vs.					
Laterborn	N	13	11	18	20
	Range	<1-2	2-4	4-8.5	86-125
	Median	2	3	6	102.5
Firstborn					
E_1	N	7	7	7	7
	Range	1-3	2-3	7-8	103-137
	Group median	2	2	8	118
$C_{1,1}$	N	7	8	8	8
	Range	1-3	2-3	5-8	118-132
	Group median	2	2.5	7	122
$C_{2,1}$	N	Not tested	Not tested	6	8
	Range			4-7	83-129
	Group median			7	111.5
Later-born					
E_2	N	7	5	6	7
	Range	1-2	2-4	4-7	88-118
	Median	2	3	5.5	98
$C_{1,2}$	N	6	6	6	6
	Range	1-2	2-3	4-7	86-118
	Median	2	2	6.5	99
$C_{2,2}$	N	Not tested	Not tested	6	7
	Range			4-8.5	90-125
	Median			5.5	113

24 months of age. We therefore use the object permanence scale of Uzgiris and Hunt (1975) for testing for precursors of higher mental ability during the second year of life. Between 2 and 3 years of life, when the Stanford-Binet could first be used, we adapted the work of C.E. Meyers to our purposes.

Our test has adequate reliability, but our normative data are very limited. As a result, interpretations of scores are limited primarily to analyses of changes over time and differences among groups.

All Children. From 12 to 14½ months of age our subjects showed little improvement and a narrow range of achievement with regard to sensorimotor intelligence. As expected, between 14½ and 24 months of age there were marked

Table 6-20
Intellectual Development, Statistics: Mann-Whitney U Test, Group
Comparisons, Preschool Project Test of Abstract Abilities,
(12 to 14 Months) and Stanford-Binet Test (36 Months)

Groups		12 Months	14½ Months	24 Months	36 Months
All firstborns	N	14	15	21	23
	Group median	2	2	7	118
vs.					
All later-borns	N	13	11	18	20
	Group median	2	3	6	102.5
	p	N.S.	N.S.	N.S.	<0.0004
Firstborn treatment					
E_1	N	7	7	7	7
	Group median	2	2	8	118
$C_{1,1}$	N	7	8	8	8
	Group median	2	2.5	7	122
$C_{2,1}$	N	–	–	6	8
	Group median	–	–	7	111.5
E_1 vs. $C_{1,1}$	p	N.S.	N.S.	0.076	N.S.
E_1 vs. $C_{2,1}$		–	–	0.17	N.S.
$C_{1,1}$ vs. $C_{2,1}$		–	–	N.S.	0.010 (two-tailed)
Later-born treatment					
E_2	N	7	5	6	7
	Group median	2	3	5.5	98
$C_{1,2}$	N	6	6	6	6
	Group median	2	2	6.5	99
$C_{2,2}$	N	–	–	6	7
	Group median	–	–	5.5	113
E_2 vs. $C_{1,2}$	p	N.S.	0.089	N.S.	N.S.
E_2 vs. $C_{2,2}$		–	–	N.S.	N.S.
$C_{1,2}$ vs. $C_{2,2}$		–	–	N.S.	N.S.

increases in both dimensions. At 3 years of age Binet testing revealed that our subjects (on the whole) had attained a high level of intellectual achievement. Their performance was slightly under the eightieth percentile (on national norms).

This clear indication of superior intellectual development was not unexpected. Several recent studies of children of lower socioeconomic status families have shown that participation in intervention studies seems to be associated with improved intellectual test performance even in children in control groups. This latter effect has come to be known as "the climbing control group effect" (Bronfenbrenner 1974). It is not clear what causes such an effect. It may be sample selection, with more interested families more likely to participate in such work. It may be test sophistication resulting from repeated testing of infants and toddlers. It could be a consequence of more attention paid to a child because the parents have become more sensitized to early development as a result of their contact with a research project.

In this study we attempted to work with families who were most likely to have average results with their children. Half the families had older children who had indeed been developing in unremarkable ways (see chapter 4). The parents were in the middle of the national socioeconomic range. The language skills of all the mothers were also average. In addition, the families under discussion were randomly and simultaneously assigned to their respective groups. Yet, on the whole, the children in the study seemed to develop intellectual ability considerably beyond what was likely had they not participated in the study.

Firstborn versus Later-Born Children. The next point revealed by the data seems of special importance. The general effect on the intellectual development of our subjects seems to be linked to birth order. Firstborn children in our study surpass later-born children by a huge margin. Indeed, for later-born children there does not seem to be any general gain from participation in the study. The simplest explanation for this result is that the childrearing practices of first-time parents are more sensitive to change than those of parents of two or more children.

This differential impact on intellectual test scores reinforces our earlier findings that firstborn infants and toddlers are treated differently by their parents and have different patterns of experience than later-born children. It reinforces the notion that research studies on early development should not lump data from families with one child with data from families with more than one child. It also reinforces our conviction that parent education programs will probably have a considerably greater chance for success when provided for first-time parents rather than for others in spite of the lack of experience in childrearing by the former group.

SES was a matched variable across families of firstborn and later-born children. The language ability of the mothers was not a matching variable, although we assumed our other procedures for matching would result in comparable group scores on this factor. In fact, it turned out that the median value on the Ammons Quick Word Test for the mothers of the firstborn children was slightly lower (67) than that of the mothers of the later-born children (71.5). It would appear therefore that neither SES nor mother's language ability accounts for the superior intellectual development of the firstborn children.

Firstborn Children Compared across Groups. All firstborn children did well. Those in the experimental (E_1) and monitored control ($C_{1,1}$) did the best, with the monitored controls having a slight edge over the experimentals. This finding suggests that the effects on the intellectual development of firstborn children of repeated contacts with our staff were stronger than the effects of merely being part of the study (C_2) or of receiving detailed guidance in childrearing from our training personnel. Was the general unguided increase in effort by the $C_{1,1}$ parents more effective than the tutored behavior of the E_1 parents, or did more of the $C_{1,1}$ parents successfully duplicate the patterns of childrearing we were trying to help the E_1 parents employ, or was there some other reason for these results such as sampling differences among the twenty-three mothers and children involved? An analysis of the task patterns of the E_1 and $C_{1,1}$ children may shed some light on this problem. A look at the verbal abilities of the mothers indicates that there were no differences of consequence across the groups.

Later-Born Children Compared across Groups. There were no significant differences across groups of later-born children. Even at 3 years of age, when the $C_{2,2}$ children had a high central tendency score, the distributions of individual scores were not significantly different. These results suggest that the parents of second or third children were considerably less sensitive to the general effects of participation in research and also perhaps less responsive to advice. Again, it should be noted that with such very small samples the possibility of other factors confounding the results is substantial. There were no significant differences in language ability of the mothers of the three groups, although the mothers in group $C_{2,2}$ generally scored higher than the others.

General Development

Partly for purposes of matching subjects and partly for comparison with other studies, we tested our children with the Bayley test of mental and motor development. Tables 6-21 and 6-22 contain the results for the most interesting index, the "mental" test score. It should be pointed out that the Bayley mental test score resembles the development quotient (DQ) score more than any index of intelligence. We treat it as a nonspecific index of general ability during infancy.

All Children. At 4½ months of age, the central tendency for the forty-three subjects was an unremarkable score of 105. At 1 year of age, the score was 106. By 2 years of age, the children had moved considerably ahead of national averages (median group value 112). This trend is consistent with the data on intellectual development.

Firstborn versus Later-Born Children. By 2 years of age, the superiority of the firstborn children seems to be surfacing, although it has reached only modest proportions. Once again, this result is consistent with earlier findings.

Table 6-21
General Development: Bayley Mental Index Scores

Group		Bayley Mental Index (DQ)		
		4½ Months	12 Months	24 Months
All	N	43	28	43
($E_1 + C_1 + C_2$)	Range	81-145	81-126	75-143
	Median	105	106	112
Firstborn	N	23	15	23
	Range	83-123	90-122	75-143
vs.	Median	104	103	114
Later-born	N	20	13	20
	Range	93-145	81-126	83-132
	Median	106	106	112
E_1	N	7	7	7
	Range	83-123	90-122	99-137
vs.	Median	109	112	116
$C_{1,1}$	N	8	8	8
	Range	94-111	93-112	96-143
	Median	102.5	98	115
$C_{2,1}$	N	8	–	8
	Range	89-107	–	107.5
vs.	Median	7	–	7
$C_{2,2}$	N	7	–	7
	Range	94-123	–	83-132
	Median	107	–	112
E_2	N	7	7	7
	Range	93-145	91-117	83-123
vs.	Median	106	106	112
$C_{1,2}$	N	6	6	6
	Range	102-113	81-126	102-119
	Median	106	109	106

Firstborn Children Compared across Groups., The children in the experimental group (E_1) seemed to have a slight edge over their counterparts in the monitored control group ($C_{1,1}$) at 14½ months, but it is no longer there at 2 years of age. By that time, both groups are scoring at about the eighty-fifth percentile and somewhat higher than the children in $C_{2,1}$. This is a rather strong performance by children whose parents average slightly higher than a high school education. Combined with the Binet scores of these children, it reinforces our judgment that most American families are quite capable of rearing children very effectively (at least in regard to intellectual development) during the first 3 years of life. As a reminder it should be pointed out that these high achievements were attained only by the firstborn children.

Later-Born Children Compared across Groups. There were no significant differences seen across the groups of later-born children at either the beginning of the study or when the children were 2 years old.

Table 6-22
General Development: Bayley Mental Index Scores, Statistical Information on Group Comparisons (Mann-Whitney U Test)

Compared Groups		4½ Months	12 Months	24 Months
All firstborn S's	N	23	15	23
vs.	Group median	104	103	114
All later-born S's	N	20	13	20
	Group median	106	106	112
	p_1(two-tailed)	N.S.	N.S.	0.078
Firstborn S's				
Experimental (E_1)	N	7	7	7
	Group median	109	112	116
Monitored control (C_1)	N	8	8	8
	Group median	102.5	98	115
Pre-post control ($C_{2,1}$)	N	8	–	8
	Group median	103	–	107.5
E_1 vs. $C_{1,1}$	p(one-tailed)	N.S.	0.060	N.S.
E_1 vs. $C_{2,1}$		N.S.	–	0.060
C_1 vs. $C_{2,1}$		N.S.	–	N.S.
Later-born S's				
Experimental (E_2)	N	7	7	7
	Group median	106	106	112
Monitored control ($C_{1,2}$)	N	6	6	6
	Group median	106	109	106
Pre-post control ($C_{2,2}$)	N	7	–	7
	Group median	107	–	112
E_2 vs. $C_{1,2}$	p (one-tailed)	N.S.	–	N.S.
E_2 vs. $C_{2,2}$		N.S.	–	N.S.
$C_{1,2}$ vs. $C_{2,2}$		N.S.	–	N.S.

Language Development

Our data on general and intellectual development (at 3 years of age) were gathered with standardized instruments, the Bayley and Stanford-Binet tests. As a result, scores for the total population could be meaningfully compared with national norms. Such is not the case with our language data. We used our own language test since, in our judgment, it was more suited to the task of monitoring the growth in *receptive language* ability during infancy than any other available measure.

The fact that our subjects scored at levels well above their chronological age cannot be taken at face value since we have not established norms for the test. In general, the norms we use are probably not far off, but for the time being their most appropriate use is for between group comparisons and as an index of change over time.

All Children. In tables 6-23 and 6-24 it can be seen that only small increases in test scores appeared between the 12- and 14½-month test dates, whereas considerably larger gains were found between the 14½- and 24-month and 24- and 36-month test results. The range of language ability appeared quite broad, especially as the children reached their second birthdays. Such a finding is consistent with a substantial amount of previous work describing the growth of language ability during the first years of life (McCarthy 1960).

Firstborn versus Later-Born Children. Our expectation from the data on parental behavior, experiences of the children, and mental and general ability tests was that firstborn children would achieve substantially higher levels of language skill as well. This expectation was only partially borne out. After equal

Table 6-23
Preschool Project Language Test Scores

Group		12 Months	14½ Months	24 Months	36 Months
All	N	28	27[a]	35	43
$(E_1 + C_1 + C_2)$	Range	10-18	12-18	18-45	27-57
	Median	14	16	33	45
All firstborn S's	N	15	15	19	23
$(E_1 + C_{1,1} + C_{2,1})$	Range	10-18	14-18	18-45	27-57
	Median	14	16	36	45
All later-born S's	N	13	12	16	20
$(E_2 + C_{1,2} + C_{2,2})$	Range	10-16	12-18	24-36	33-48
	Median	14	16	30	45
Firstborn treatment					
E_1	N	7	7	7	7
	Range	10-16	14-18	33-45	42-57
	Median	16	16	39	48
$C_{1,1}$	N	8	8	7	8
	Range	12-17	16-18	24-39	42-51
	Median	14	17	36	46.5
$C_{2,1}$	N	–	–	5	8
	Range	–	–	18-36	27-48
	Median	–	–	33	42
Later-born treatment					
E_2	N	7	6	7	7
	Range	10-16	12-18	24-36	36-45
	Median	14	16	36	39
$C_{1,2}$	N	6	6	5	6
	Range	10-16	12-16	24-36	36-48
	Median	12	16	30	42
$C_{2,2}$	N	–	–	4	7
	Range	–	–	24-33	33-48
	Median	–	–	30	45

[a]At time subjects were untestable, therefore group size varies from cell to cell.

Table 6-24
Preschool Project Language Test Scores, Statistical Information on Group Comparisons

Compared Groups		12 Months	14½ Months	24 Months	36 Months
All firstborn S's	N	15	15	19	23
	Group median	14	16	36	45
vs.					
All later-born S's	N	13	12	16	20
	Group median	14	16	30	45
	p	N.S.	>0.02 <0.05*	>0.002 <0.02*	N.S.
Firstborn treatment					
E_1	N	7	7	7	7
	Group median	16	16	39	48
$C_{1,1}$	N	8	8	7	8
	Group median	14	17	36.0	46.5
$C_{2,1}$	N	–	–	5	8
	Group median	–	–	33	42
E_1 vs. $C_{1,1}$	p	N.S.	N.S.	0.082 (one-tailed)	0.191 (one-tailed)
E_1 vs. $C_{2,1}$		X	X	0.015 (one-tailed)[a]	0.047 (one-tailed)[a]
$C_{1,1}$ vs. $C_{2,1}$		X	X	N.S.	0.080 (one-tailed)
Later-born treatment					
E_2	N	7	6	7	7
	Group median	14	16	36	39
$C_{1,2}$	N	6	6	5	6
	Group median	12	16	30	42
$C_{2,2}$	N	–	–	4	7
	Group median	–	–	30	45
E_1 vs. $C_{1,1}$	p	0.147 (one-tailed)	N.S.	N.S.	N.S.

E_1 vs. $C_{2,1}$	X	N.S.	0.082 (one-tailed other direction)
C_1 vs. $C_{2,1}$	X	N.S.	0.147 (one-tailed other direction)

*0.156, two-tailed a trend.
[a]Trouble testing C_2's at 24 months.

performances at 12 months of age, the firstborn children did move ahead during the second year, moderately so at 14½ months, and substantially by the second birthday. Their advantage decreased, however, during the third year to a nonsignificant margin.

Firstborn Children Compared across Groups. At 12 and 14½ months of age, E_1 and $C_{1,1}$ children performed equally well. (Both had been experiencing huge quantities of maternal attention.) By the second birthday, E_1 children showed an edge over $C_{1,1}$ children and a clear superiority over $C_{2,1}$ children. By their third birthdays, E_1 children still led both other groups, but by a slightly smaller margin, while the $C_{1,1}$ children were somewhat more ahead of the $C_{2,1}$ children than they were at 2 years of age.

In this specific area of language learning, then, the experimental conditions seemed to have had the desired impact. In addition, as was the case with intellectual development, the firstborn children in the two more heavily involved groups moved ahead of their counterparts in C_2.

Later-Born Children Compared across Groups. Here our expectations were for few differences of consequences. In general, that is what we found. Two points, however, deserve attention. We had considerable difficulty testing our 2-year-olds because of negativism, so much so, in fact, that we could gather trustworthy data only on sixteen of the twenty subjects. In a small-sample study, once again, such problems became significant. In addition, although the group differences did not reach significance, there was a clear reversal of progress between the children's second and third birthdays, when $C_{2,2}$ children apparently acquired language at a much more rapid pace than E_2 children. Once again the explanation of this trend is not to be found in SES or the mothers' language ability, since these groups were quite comparable on both factors.

The Ability to Sense Dissonance

Once again, using a test of our own construction and without substantial normative data, we tested our children for their observational ability. The capacity to notice small differences was one of the several attributes we found particularly well developed in competent 3- to 6-year-olds. Tables 6-25 and 6-26 contain data on our subjects for this ability.

All Children. Once again we find a spurt in the growth of this ability during the second half of the second year of life, as well as a broadening of the range of achievement among our subjects.

Firstborn versus Later-Born Children. Firstborn children developed somewhat faster than later-born children at the beginning of their second year, but the gap

Table 6-25
Preschool Project Dissonance Test Scores

		12 Months	14½ Months	24 Months
All subjects	N	27	27	40
	Median	2	2	7
	Range	0-3.5	1-3	4-8
Firstborns	N	15	15	20
	Median	2	2	7
	Range	0-3	1-3	4-8
Others	N	12	12	20
	Median	2	2	6.5
	Range	0-3.5	1-3	4-8
Experimental firstborns	N	7	7	4
	Median	2	3	7
	Range	0-2	1-3	6-8
Control 1 firstborns	N	8	8	8
	Median	2	2	7
	Range	0-3	2-3	5-8
Control 2 firstborns	N	Not tested	Not tested	8
	Median			6
	Range			4-8
Experimental others	N	6	6	7
	Median	2	2	5
	Range	1-3.5	1-3	4-7
Control 1 others	N	6	6	6
	Median	2	2	6.5
	Range	0-2	1-2	4-8
Control 2 others	N	Not tested	Not tested	7
	Median			7
	Range			5-7

seems to have narrowed by the second birthday. We say "seems to have narrowed" because our testers commented that the test seemed to have too low a ceiling to continue to allow a discrimination between very able children and others at 24 months of age. Indeed, several of our brighter subjects refused to complete the test.

Firstborn Children Compared across Groups. At 14½ months of age, firstborns appeared slightly more advanced in this ability, but by 2 years of age, there were no differences worthy of notice.

Firstborn Children Compared by Treatment. No differences were noted among these groups.

Later-Born Children Compared by Treatment. At 2 years of age, the later-born children of the nonmonitored control group $(C_{2,2})$ performed better on this test than the E_2 children. This finding is consistent with trends in the language development data, but because of possible ceiling effects in this test, it would be unwise, in our view, to read much into this finding.

Table 6-26
Preschool Project Dissonance Test, Statistical Information,
Group Comparisons

Groups		12 Months	14½ Months	24 Months
All firstborn	N	15	15	20
vs.	Group median	2	2	7
All later-born	N	12	12	20
	Group median	2	2	6.5
	p	N.S.	>0.05 <0.10 (two-tailed)	N.S.
Firstborn treatment				
E_1	N	7	7	7
	Group median	2	3	8
$E_{1,1}$	N	7	8	8
	Group median	2	2	7
$C_{2,1}$	N	–	–	8
	Group median			6
E_1 vs. $C_{1,1}$	p	N.S.	N.S.	N.S.
E_1 vs. $C_{2,1}$		–	–	N.S.
$C_{1,1}$ vs. $C_{2,1}$		–	–	N.S.
Later-born treatment				
E_2	N	6	6	7
	Group median	2	2	5
$C_{1,2}$	N	6	6	6
	Group median	2	2	6.5
$C_{2,2}$	N	–	–	7
	Group median			7
E_2 vs. $C_{1,2}$	p	N.S.	N.S.	N.S.
E_2 vs. $C_{2,2}$		–	–	0.13 (opposite direction)
$C_{1,2}$ vs. $C_{2,2}$		–	–	N.S.

Interrelations among Achievement Scores

Longitudinal research utilizing a variety of assessment procedures offers an opportunity to explore issues of predictive capacities of tests and relations among abilities and other factors of theoretical interest. In our longitudinal natural experiment (see Volume 2), we found (as did many others) that scores at 1 year of age on the Bayley mental scale did not predict to performance on the same test at 2 years of age, or to performance on the Stanford-Binet test at 3 years of age, or the Wechsler at 5 years of age. Likewise, scores on the Bayley mental scale by 2-year-old children predicted Binet and Wechsler scores at 3 and 5 years reasonably well.

In addition, we found some predictive power from scores on our own experimental assessment tests of language and social competence from performance shortly after the first birthday. In particular, receptive language ability at 14½ months of age and use of an adult as a resource from 12 to 15 months of age seem to hold real promise as early indicators of educational development. We found also that individual experiences (such as live language directed to the child), clusters of experiences (namely, the quantity of all social experiences), and certain patterns of experiences at 12 to 15 months of age predicted achievement at 3 and at 5 years of age with surprising power.

These predictions were in the form of correlation coefficients. The fact that we selected unusually successful and unsuccessful families (in their previous childrearing efforts) increased the sensitivity of our correlational analyses. Conversely, in this study the fact that we selected families that were all likely to be about average in childrearing abilities reduced the sensitivity of our correlational analyses. The intention of the study, however, was to improve the childrearing styles of trained groups of families as much as possible and hopefully thereby produce higher achievement scores by their children. It was not likely, however, either that our trained group would become as effective as the most successful families we had studied previously or that our control groups would be as unsuccessful as the least effective families previously studied.

Table 6-27 provides data on interrelations among test scores and demographic factors for the forty-three children in the E, C_1, and C_2 groups. Blank spaces in the array indicate r values lower than plus or minus 0.10.

Socioeconomic Status (SES). In general, we expected low positive correlations between SES and child achievement scores in this study because of the limited range of SES allowed by the design. This expectation was borne out.

Mothers' Education. In the sample, mothers' education varied with SES to a moderate degree. Since the design of the study required a narrow range of maternal education, this result was expected.

Quick Word Test (QWT). Similarly, QWT, a measure of verbal ability, also varied positively with SES.

Fathers' Education. Fathers' education was highly correlated with family SES. The finding is due to the fact that fathers' education is a major factor in the composition of the Hollingshead and Redlich SES value.

Bayley Mental Index Scores

4½ Months: As expected there was no relationship between SES and performance on the Bayley mental scale at this age.

12 Months: Again, no relationship was expected or found.

24 Months: As in many previous studies, the first linkage between SES and the Bayley mental index scores occurred at the second birthday.

Language Ability

12 Months: We did not expect a significant relationship at 12 months, but we found a clear positive trend.

14½ Months: At this age, because of the restricted SES range, we expected no relationship. There was none found.

24 Months: If a relationship was to surface, 2 years would be an expected time. There was none found, and this turned out to be one of the few surprises in the matrix. Its possible meaning is dealt with in later sections.

Abstract Ability. Expectations here were the same as those for language.

12 Months: No relationship was expected. None was found.

14½ Months: No relationship was found.

24 Months: A positive trend was indicated.

Sensing Dissonance. Expectations here were the same as those for language and abstract abilities. No substantial relationships were found.

Stanford-Binet Mental Test Scores. We expected a small positive relationship, and it was present.

Language Ability at 3 Years. We expected a small positive relationship, and it was present.

Rank versus Nonsocial Competence. We expected a small positive relationship, and it was present.

Summary

The only surprise was in regard to language scores at 2 years of age. The next two sections will deal with this issue.

Mothers' Education. We expected mothers' education to relate positively to mothers' language ability and to children's achievements from 2 years on. Mothers' education did indeed relate to their language ability, but did not relate in any substantial way to the child's achievement. Merely possessing a higher

Table 6-27
Demographic and Test Matrix

	SES Standinga	Mother's Ed.	Mother's Quick Word Test	Father's Ed.	Bayley (mos.) 4	Bayley (mos.) 12	Bayley (mos.) 24	Language (mos.) 12	Language (mos.) 15
SESa									
Mother's Ed.	+0.30								
M. Quick Word Test	+0.27	+0.43****							
Father's Ed.	+0.71*****	+0.26*	<0.10						
Bayley									
4 mos.	+0.10	+0.20	+0.23	+0.11					
12 mos.	-0.15	<0.10	-0.24	<0.10					
24 mos.	+0.27*	<0.10	-0.11	+0.15		+0.27			
Language									
12 mos.	+0.34	<0.10	+0.26	+0.24	<0.10	+0.26	+0.21		
15 mos.	<0.10	<0.10	-0.10	<0.10	<0.10	<0.10	+0.50****	+0.50****	
24 mos.	+0.15	<0.10	-0.20	<0.10	<0.10	+0.17	+0.62	+0.10	+0.41**
Abstract Abilities									
12 mos.	<0.10	<0.10	+0.11	+0.17	<0.10	-0.24	<0.10	+0.15	+0.35*
15 mos.	<0.10	-0.61***	-0.22	-0.13	+0.33	-0.22	<0.10	-0.14	<0.10
24 mos.	+0.28	+0.17	-0.20	+0.32*	-0.12	+0.29	+0.54****	<0.10	+0.26
Dissonance									
12 mos.	+0.19	<0.10	+0.19	+0.36*	-0.12	<0.10	-0.12	+0.25	<0.10
15 mos.	+0.13	-0.33*	<0.10	<0.10	-0.26	+0.45	+0.34*	+0.41**	+0.46***
24 mos.	<0.10	-0.17	<0.10	<0.10	<0.10	+0.29	+0.34*	<0.10	+0.12
Binet									
36 mos.	+0.28*	<0.10	+0.15	+0.11	<0.10	<0.10	+0.41****	+0.12	+0.33*
Language									
36 mos.	+0.33**	<0.10	-0.11	+0.11	<0.10	+0.29	+0.63*****	+0.24	+0.44**
Rankb									
36 mos.	+0.36***	<0.10	+0.13	+0.16	<0.10	+0.19	+0.50****	+0.19	+0.39**

Table 6-27 continued

	Language (mos.) 24	Abstract Abilities (mos.) 12	15	24	Dissonance (mos.) 12	15	24	Binet (mos.) 36	Language (mos.) 36
SES^a									
Mother's Ed.									
M. Quick Word Test									
Father's Ed.									
Bayley									
4 mos.									
12 mos.									
24 mos.									
Language									
12 mos.									
15 mos.									
24 mos.									
Abstract Abilities									
12 mos.	<0.10								
15 mos.	<0.10	−0.32							
24 mos.	+0.39**	+0.11	−0.24						
Dissonance									
12 mos	−0.32	<0.10	−0.27	<0.10					
15 mos.	+0.14	+0.22	−0.59	+0.40*	+0.24				
24 mos.	+0.45****	+0.17	−0.29	+0.40***	−0.12	+0.14			
Binet									
36 mos.	+0.50****	+0.22	<0.10	+0.36**	−0.12	+0.15	+0.36**		
Language									
36 mos.	+0.72****	−0.11	<0.10	+0.54***	<0.10	+0.26	+0.52****	+0.64****	
Rank^b									
36 mos.	+0.58****	<0.10	<0.10	+0.53***	<0.10	+0.23	+0.51****	+0.88	+0.86

^{a}SES Standing = SES score; SES score of 1 = highest standing, SES score of 5 = lowest standing.

^{b}Rank = rank score; rank score of 1 = highest rank, rank score of 43 = lowest rank.

  * = 0.05.

  ** = 0.025.

  *** = 0.01.

  **** = 0.005.

than average level of education did not ensure a mother that her child would develop better language and intellectual skills than a child of someone with less education.

Mothers' Verbal Ability. We found the same pattern to be true with respect to verbal ability. The common-sense notion that a more verbally able mother will have a more verbally and intellectually able child was not confirmed in this study.

Fathers' Education. We did not expect this factor to appear to be a powerful influence on a child's development, and our expectations were confirmed.

The Bayley Mental Index Score (MDI)

4½ Months: Scores on the Bayley mental scale had never been found to predict achievement except in the case of children scoring below 85 repeatedly. Our population was by design free from serious pathology, and as expected, these scores predicted nothing.

12 Months: At 12 months of age, the predictive power of this test is considered to be similar to what it was at 4½ months. We found, however, some understandable trends in our data with respect to Bayley mental index scores at 24 months, language ability at 12 months, abstract ability at 24 months, sensing dissonance at 14½ and 24 months, and language ability at 3 years.

24 Months: By 2 years of age, this test has traditionally become more useful. Our study is no exception in this regard. Bayley MDI correlates very well (in spite of the restricted range of our sample) with most of our achievement scores from 14½ months on.

Language Ability. We expected scores on language ability to be correlated with other scores of achievement from 2 years and possibly from 15½ months of age.

12 Months: Even at this early point in development, scores on the Preschool Project receptive language test related positively to language scores at 3 years.

14½ Months: Considerably more predictive power was present by 14½ months of age. Significant relations were found with most of the later achievement scores.

24 Months: The expected very strong relationships were obtained here.

Abstract Ability. This selective home-grown test consists of object permanence test items for the infant and toddler, pattern matching items for the toddler and 2-year-old, and some Stanford-Binet items for the child approaching his third birthday. We expected its predictive power to emerge when children were about 2 years of age. That is approximately what we found.

Sensing Dissonance. This home-grown test of pattern discrimination ability was found to have a somewhat low ceiling for bright 2-year-old children. Nevertheless, we expected some predictive capacity to emerge when the children were 2 years old. Again, this expectation was confirmed.

Stanford-Binet Intelligence Test Score. We expected high correlations between this test and the Preschool Project language test. The results were as expected.

Discussion

By and large, this matrix was remarkably within our expectations, with a few notable exceptions. The consistent relationships in expected directions of the home-grown Preschool Project tests with standard instruments was an important finding, justifying increased confidence in these procedures. The fact that the relationships of the Bayley and Stanford-Binet test scores to age of child and demographic factors were consistent with much previous work further reflects well on the experimental procedures. These results also help the reader to interpret this study by indicating levels of achievement of the subjects in the study on nationally standardized scales.

It seems especially noteworthy that our receptive language test, given when the child was only 12 months old, predicted rather well his language and intelligence scores at 3 years of age.

It is perhaps even more interesting to note the *lack of association* between maternal factors such as education and verbal ability and the child's achievements. Once again, the notion is that it is what you *do* with parenting skills rather than what you *can* do that is important. Research focused on the quality of a parent's teaching style, such as the pioneering studies of Hess and Shipman (1965) and Bernstein (1960), has to be supplemented by information on typical day-to-day behavior in order to be effective as an indicator of parent effectiveness.

Early Experiences and the Development of Competence

It is our belief that the experiences children have between their seventh and twenty-fourth months of life are of especial importance for the lifelong developmental process. In our natural longitudinal experiment we looked for patterns of experience during the 12- to 15-month data-collection period which related powerfully to competence at 3 years of age. We were studying a population selected because its members were likely to develop either very well or not as well as average. We therefore had hopes of finding a broad range of achievement by 3 years of age. The achievements of the nineteen children (of the thirty-nine in the study) we studied from their first birthdays were indeed quite variable. Multiple regression analyses identified several groups of experiences at 12 to 15 months of age that correlated at very high levels (from +.76 to +.93) with achievement at 3 years of age (see table 6-28) and also at 5 years of age (see table 6-29).

Our analyses seemed to indicate that a rich social life (many social tasks) was likely to be associated with high levels of achievement. In particular, *procuring a service* and *gaining attention* seemed of special significance in this observation study of natural styles of childrearing. The *amount of live language directed to a child* was perhaps the strongest single indicator of later intellectual and linguistic and social achievement. Restriction of a child's activities (*pass time*) was another factor that surfaced repeatedly in these analyses.

These statistical analyses, combined with our subjective views about the general shape of the childrearing styles of the most and least successful families, were the bases for our hypotheses about effective early educational practices. They served also as the guidelines for the training programs we have created, including the experimental treatment for this study.

We have seen already that the effects of being a firstborn child and being involved in a research study of this kind were stronger than the effect of merely being a member of our experimental group (E). Firstborn children in the monitored control group $(C_{1,1})$ developed about as well as firstborn children in our trained (and monitored) group (E_1), with both groups developing considerably better (beyond the eighty-seventh percentile) in intellectual and linguistic areas than average children. We have seen from our analyses of parental behavior (earlier in this chapter) that the mothers of firstborn children $(E_1$ and $C_{1,1})$ in this study dealt with their children generally in styles much like what we had hypothesized would be effective. Although the mothers in the experimental group seemed to behave closest to the desired manner, both groups resembled our previously successful parents more than did the mothers of later-born children in this study. We were not able to separate to any substantial degree the childrearing practices or our experimental group mothers from those of the monitored control group. Furthermore, the effect of birth order seemed much more powerful than that of training.

The next question to address is: What were the relations among patterns of experience at 12 to 15 months of age in this study to achievement at 3 years of age? Were the patterns associated with outstanding development in the previous study found to be similarly linked to good development in this study?

The loss of our social competence outcome data, along with the deletion of tests for abstract ability and sensing dissonance at 3 years of age, reduced our regression analyses to only three, those dealing with nonsocial competence (combining rank on the Binet test with rank on the Preschool Project language test), the Stanford-Binet score, and the Preschool Project language test.

Table 6-28
Task Experiences (12 to 15 Months), Predicting Outcome Variables (36 Months), Regression Analysis (from Previous Study)

Dependent Variables	Multiple R	p*	Regression Equation
Overall competence rank (1 = high, 39 = low)	0.8438	0.049	Predicted overall rank = 23.0248 + percent duration (0.1882) + percent duration (−2.9090) Procure a service Gain attention + percent duration (0.3765) + percent duration (−1.2073) + percent duration (0.3407) Gross motor mastery Eat and gain info. (v) Gain info. (v) + percent duration (−1.9713) + percent duration (0.0414) + percent duration (0.6750) Live language directed to S Pass time Procure an object
Social competence rank (1 = high, 39 = low)	0.7691	0.107	Predicted social rank = 54.0601 + percent duration (−2.8875) + percent duration (−1.1046) Procure a service Maintain social contact + percent duration (−1.6720) + percent duration (−1.7093) + percent duration (−0.3008) Eat and gain info. (v) Live language directed to S Pass time + percent duration (−0.7232) + percent duration (−1.1852) Procure an object Explore
Nonsocial competence rank (1 = high, 39 = low)	0.9176	0.001	Predicted nonsocial rank = 37.7065 + percent duration (−0.6243) Procure a service + percent duration (−2.2283) + percent duration (−0.3873) + percent duration (−1.6141) Gain attention Gain info. (v) Live language directed to S + percent duration (0.0358) + percent duration (−1.1897) + percent duration (0.2713) Pass time Prepare for activity Procure an object
Stanford-Binet Intelligence Test	0.8920	0.001	Predicted Binet score = 67.0602 + percent duration (1.5902) + percent duration (6.5512) Procure a service Gain attention + percent duration (0.6994) + percent duration (2.9799) + percent duration (−0.2671) Gain info. (v) Live language directed to S Pass time + percent duration (3.1625) Prepare for activity

Preschool Project Language Test	0.9274	0.001	Predicted language score = 46.3204 + percent duration (−1.4235) Procure a service + percent duration (1.9750) Gain attention + percent duration (0.0715) Gain info. (v) + percent duration (1.1439) Live language directed to S + percent duration (0-.4920) Pass time + percent duration (1.7519) Prepare for activity + percent duration (−2.1737) Procure an object
Preschool Project Abstract Abilities Test	0.8568	0.006	Predicted abstract abilities score = 6.5754 + percent duration (0.0782) Gain info. (v) + percent duration (0.1240) Gain attention + percent duration (0.1199) Live language directed to S + percent duration (0.1149) Eat and gain info. (v) + percent duration (0.2776) Prepare for activity + percent duration (−0.0367) Pass time
Preschool Project Dissonance Test	0.7578	0.068	Predicted dissonance score = 4.8930 + percent duration (0.0382) Gain attention + percent duration (0.6075) Procure a service + percent duration (0.0654) Gain info. (v) + percent duration (−0.0644) Live language directed to S + percent duration (−0.0173) Pass time + percent duration (0.5624) Prepare for activity

*Statistical probability.

Table 6-29
Task Experiences (12-15 Months), Predicting Weschler Preschool and Primary Scale of Intelligence (60 Months), Regression Analysis (from Previous Study)

Dependent Variable	Multiple R	p*	Regression Equation
WPPSI	0.8331	0.008	Predicted WPPSI = 118.7795 + percent duration (1.8797) Gain attention + percent duration (0.5974) + percent duration (−0.1365) + percent duration (−0.5769) Nontask Gain info. (v) Live language directed to S + percent duration (−0.4996) Explore

*Statistical probability.

Correlational Analyses of the Effects of Experience
at 11 to 16 Months of Age on the Development of
Competence at 3 Years of Age

Table 6-30 presents data on the correlation of individual tasks at 11 to 16 months of age with each of the three outcomes at 3 years of age.

Performance on the Stanford-Binet Test. We did not expect any single type of experience between 11 and 16 months of age to be highly predictive of achievement at 3 years of age. We hoped to find strong associations between patterns of tasks and later achievements (as we did in the natural experiment).

Table 6-30
Spearman Rank Correlation among Tasks at 11 to 16 Months and Achieved
Levels of Competence at 3 Years of Age ($N = 27$)

		Correlation with		
Social Tasks	Percent Time Spent in Activity	Stanford-Binet Scores	Preschool Project Language Test Scores	Nonsocial Competence Rank
All social tasks	11.0	−0.15	−0.54****	−0.41*
To cooperate	2.0	−0.17	−0.31	−0.33
To procure a service	1.0	+0.39**	+0.14	+0.27
To gain attention	2.0	0.00	−0.27	−0.10
To maintain social contact	3.2	−0.25	−0.38*	−0.38*
To assert self	0.0	0.00	−0.43*	−0.25
Nonsocial Tasks				
To eat	2.7	−0.25	−0.31	−0.32
To gain information (visual)	6.4	0.00	0.00	0.00
To gain information (visual and auditory)	11.0	+0.32	+0.39**	+0.35*
Live language directed to child	7.1	+0.36*	0.42**	0.40**
Overheard language	0.0	−0.24	−0.27	−0.29
Mechanical language	0.0	0.00	+0.18	+0.15
Nontask	11.6	−0.23	−0.28	−0.23
To pass time	1.6	0.00	−0.14	0.00
To procure an object	1.8	0.00	0.00	0.00
To gain pleasure	0.0	0.00	+0.23	+0.18
To ease discomfort	0.4	0.00	0.00	0.00
To explore	13.5	+0.25	+0.25	+0.30
Mastery	11.0	+0.26	+0.33*	+0.33*
Gross	3.4	+0.15	0.00	0.00
Fine	5.6	+0.20	+0.36*	+0.34*

One-tailed probabilities.
  *$p \leqslant 0.05$.
  **$p \leqslant 0.025$.
  ***$p \leqslant 0.01$.
****$p \leqslant 0.001$.

Nevertheless, two of the seven types of experience that related significantly to performance on the Binet test in our previous study did so again in this study. *Procuring a service* (usually from the mother) and *listening to live language directed to the child* (also usually from the child's mother) are experiences found most frequently in homes where parents lavish attention on their infants. Both experiences mesh well with our previously stated hypotheses about effective childrearing practices.

It is important to note that we classify *live language directed to the child* as a nonsocial task. We do this because our coding system is designed to reflect the child's *purposes*. We limit social tasks, therefore, to episodes in which a child's primary purpose is to create an effect on another person. Unfortunately, confusion may result with regard to conversations and other language experiences which are obviously social in a sense yet labeled nonsocial in our analyses. The distinction between the child's *purpose* and the *means* by which he achieves it must be made if one is to be able to inerpret these data accurately. We apologize to the reader for any extra difficulties that result from this approach.

In the natural experiment we expected and obtained more and larger correlations between individual tasks and performance on the Binet at 3 years of age (*Experience and Environment*, Volume 2, pp. 81-88). Among social tasks, *to please* and *gaining attention* were positively and highly associated with Binet scores at 3 years of age. *Procuring a service* and total social experience were also positively associated with Binet scores, although at a lower level.

In the current study, total social experience was not associated with Binet scores. The reason seems to reside in the marked increase in *live language directed to the child* at the expense of other tasks, including social tasks such as *gaining and maintaining social contact*. Especially among our firstborn children, there was much less of a need for the child to initiate or maintain contact with his mother. For both the E_1 and the $C_{1,1}$ children, the mothers were very often present and talking to them about something they were attending to. Indeed, firstborn children in this study sought attention much less than the later-born children and also much less often than those in the previous study. More strikingly, firstborn scores in looking and listening (*gain information, visual and auditory*) and in *live language directed to them* were three and six times as great, respectively, as those of the children in the previous study and more than twice as great as later-born children in the current study. In previous observations we saw a great deal of steady staring (unaccompanied by comments by parents). In this study there seems to have been a conversion of such experiences (*gain information, visual*) into *gain information, visual and auditory*, and *live language directed to the child* because of the large increases in attention to the infant, especially in the case of firstborn children. If, for example, we had classified language experiences as social, the total social task scores for the children in the previous study (all later-borns) would have been about 16.6 percent; for later-borns in this study, about 22.2 percent; and for firstborns in this study, about 30.0 percent. Interestingly, *procure a service* remains highly associated with good Binet performance in both studies.

In spite of the negative correlations of social tasks with achievement, it still seems clear that a *rich social life during infancy* is important for the development of intelligence (as indicated by performance on the Binet test at 3 years of age). We can add that when contact with a caring adult involves a good deal of language directed by that adult to what the child is focused on at the moment, the experience seems to be even more beneficial than other social interchanges.

The huge increase in *live language directed to the child* in the current study also seems to modify the nonsocial task array as well. There is a striking decline in *gaining information through steady staring* in this study as compared with the last one. In the previous study, the group value was 16.0 percent. In this study, later-borns had 7.2 percent, while firstborns had but 6.0 percent. Again, we believe the differences are due to a substitution of language accompanying staring episodes for the purely visual experience.

Two tasks previously found to be related to Binet achievement did not occur often enough in this study to merit analysis (*to please* and *preparing for an activity*). In addition, there is an interesting trend in the data in the case of the category *to eat*. We have previously noted an inverse relationship between time spent eating at 18 to 21 months of age and achievements at 3 years of age. One of the ways loving parents keep infants from hounding them is to keep them busy with food between meals.

The previously reported negative relationships of Binet performance at 3 years to procuring objects and gross motor mastery did not reappear in this study.

Language Capacity. Not surprisingly, most of the early experiences that were correlated with Binet test scores were also correlated with language achievement in the earlier study (*Experience and Environment*, Volume 2, pp. 86-87).

In the current study, once again the dominant factor seemed to be the amount of *live language directed to the child*. In addition, several low-frequency social tasks did relate strongly to late language scores. They were *assert self, maintain social contact*, and *to cooperate*. *Assert self* appeared only in the lives of later-born children and then quite infrequently. The others were considerably more common experiences during infancy. How they might relate to language development is unclear to us.

In the area of nonsocial tasks, we found *live language directed to the child* very strongly associated with language skill at 3 years of age. There was a trend for *eating time* to be negatively associated with language achievement. *Steady staring* seemed to be supplanted by *staring and listening to live language*. *Nontask* behavior was not significantly related to achievement but trended negatively in that direction. Finally, there was a reversal from the expected direction of association between *motor mastery* experiences and language achievement, with *fine motor mastery* positively related to language development. Once again, no obvious explanations aside from chance sampling variations suggest themselves to us at this time.

Nonsocial Competence. In the previous study, nonsocial competence was compiled by averaging the ranks for each child on the Preschool Project language, sensing dissonance, and abstract abilities tests and then averaging that composite rank with the child's rank on the Binet test. In this study, we simply averaged the child's rank in the language area and his rank on the Binet test. There was reason to believe that the correlation of these two composite scores would be very high.

Only two tasks correlated substantially with nonsocial competence in the previous study: *steady staring* and *live language directed to the child.* In this study, *live language directed to the child* once again was significantly correlated with achievement. In addition, *maintain social contact* was negatively associated with achievement, as was *eating* and *to cooperate. Explore* and *fine motor mastery* were positively related to achievement. Once again, we cannot with confidence offer explanations for these relationships.

Summary

From these data and from our previous study (*Experience and Environment*, Volume 2), it would appear that *live language directed to the child* is the most consistently favorable kind of educational experience an infant can have during the 11- to 16-month period. Neither language from a television set nor language engaged in by nearby people and overheard by an infant seem to play a substantial role in the process of acquisition of intellectual or linguistic skill. Since live language directed to the infant during the 11- to 16-month period seems quite important for good early educational development, it should be noted that such experience, though not coded as *social* by us, presupposes large amounts of social contact. Our previous statements about the importance of a rich social life still stand.

A second major point (from both sets of data) is that episodes where an infant seeks assistance from an adult (*procure a service*) seem especially beneficial. This type of experience during the period of life surrounding the first birthday is very likely to determine how well an infant learns *to use an adult as a resource*, a characteristic we found especially well developed in very able 3- to 6-year-olds. Above-average amounts of between-meal eating and nontask (idling) behavior seem to be symptoms of a less than ideal early educational curriculum. Certain other ideas suggested by our earlier study were not borne out in the current data and probably reflect the immaturity of our efforts at that time.

*Pattern Analysis: Experience at 11 to 16 Months
and Competence at 3 Years of Age*

Table 6-30 contains correlations among all common experiences of our subjects at 11 to 16 months of age and three major achievement indices at 3 years of age. We now present multiple regression analyses based on table 6-30.

In the previous study, we worked with children who at 3 years of age ranked from substantially below average achievement up to several who were above the ninety-fifth percentile. We found very substantial relationships among patterns of early experience and later achievement in every area except social competence.

In the current study, working with average families, we did not expect correlations to reach such high levels. Furthermore, the huge amounts of language experience made it clear that the same regression equations would not be found in these data. This meant also that we could expect somewhat different patterns of experience to relate to achievement.[4]

Once again we identified the individual tasks that correlated most highly with outcomes. We then fed them in increasing numbers into the computer. The results can be seen in tables 6-31, 6-32, and 6-33.

Performance on the Stanford-Binet Test. Table 6-31 indicates how well one could predict scores on the Binet test at 3 years of age for our population of twenty-seven children from only two variables: the amounts of *procure a service* and *live language directed to the children* experiences which they had at 11 to 16 months of age. The multiple *r* of +0.491 with a statistical significance of 0.037 seems to underline the special importance of these experiences. Both variables were implicated in the regression analyses of the previous study. Presumably, data from a normally distributed population would show somewhat greater predictive power. Clearly, such studies as these are too few and too crude to merit great confidence, yet this finding is consistent with our data from both this study and our preceding natural experimental work.

Table 6-31 also indicates how well one could predict scores on the Binet test at 3 years of age for our population when five additional experiences are added to the analysis. These five were *maintain social contact, to eat, to explore*, and *motor mastery* (fine and gross). While the multiple *r* increases to 0.622, the significance drops to 0.098.

Table 6-31 also indicates how well one could predict scores on the Binet test at 3 years of age for our population when one additional experience *live language, overheard*) is added to the analysis. The multiple *r* remains the same, but the significance drops even further.

Further analyses might produce other interesting ideas, but we felt little inclination to proceed further on this track. The most important feature of these data seems to be indicated by the first two variable analysis.

Table 6-31
Predicting Stanford-Binet Performance at 3 Years of Age from Earlier Experience

```
TASK REGRESSION E AND C 11-16 MOS

MULTIPLE REGRESSION USING FILES        R.DATA AND        DATA.DES

DEPENDENT VARIABLE IS NUMBER    1  (    BINET.36.MO )

INTERCEPT =      101.8486
MULTIPLE R SQUARE =    0.2407
MULTIPLE R =           0.4906
DETERMINANT =          0.7414

        ANALYSIS OF VARIANCE FOR THE MULTIPLE
                LINEAR REGRESSION

              D.F.     SUM OF        MEAN          F
                        SQ/  26     SQ/  26      VALUE    PROB.
REGRESSION      2      50.7815      25.3908      3.80     0.037
RESIDUAL..     24     160.1672       6.6736
TOTAL.....     26     210.9487
```

VAR.	LABEL	MEAN	S.D.	INTER	RAW WEIGHTS	STAND. WEIGHTS	STD. ERROR OF WTS.	T OF WEIGHTS	PARTIAL COR.
5	PROC.SERV	0.7111	0.6571	0.3870	7.5179	0.3401	3.9786	1.8896	0.3599
12	LIVE.LANG	9.7259	8.5755	0.3574	0.5169	0.3052	0.3049	1.6956	0.3271
1	BINET.36.MO	112.2222	14.5241						

TASK REGRESSION E AND C 11-16 MOS

MULTIPLE REGRESSION USING FILES   R.DATA AND   DATA.DES

DEPENDENT VARIABLE IS NUMBER   1 (BINET.36.MO)

INTERCEPT =   103.2438
MULTIPLE R SQUARE =   0.3872
MULTIPLE R =   0.6223
DETERMINANT =   0.2762

ANALYSIS OF VARIANCE FOR THE MULTIPLE
LINEAR REGRESSION

	D.F.	SUM OF SQ/	MEAN SQ/	F VALUE	PROB.
REGRESSION	6	81.6823	13.6137	2.11	0.098
RESIDUAL..	20	129.2664	6.4633		
TOTAL.....	26	210.9487			

VAR.	LABEL	MEAN	S.D.	INTER	RAW WEIGHTS	STAND. WEIGHTS	STD. ERROR OF WTS.	T OF WEIGHTS	PARTIAL COR.
5	PROC.SERV	0.7111	0.6571	0.3870	7.5508	0.3416	4.4985	1.6785	0.3514
7	MSC	4.0852	3.0952	-0.2495	-1.1657	-0.2484	0.8371	-1.3925	-0.2973
9	EAT	5.3074	5.2677	-0.2483	-0.5174	-0.1877	0.6491	-0.7971	-0.1755
12	LIVE.LANG	9.7259	8.5755	0.3574	0.4620	0.2728	0.3309	1.3961	0.2980
20	EXPLORE	12.3074	4.5447	0.2488	0.4213	0.1318	0.6850	0.6151	0.1363
21	MASTERY	12.0333	7.6624	0.2556	0.1195	0.0630	0.3774	0.3167	0.0706
1	BINET.36.MO	112.2222	14.5241						

Table 6-31 continued

TASK REGRESSION E AND C 11-16 MOS

MULTIPLE REGRESSION USING FILES   R.DATA AND   DATA.DES

DEPENDENT VARIABLE IS NUMBER   1   (BINET.36.MO)

INTERCEPT =   108.0756
MULTIPLE R SQUARE =   0.3951
MULTIPLE R =   0.6286
DETERMINANT =   0.1579

ANALYSIS OF VARIANCE FOR THE MULTIPLE
LINEAR REGRESSION

	D.F.	SUM OF SQ/	MEAN SQ/	F VALUE	PROB.
REGRESSION	7	83.3408	11.9058	1.77	0.152
RESIDUAL..	19	127.6079	6.7162		
TOTAL.....	26	210.9487			

VAR.	LABEL	MEAN	S.D.	INTER	RAW WEIGHTS	STAND. WEIGHTS	STD. ERROR OF WTS.	T OF WEIGHTS	PARTIAL COR.
5	PROC.SERV	0.7111	0.6571	0.3870	7.8542	0.3553	4.6262	1.6978	0.3629
7	MSC	4.0952	3.0952	-0.2495	-1.1352	-0.2419	0.8556	-1.3269	-0.2912
9	EAT	5.3074	5.2677	-0.2483	-0.7045	-0.2555	0.7613	-0.9254	-0.2077
12	LIVE.LANG	9.7259	8.5755	0.3574	0.3590	0.2120	0.3959	0.9068	0.2037
13	OVERHEARD	1.6000	2.4847	-0.2380	-0.6810	-0.1165	1.3705	-0.4969	-0.1133
20	EXPLORE	12.3074	4.5447	0.2488	0.3427	0.1072	0.7160	0.4786	0.1091
21	MASTERY	12.0333	7.6624	0.2556	0.0265	0.0140	0.4278	0.0619	0.0142
1	BINET.36.MO	112.2222	14.5241						

Table 6-32
Predicting Language Ability at 3 Years of Age from Earlier Experience

```
TASK REGRESSION E AND C 11-16 MOS

MULTIPLE REGRESSION USING FILES      R.DATA AND      DATA.DES

DEPENDENT VARIABLE IS NUMBER    2  (  LANGUAGE.36.MO  )

INTERCEPT =        43.6048
MULTIPLE R SQUARE =  0.4026
MULTIPLE R =         0.6345
DETERMINANT =        0.5843

          ANALYSIS OF VARIANCE FOR THE MULTIPLE
                  LINEAR REGRESSION

               D.F.    SUM OF      MEAN
                        SQ/  26   SQ/  26    VALUE    PROB.
REGRESSION      3      11.8394    3.9465      5.17    0.007
RESIDUAL..     23      17.5708    0.7639
TOTAL......    26      29.4102
```

VAR.	LABEL	MEAN	S.D.	INTER	RAW WEIGHTS	STAND. WEIGHTS	STD. ERROR OF WTS.	T OF WEIGHTS	PARTIAL COR.
7	MSC	4.0852	3.0952	-0.3835	-0.6339	-0.3618	0.2835	-2.2360	-0.4226
12	LIVE.LANG	9.7259	8.5755	0.4202	0.2460	0.3889	0.1027	2.3955	0.4469
23	FINE.M	6.6852	5.9654	0.3581	0.2548	0.2803	0.1482	1.7199	0.3376
2	LANGUAGE.36.MO	45.1111	5.4231						

Table 6-32 continued

TASK REGRESSION E AND C 11-16 MOS

MULTIPLE REGRESSION USING FILES   R.DATA AND   DATA.DES

DEPENDENT VARIABLE IS NUMBER   2   (LANGUAGE.36.MO)

INTERCEPT =   44.8645
MULTIPLE R SQUARE =   0.5297
MULTIPLE R =   0.7278
DETERMINANT =   0.2285

ANALYSIS OF VARIANCE FOR THE MULTIPLE LINEAR REGRESSION

	D.F.	SUM OF SQ/	MEAN SQ/	F VALUE	PROB.
REGRESSION	7	15.5780	2.2254	3.06	0.025
RESIDUAL..	19	13.8322	0.7280		
TOTAL.....	26	29.4102			

VAR.	LABEL	MEAN	S.D.	INTER	RAW WEIGHTS	STAND. WEIGHTS	STD. ERROR OF WTS.	T OF WEIGHTS	PARTIAL COR.
4	COOPERATE	2.2296	1.7871	-0.3051	-0.7265	-0.2394	0.5198	-1.3977	-0.3053
6	GAIN.ATT	1.9148	0.9037	-0.2687	-0.5087	-0.0848	1.0333	-0.4923	-0.1122
7	MSC	4.0852	3.0952	-0.3835	-0.6579	-0.3755	0.2836	-2.3198	-0.4698
9	EAT	5.3074	5.2677	-0.3070	-0.0682	-0.0663	0.1875	-0.3640	-0.0832
12	LIVE.LANG	9.7259	8.5755	0.4202	0.2509	0.3967	0.1118	2.2442	0.4577
20	EXPLORE	12.3074	4.5447	0.2546	0.1964	0.1646	0.2255	0.8709	0.1959
23	FINE.M	6.6852	5.9654	0.3581	0.1545	0.1700	0.1535	1.0070	0.2251
2	LANGUAGE.36.MO	45.1111	5.4231						

TASK REGRESSION E AND C 11-16 MOS

MULTIPLE REGRESSION USING FILES   R.DATA AND   DATA.DES

DEPENDENT VARIABLE IS NUMBER   2   (LANGUAGE.36.MO)

INTERCEPT   = 43.5114
MULTIPLE R SQUARE = 0.5641
MULTIPLE R   = 0.7510
DETERMINANT   = 0.1517

ANALYSIS OF VARIANCE FOR THE MULTIPLE LINEAR REGRESSION

	D.F.	SUM OF SQ/ 26	MEAN SQ/ 26	F VALUE	PROB.
REGRESSION	8	16.5893	2.0737	2.91	0.028
RESIDUAL..	18	12.8209	0.7123		
TOTAL.....	26	29.4102			

VAR.	LABEL	MEAN	S.D.	INTER	RAW WEIGHTS	STAND. WEIGHTS	STD. ERROR OF WTS.	T OF WEIGHTS	PARTIAL COR.
4	COOPERATE	2.2296	1.7871	-0.3051	-0.5456	-0.1798	0.5360	-1.0179	-0.2333
6	GAIN.ATT	1.9148	0.9037	-0.2687	-0.0674	-0.0112	1.0871	-0.0620	-0.0146
7	MSC	4.0852	3.0952	-0.3835	-0.6523	-0.3723	0.2806	-2.3250	-0.4806
8	ASSERT.SELF	0.5444	0.8872	-0.4255	-1.3395	-0.2191	1.1241	-1.1916	-0.2704
9	EAT	5.3074	5.2677	-0.3070	-0.0082	-0.0079	0.1921	-0.0426	-0.0100
12	LIVE.LANG	9.7259	8.5755	0.4202	0.2403	0.3800	0.1109	2.1661	0.4547
20	EXPLORE	12.3074	4.5447	0.2546	0.2547	0.2134	0.2283	1.1154	0.2543
23	FINE.M	6.6852	5.9654	0.3581	0.1363	0.1499	0.1526	0.8933	0.2060
2	LANGUAGE.36.MO	45.1111	5.4231						

Language Capacity. Table 6-32 indicates how well one could predict scores on the Preschool Project language test at 3 years of age for this population from the amounts of the three experiences at 11 to 16 months of age that individually correlated most strongly with language achievement. Those experiences were *live language directed to the child, maintain social contact*, and *fine motor mastery*. (*Maintain social contact* was negatively correlated with language achievement.) The multiple *r* is +0.635, with a statistical probability of 0.007. Once again, this is a rather striking outcome, although only one of the key predictive variables in this study was isolated in the analyses of the previous study.

Table 6-32 also indicates predictive power when the five next most related experiences are added to the analysis. The *r* increases to +0.728, and statistical significance remains substantial at 0.025. Two social tasks, *gain attention* and *maintain social contact*, are negatively correlated with language achievement. The infant receiving a good deal of live language from his mother did not seem to need to seek to achieve or maintain her attention as often as one who was receiving less of such language input.

Table 6-32 also indicates what happens to the predictive power of the analysis when one additional task (*to assert self*) is added. The multiple *r* increases a bit to +0.751, while the probability remains about the same at 0.028.

In general, prediction of language achievement at 3 years of age was a bit more reliable than prediction of achievement on the Binet test from these data. *Exploring* and practicing hand-eye skills (*fine motor mastery*) were positively related to language achievement in this population. While this finding seems reasonable, it must be remembered that this relationship was not found in our previous study. Such variations remind us that correlational studies, especially those performed only once, should be interpreted with caution. While it seems reasonable to point out how steady staring (*gain information visual*) can become transformed into *live language directed to the child (gain information, visual and auditory)* when a mother is motivated to talk a great deal to her infant, such reasonable explanations are not available for other shifts in our data.

Clearly the greatest single influence on language achievement in this and in our previous analyses is the amount of live language directed to the child.

Nonsocial Competence. Table 6-33 indicates how well one could predict the rank of a child on nonsocial competence at 3 years of age from the amounts of two experiences at 11 to 16 months of age: *live language directed to the child* and *maintain social contact. Maintain social contact* was negatively associated with achievement. The more the child sought to maintain contact, the lower his rank. The multiple *r* was +0.555, and the probability was 0.012. Once again, this is a rather impressive finding under the circumstances. While language is obviously central to this discussion, we would like to underline the fact that we have found social experience to be at the heart of good early development. We could have found that experiences with small objects were prepotent, or that time spent alone staring at scenes was highly associated with good development. Indeed, there were quite a number of other possibilities given the complexity and comprehensiveness of our data. Yet repeatedly, it has been language of a particular kind that required intimate and frequent social experience that has shown up in association with linguistic and intellectual achievement.

Table 6-33 also indicates the consequences for prediction of adding the next five experiences to the analysis. The multiple r improves substantially to +0.729, as does the probability to 0.011. As before, the amount of between-meal eating is negatively related to achievement.

Table 6-33 also indicates the consequences for prediction of adding one additional experience to the analysis. The multiple r increases slightly to +0.741, while the probability drops slightly to 0.018.

Discussion

We did not find that the patterns of tasks in the 11- to 16-month period in this study most highly associated with nonsocial achievement at 3 years of age were identical to those found in our previous study. We were not studying quite the same population, nor were the conditions the same. In the previous study, all nineteen infants were later-born, SES varied more, the children were expected to develop either very well or considerably less well, and the families were being observed but not assisted in any way. In the current study, about one-half the children were firstborn, about one-half were in a training program, and the range of SES was limited.

In spite of these differences, we were still dealing with physically healthy children that were being reared by their own families in their own homes. The children who developed the best did share certain kinds of experiences in the 12- to 15-month range. Most conspicuously, they were in the company of a person who cared very deeply for them for a good deal of their waking time every day. In the previous study, the sum total of all social tasks was highly correlated with achievement. In the current study, such was not the case. This apparent difference, however, was due to a remarkable emphasis, by the mothers in the current study, on talking to their children. A better index of total social experience than all social tasks is the combination of social tasks and *live language directed to the child*. Using that index, it is quite clear that the positive correlation between the amount of social experience in the 12- to 15-month period and achievement of language and intellectual ability is the central finding of these studies.

Indeed, from our multiple regression analyses, it appears likely that sampling the experiences of 1-year-old infants for the amount of live language directed to them throughout the day may turn out to be one of the simplest and most effective ways to assess their early learning opportunities.

Table 6-33
Predicting Nonsocial Competence at 3 Years of Age from Earlier Experience

```
TASK REGRESSION E AND C 11-16 MOS

MULTIPLE REGRESSION USING FILES      R.DATA AND      DATA.DES

DEPENDENT VARIABLE IS NUMBER   3  (   ECRANK.36.MO  )

INTERCEPT =        19.5009
MULTIPLE R SQUARE =  0.3077
MULTIPLE R =         0.5547
DETERMINANT =        0.6923
```

ANALYSIS OF VARIANCE FOR THE MULTIPLE
LINEAR REGRESSION

	D.F.	SUM OF SQ/	MEAN SQ/	F VALUE	PROB.
REGRESSION	2	50.9063	25.4531	5.33	0.012
RESIDUAL..	24	114.5552	4.7731		
TOTAL.....	26	165.4615			

VAR.	LABEL	MEAN	S.D.	INTER	RAW WEIGHTS	STAND. WEIGHTS	STD. ERROR OF WTS.	T OF WEIGHTS	PARTIAL COR.
7	MSC	4.0852	3.0952	0.3821	1.5988	0.3847	0.7059	2.2650	0.4197
12	LIVE.LANG	9.7259	8.5755	-0.3996	-0.6031	-0.4021	0.2548	-2.3672	-0.4351
3	ECRANK.36.MO	20.1667	12.8632						

```
TASK REGRESSION E AND C 11-16 MOS

MULTIPLE REGRESSION USING FILES        R.DATA AND        DATA.DES

DEPENDENT VARIABLE IS NUMBER    3  (    ECRANK.36.MO )

INTERCEPT =         24.9497
MULTIPLE R SQUARE =  0.5307
MULTIPLE R =         0.7285
DETERMINANT =        0.2731

        ANALYSIS OF VARIANCE FOR THE MULTIPLE
                 LINEAR REGRESSION

              D.F.    SUM OF      MEAN       F
                      SQ/ 26      SQ/ 26    VALUE    PROB.
                                 14.6358    3.77    0.011
REGRESSION      6    87.8145     14.6358
RESIDUAL..     20    77.6470      3.8823
TOTAL......    26   165.4615
```

VAR.	LABEL	MEAN	S.D.	INTER	RAW WEIGHTS	STAND. WEIGHTS	STD. ERROR OF WTS.	T OF WEIGHTS	PARTIAL COR.
4	COOPERATE	2.2296	1.7871	0.3267	1.7236	0.2395	1.1913	1.4468	0.3078
7	MSC	4.0852	3.0952	0.3821	1.6437	0.3955	0.6416	2.5619	0.4971
9	EAT	5.3074	5.2677	0.3201	0.1521	0.0623	0.4307	0.3532	0.0787
12	LIVE.LANG	9.7259	8.5755	-0.3996	-0.6203	-0.4135	0.2445	-2.5367	-0.4934
20	EXPLORE	12.3074	4.5447	-0.3005	-0.6644	-0.2347	0.5043	-1.3175	-0.2826
23	FINE.M	6.6852	5.9654	-0.3394	-0.2899	-0.1345	0.3541	-0.8187	-0.1801
3	ECRANK.36.MO	20.1667	12.8632						

Table 6-33 continued

TASK REGRESSION E AND C 11-16 MOS

MULTIPLE REGRESSION USING FILES   R.DATA AND   DATA.DES

DEPENDENT VARIABLE IS NUMBER   3 (ECRANK.36.MO)

INTERCEPT = 20.4468
MULTIPLE R SQUARE = 0.5487
MULTIPLE R = 0.7407
DETERMINANT = 0.1829

ANALYSIS OF VARIANCE FOR THE MULTIPLE LINEAR REGRESSION

	D.F.	SUM OF SQ/	MEAN SQ/	F VALUE	PROB.
REGRESSION	7	90.7846	12.9692	3.30	0.018
RESIDUAL..	19	74.6769	3.9304		
TOTAL.....	26	165.4615			

VAR.	LABEL	MEAN	S.D.	INTER	RAW WEIGHTS	STAND. WEIGHTS	STD. ERROR OF WTS.	T OF WEIGHTS	PARTIAL COR.
4	COOPERATE	2.2296	1.7871	0.3267	1.8565	0.2579	1.2083	1.5364	0.3324
7	MSC	4.0852	3.0952	0.3821	1.5709	0.3780	0.6509	2.4132	0.4844
9	EAT	5.3074	5.2677	0.3201	0.2957	0.1211	0.4637	0.6376	0.1447
12	LIVE.LANG	9.7259	8.5755	-0.3996	-0.5021	-0.3348	0.2811	-1.7865	-0.3792
13	OVERHEARD	1.6000	2.4847	-0.2892	-0.8312	0.1606	0.9561	0.8693	0.1956
20	EXPLORE	12.3074	4.5447	-0.3005	-0.5850	-0.2067	0.5155	-1.1349	-0.2520
23	FINE.M	6.6852	5.9654	-0.3394	-0.2471	-0.1146	0.3597	-0.6868	-0.1556

```
3    ECRANK.36.MO    20.1667    12.8632

END$

    NUMBER OF ERRORS DURING THIS RUN WAS    0

    --------- P-STAT I/O SUMMARY ---------

    PRODUCTIVE FULL BLOCK READ/WRITES =    32
FIND / SAVE, ETC, FULL BLOCK READ/WRITES =    0
INTERNAL JUGGLING FULL BLOCK READ/WRITES =    0

            PER CENT PRODUCTIVE = 100.0

BACKSPACES =    0
  REWINDS =   30
PARTIAL READS =    0
```

Our analyses, both formal and subjective, suggest also that larger than average amounts of idling time (*nontask behavior*) and between-meal eating (*to eat*) are symptomatic of a less than ideal early learning situation. We also remained convinced that routine restriction of the infant's exploratory efforts is a poor idea. Not only do episodes of *pass time* increase, but the opportunity for a variety of apparently important social experiences is also reduced.

Various other relationships between experience and achievement have surfaced in our data, but not with as much consistency as those already discussed. Considering the complexity of these issues and the crudeness of our early efforts, we would prefer to resist engaging in additional speculation.

It is most unfortunate that we lost our social competence outcome data in this study, but in retrospect, we seemed to have been somewhat overambitious. A serious effort at process analysis in early human development turns out to be more multifaceted and scientifically complex than we can at least currently handle without a significant number of errors.

Notes

1. It is important to note that we visit each home on many more occasions, before, during, and after these observations. Observer effects seem greatest on the first few visits by a professional data gatherer. As a result, we never gather quantitative data during our first few visits to a home.

2. This number includes fifteen families in the pediatric control group to be reported on separately in this volume.

3. This statement is not true of the pediatric control group (PC). They were recruited in a separate process by the pediatric staff. Their socioeconomic status was higher than what we had stipulated and thirteen of the fifteen families had only one child. Because of the importance of these differences, the pediatric control group cannot be considered as matched with the others and will therefore be treated separately.

4. It should be noted that since our task data constitute samples of *all* of a child's daily experiences, changes in any category will affect other categories. The marked increase in language experience in this study seems to have resulted in a substantial decrease in steady staring (without language input).

7

The Pediatric Control Group

The design of this study involved three separate control groups. Had we none, high levels of achievement by our subjects could not be simply attributed to our ideas about effective childrearing practices for several classical reasons. Other factors that have been found to affect test performance of young children in studies such as this are: test sophistication due to repeated experiences in test situations, changed behavior toward the children because their parents become more child-oriented because of participation in this kind of study, and the tendency of families with unusually high interest in young children and early education to make themselves more available for studies of this kind than other families from similar backgrounds.

We planned to control for all these factors to the extent possible, knowing well that perfect control was not possible. After all, to some extent, a group of sixty families that would participate regularly in a university-based research project for several years cannot be considered truly representative of the national population.

Differences in achievement between the pretest and posttest control group (C_2) and the monitored controls (C_1) would presumably give an indication of the impact of repeated testing of the children and sensitization of the parents to the behavior of their infants. Differences in achievement between the tutored groups (E and PC) and the monitored control group (C_1) would presumably provide an indication of the general impact of training and supporting the parents. Finally, differences in achievement between the children in the pediatric control group (PC) and the experimental group (E) would presumably provide an indication of the differential power of the two training efforts.

Unfortunately, the design was not fully utilized. Our pediatric colleague believed that he could recruit families that met our criteria (for average families), but in fact, try as he might, he could not. He was limited by his conviction that he had to provide medical care to his group as well as educational services. He felt there was no feasible way he could provide only educational services to a young family. Although we realized we would be violating our design in that his relation to the families would no doubt be valued more than ours, we agreed to this condition. After a rather protracted recruiting period during which our pediatrician tried a variety of procedures to find less affluent, less well-educated families than his usual clients, we had to settle for a group which deviated rather markedly from our specifications.

Tables 7-1 and 7-2 present information on the characteristics of the

Table 7-1

Distribution of Subjects on Matched Dimensions

	E Experimental (N = 14)	C₁ Control I (N = 15)	C₂ Control II (N = 15)	PC Medical (N = 15)
Birth Order				
1	7	8	8	13
2	5	5	5	2
3	2	2	2	0
Mother's education				
Less than high school	0	0	0	1
High school	8	9	9	4
High school, plus	6	6	6	10
SES				
II	2	2	3	6
III	10	10	8	9
IV	2	3	4	0
Sibling Gap				
Median	48 mos.	41 mos.	34 mos.	16 mos.
Sex				
M	7	6	8	9
F	7	9	7	4

Table 7-2

Distribution of Subjects on Unmatched Dimensions

	E Experimental (N = 14)	C₁ Control I (N = 15)	C₂ Control II (N = 15)	PC Medical (N = 15)
Mother's Quick Word Test				
Median	67	72	68	85
Range	52-78	51-89	57-85	69-88
Father's education				
Less than high school	1	1	0	0
High school	7	5	8	2
High school, plus	4	6	4	6
College	2	3	2	3
Graduate training	0	0	1	4

pediatric control group compared with our other groups. The most striking deviation (in the light of our data on the first three groups) is that thirteen of the fifteen families had only one child. In addition, however, the PC families were substantially better off educationally and with respect to the language abilities of the mothers. Clearly, if our experimental children outperformed the children of this group, it would have been quite an achievement.

Our cooperating pediatrician was given funds to provide childrearing assistance to fifteen families in what he perceived to be an ideal manner. The pediatrician concluded that medical management was already satisfactory but that "gaps were greatest in parental knowledge and understanding of the physical and emotional needs of the new member of the family." To remedy this situation, he formed a team consisting of a pediatric nurse practitioner, a child psychologist, and himself.

Schedule

Contacts with the families were frequent. The pediatrician saw the child and parents within 24 hours of the delivery of the baby and then each day until mother and child were discharged from the hospital. He then saw each of the infants and mothers for a well-baby checkup at 6-week intervals until the child was 10 months of age and again at 12, 15, 19, and 24 months.[1] Each visit took place at the doctor's office, and he spent approximately 30 minutes with each family each visit (range 20 to 45 minutes). In addition, the pediatrician was available for telephone consultations during his daily call hour.

The nurse practitioner made her first contact with each family approximately 2 weeks after the birth of the child and then made home visits at 3-month intervals. Each contact lasted approximately 60 minutes (range 45 minutes to 2 hours). Following this schedule, she saw each family a minimum of nine times. Five of the fifteen families received additional visits: three received one additional visit, one received two additional visits, and one received three additional visits. In addition, the nurse practitioner was available for telephone consultations. This service was used infrequently by eleven of the families (less than five phone contacts during the 24 months), modestly by three families (seven to eleven phone contacts), and frequently by one family (thirty-three phone contacts).

The child psychologist also followed the preceding schedule for home visiting. The number of visits ranged from eight to fifteen during the 24 months (five families had eight contacts, three had nine, three had ten, one had eleven, one had twelve, one had thirteen, and one had fifteen). Each visit lasted for approximately 1 hour, and additional phone contacts were available although rarely used with the psychologist. (During the first 12 months, eleven families did not call the psychologist at all, one called once, and three called twice.) Figure 7-1 provides a schedule for all PC group services.

Curriculum

Ideally, it was felt that the nurse practitioner would concentrate largely on physical care and the psychologist would concentrate on emotional and

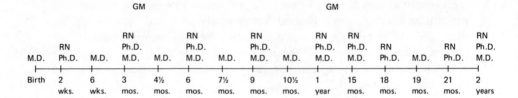

Key: M.D. = pediatrician; Ph.D. = psychologist; R.N. = registered nurse; and G.M. = group meeting.

Figure 7-1. Pediatric Control Group (PC) Schedule of Services.

intellectual development. In practice, there was an overlapping of roles. Both the nurse and the psychologist defined their primary function as one of offering *support to the families*. They refrained from offering unsolicited advice or any direct program of instruction. Rather they chose to inform the parents about "different aspects of child care in response to their [parents'] own stated concerns." The topics most frequently discussed by the nurse practitioners were feeding, sleep patterns, physical development, sibling relationships, accident prevention, illnesses, and marital and financial problems (not listed in terms of actual frequencies). The topics most frequently discussed with the psychologist were spoiling, appropriate kinds of stimulation, stranger anxiety, strivings for autonomy, safety, setting limits, toilet training, and a wide range of personal and marital concerns.

In addition, two informal group meetings were scheduled for the parents with the three members of the team. The first meeting, when the baby was approximately 4 months old, was spent discussing the purpose of the project and the roles of the three professionals involved. The second meeting, when the children were approximately 12 months old, was not well attended. The few couples who came spent most of the evening discussing the issue of discipline.

It was also suggested that three books be read: *Baby and Child Care*, by Benjamin Spock, 1968; *How to Parent*, by Fitzhugh Dodson, 1971; and *Infants and Mothers,* by T. Berry Brazelton, 1969. Ten of the families reported reading Spock, two reported reading Brazelton, and seven reported reading Dodson.

The following pages contain a brief description of the nature of the program employed by the pediatric staff.

Plan of Operation for Private Segment
of Pediatric Care Project   *by Dr. Albert Cohen*

My portion of the Pediatric Care Project evolved from discussions with Dr. Burton White on the nature of pediatric private practice, and how the practitioner could be helped to function more effectively.

It has become steadily more apparent in recent years that the nature of the problems pediatricians confront has changed radically. In the early decades of this century, the primary concerns were with physical problems. However, with improved standards of living, better diagnostic tools, potent vaccines, and effective antibiotics there has been a significant diminution in the number and severity of these problems. However, the changing character and quality of life have brought on a new and different set of dilemmas. The change from a rural to an urban society, a more mobile society, the disappearance of the extended family, and changing parental roles have affected children profoundly and not always well. Until very recently the pediatrician has tended to shun this very important part of child care for several reasons. He is ill equipped by training to understand and treat emotional problems. In addition the amounts of time required are large, and often not available in a busy practice.

Subsequent to numerous discussions on ways of dealing with these problems, Dr. White made available funds for the management of fifteen families in what I conceived to be an ideal fashion. The families were chosen on the basis of criteria devised by him as part of a larger study. It was intended that the families would represent a cross-section of middle class America and exclude the underprivileged and the well-to-do and highly educated. The exact criteria have been set out elsewhere by Dr. White.

In devising a plan I concluded that medical management was already satisfactory. Gaps were greatest in parental knowledge and understanding of the physical and emotional needs of the new member of the family. Heretofore support and education came largely from the extended family in immediate physical proximity. In today's mobile society, the new mother is largely on her own. To remedy these deficits, funds were made available for helping in dealing with both physical and emotional problems. I decided to enlist the help of a pediatric nurse practitioner and a child psychologist with special training in problems of the early years. We were fortunate in obtaining the services of Mrs. Grace McMann, who has had extensive nursing experience at the Massachusetts General Hospital and at church missions in Peru in dealing with families with newborns. Miss Miriam Gofseyeff, a staff member in the Department of Child Psychology at the Beth Israel Hospital at Boston, was available to help us deal with the psychological phase of the project. Following a number of meetings, a program of management was evolved for the 24 months of the study.

Mother and child were seen by me within 24 hours of the delivery, and daily till discharge from the hospital. Prior to leaving, care and management of the neonate was discussed at length and reading material, which I had prepared, was made available. Mothers were told of a daily telephone call hour for the discussion of routine problems as well as an open line at all times for acute problems. Office visits were scheduled at six weekly intervals until the tenth month and at 12, 15, 19, and 24 months.

Initial contacts by both nurse and psychologist were scheduled for the first two weeks of life and thereafter at three monthly intervals. All meetings would be at home, and an attempt would be made to schedule them at times when fathers were available. Obviously some families would need additional support, and both workers agreed to be freely available by phone and in person. The nurse practitioner would concentrate largely on physical problems and the psychologist on emotional difficulties.

Undoubtedly there would be overlapping in our roles. To ensure smooth functioning, regular staff meetings would be held, and there would be frequent telephone communication to keep the three of us abreast of each family's progress.

There would also be regularly scheduled meetings of parents with the staff in a setting out of the home and away from the children. We felt that the opportunity to discuss common problems and the way different parents confronted them would be helpful and reassuring to all the participants.

Table 7-3 contains data on the interactions between the thirteen mothers and the firstborn children in the PC group and comparable data on the fifteen mothers and their firstborn children in other monitored groups (E_1 and $C_{1,1}$).

The data are remarkably similar. The infants in the PC group made slightly more overtures to their mothers than did those in the E_1 and $C_{1,1}$ groups. The mothers in the E_1 group initiated more interchanges with their infants than did the mothers in the medical group. Total time spent initiating and responding and average durations of maternal behavior were quite comparable. The only differences that seem worthy of note were in the area of maternal language, where mothers in group E_1 provided slightly more appropriate language (according to our views) than did the mothers in group PC.

In all, the differences among the interaction behaviors of the PC_1 group and those of the E_1 and $C_{1,1}$ groups were dwarfed by the differences among these families as a function of number of children (one or more). Apparently, what our staff suggested to E_1 mothers and what the medical staff suggested to PC_1 mothers did not produce many substantial differences in their interaction behaviors with their infants as compared with what mothers in the $C_{1,1}$ group did. Only in two of the three aspects of the quality of language was there a noticeable difference favoring the mothers in the E_1 group. On the whole, however, what was striking in the behavior of these three groups was not the differences among them but rather their resemblances.

The Experiences of the PC_1 Children

Tables 7-4 and 7-5 present data on the experiences of all the firstborn children whose lives were observed periodically during the 11- to 16-month period.

Among social tasks, the infants in group PC_1 sought the services of their mothers less often but tried to maintain social contact with them more often than did the infants in the other groups.

Table 7-3

**Adult Assessment Scales Data: Pediatric Control Group Firstborn
Children Compared to Other Firstborn Children in the Study**

Behaviors		PC (N = 13)	$E_1 + C_1$ (N = 15)	E_1 (N = 7)	C_1 (N = 8)
Interactions Initiated by the Child					
Frequency of overtures/30-	Median	7.5	5.9	5.7	6.4
minute observation	Range	2.0-10.0			
Frequency of child purposes					
Procure a service	Median	2.0	1.5	1.0	2.0
	Range	0.0-5.0	-.5-3.5	1.0-3.5	0.5-3.5
Gain attention	Median	2.0	2.5	1.5	2.5
	Range	0.0-4.0	0.5-6.5	0.5-6.5	0.5-4.5
Maintain social contact	Median	1.0	0	0	0.3
	Range	0.0-5.0	0.0-1.5	0.0-0.5	0.0-1.5
Ease discomfort	Median	0.5	0	0	0.3
	Range	0.0-1.0	0.0-1.0	0.0-1.0	0.0-0.5
Quality of adults' responses (percent frequency)					
Timing of response					
Immediate (<3 s)	Median	88.6	90.3	96.2	84.9
	Range	65.4-100.0	73.7-100.0	76.2-100.0	73.7-92.6
Delayed (>5 s)	Median	6.1	6.5	3.8	9.3
	Range	0.0-34.6	0.0-20.8	0.0-9.5	5.6-20.8
No response	Median	3.3	0.0	0.0	1.4
	Range	0.0-11.1	0.0-15.8	0.0-14.3	0.0-15.8
Rejects	Median	0.0	0.0	0.0	0.0
	Range	0.0-2.6	0.0-11.1	0.0	0.0-11.1
Perception of child's need					
Accurately	Median	100.0	100.0	100.0	96.4
	Range	79.2-100.0	88.6-100.0	97.9-100.0	88.6-100.0
Partially	Median	0.0	0.0	0.0	3.5
	Range	0.0-23.1	0.0-11.4	0.0-2.1	0.0-11.4
Not at all	Median	0.0	0.0	0.0	0.0
	Range	0.0-2.6	0.0	0.0	0.0
Level of difficulty of words					
Appropriate	Median	57.1	82.6	91.3	68.7
	Range	13.2-92.9	11.8-100.0	48.9-100.0	18.7-91.4
Too complex	Median	0.0	0.0	0.0	0.0
	Range	0.0	0.0	0.0	0.0
Too simple	Median	31.1	14.3	5.3	24.3
	Range	2.6-70.0	0.0-75.0	0.0-34.0	8.6-75.0
Babytalk	Median	0.0	0.0	0.0	0.0
	Range	0.0-5.6	0.0	0.0	0.0
None	Median	9.7	5.3	3.8	6.4
	Range	0.0-21.1	0.0-17.0	0.0-17.0	0.0-11.4
Provisions of related ideas					
Yes	Median	43.7	68.6	70.6	62.8
	Range	0.0-81.6	27.8-96.2	38.3-96.2	27.8-77.1
No	Median	56.3	31.4	29.4	37.3
	Range	18.4-100.0	3.8-72.2	3.8-61.7	22.9-72.2
Complexity of language					
Complex sentence (>3 s)	Median	28.6	22.2	41.2	16.1
	Range	0.0-78.6	0.0-69.7	0.0-69.6	0.0-57.1

Table 7-3 continued

Behaviors		PC (N = 13)	$E_1 + C_1$ (N = 15)	E_1 (N = 7)	C_1 (N = 8)
Phrase/sentence (<3 s)	Median	52.3	59.1	58.8	66.2
	Range	17.9-82.8	21.7-78.3	21.7-78.3	34.3-77.8
One word	Median	8.2	4.3	0.0	5.9
	Range	0.0-23.1	0.0-27.3	0.0-12.8	0.0-27.3
None	Median	9.7	5.6	3.8	6.4
	Range	0.0-19.2	0.0-17.0	0.0-17.0	0.0-11.4
Provision of encouragement, reinforcement, or enthusiasm					
Yes	Median	70.6	83.3	84.2	80.6
	Range	30.8-94.7	57.1-100.0	76.5-100.0	57.1-93.7
No	Median	8.1	5.6	4.3	8.9
	Range	0.0-38.5	0.0-26.5	0.0-8.7	0.0-26.5
Inappropriate	Median	20.8	11.1	10.5	11.1
	Range	0.0-42.9	0.0-23.5	0.0-23.5	0.0-20.0
Teaching realistic limits					
Yes	Median	21.4	16.7	16.7	14.3
	Range	0.0-24.1	0.0-29.4	5.6-29.4	0.0-47.1
No	Median	0.0	0.0	0.0	5.0
	Range	0.0-15.4	0.0-19.2	0.0-5.6	0.0-19.2
Inappropriate	Median	77.8	77.8	82.6	76.4
	Range	61.5-100.0	47.1-95.8	70.6-94.4	47.5-95.8
Satisfaction of child's needs					
Yes	Median	91.3	87.5	88.2	85.4
	Range	57.1-100.0	66.7-100.0	70.6-100.0	66.7-96.7
No	Median	2.1	5.7	4.3	5.9
	Range	0.0-15.4	0.0-29.4	0.0-29.4	0.0-24.2
Partial	Median	4.6	5.6	4.3	5.6
	Range	0.0-35.7	0.0-14.3	0.0-13.0	0.0-14.3
Average duration of adults' responses (seconds)	Median	35.5	34.8	37.3	36.9
	Range	15.3-62.9	2.2-56.5	20.2-47.0	24.3-56.5
Time spent by adults responding (percent duration)	Median	14.1	14.9	11.9	15.6
	Range	1.7-29.7	5.9-22.3	5.9-20.3	6.2-22.3
Interactions Initiated by the Adult					
Frequency of overtures/30-minute observations	Median	10	7.5	13.7	9.1
	Range	4-21	2.0-23.0	5.8-20.2	6.2-12.0
Purpose of the interaction (percent frequency)					
Stimulating the child	Median	15.8	8.9	15.9	8.1
	Range	0.6-35.6	2.8-29.9	2.8-29.9	4.7-29.2
Use of positive techniques to control the child	Median	3.6	3.9	5.9	3.4
	Range	0.5-16.7	0.7-19.7	2.0-19.7	0.7-12.6
Use of negative techniques to control the child	Median	0.4	1.7	0.8	1.8
	Range	0.0-4.7	0.0-3.5	0.0-2.2	0.1-3.5
Routine caretaking	Median	3.3	2.2	2.6	1.9
	Range	0.0-10.6	0.0-11.7	0.4-11.7	0.6-7.4
Emotional tone of interaction (percent frequency)					
Positive	Median	91.9	87.0	93.2	83.3
	Range	68.6-98.3	40.5-99.6	80.0-99.6	40.5-99.4
Negative	Median	2.7	2.7	2.1	3.4
	Range	0.0-30.7	0.0-20.0	0.0-20.0	0.0-17.7

Table 7-3 continued

Behaviors		PC (N = 13)	$E_1 + C_1$ (N = 15)	E_1 (N = 7)	C_1 (N = 8)
Neutral	Median	4.5	3.2	1.0	9.3
	Range	0.7-22.9	0.0-43.4	0.0-13.0	0.3-43.4
Average duration of adult-initiated interactions (seconds)	Median	43.2	30.4	37.1	37.1
	Range	13.8-62.8	13.1-57.6	26.6-53.4	25.1-57.6
Time spent by adults in adult-initiated interactions (percent duration)	Median	24.4	24.0	28.7	17.0
	Range	5.5-47.2	8.5-46.7	8.5-46.7	8.7-35.2
Total time spent by adults in interactions with children (percent duration)	Median	41.0	39.7	42.4	34.5
	Range	12.2-59.0	15.0-61.9	19.1-61.9	15.0-51.6

Table 7-4
Experiences of Firstborn Children 11 to 16 Months of Age, Median Group Values

Social Tasks	PC_1 (N = 13)	$E_1 + C_{1,1}$ (N = 15)	E_1 (N = 1)	$C_{1,1}$ (N = 8)
All social tasks	16.6	11.0	9.1	11.0
To cooperate	2.4	2.2	3.1	1.1
To procure a service	0.0	0.7	0.4	0.4
To gain attention	1.7	1.4	1.6	1.5
To maintain social contact	4.2	2.8	1.4	2.1
To assert self	0.0	0.0	0.0	0.0
Nonsocial tasks				
To eat	2.1	2.4	2.2	5.1
To gain information (visual)	13.4	6.0	6.0	8.6
To gain information (visual and auditory)	8.6	18.9	24.3	13.8
Live language	7.9	10.4	17.2	8.3
Overheard language directed to child	0.0	0.0	0.0	0.0
Mechanical language	0.0	0.0	0.8	0.0
"Sesame Street"	0.0	0.0	0.0	0.0
Nontask	10.5	9.6	6.2	13.5
To pass time	1.0	0.6	0.0	0.7
To procure object	1.2	1.8	2.5	1.4
To gain pleasure	0.0	0.0	0.6	0.0
To ease discomfort	0.0	0.3	0.0	0.6
To explore	10.6	12.5	7.5	12.1
Mastery	10.3	11.2	14.2	11.9
Gross	2.8	3.1	2.4	1.4
Fine	3.8	6.0	6.8	6.0
Verbal	0.0	0.0	0.0	0.0
To imitate	0.0	0.0	0.0	0.0

Table 7-5
Additional Task Data, Medical Subjects (PC$_1$), N = 13

	Social/Nonsocial Tasks	
	Percent Social	*Percent Nonsocial*
Median	16.6	83.4
Range	11.4-21.0	7.9-88.6

	Initiation Data	
	Percent Self-Initiated	*Percent Mother-Initiated*
All tasks		
Median	75.9	25.3
Range	31.1-93.9	5.3-69.1
Nonsocial tasks		
Median	65.6	19.2
Range	22.0-74.4	4.5-54.0
Social tasks		
Median	11.3	3.4
Range	4.7-18.5	0.3-13.6

In the nonsocial area, PC$_1$ and E$_1$ infants did much less between-meal eating than did those in group C$_{1,1}$. Steady looking while listening to relevant language was markedly lower in the infants in the PC$_1$ group than in those in groups E$_1$ and C$_{1,1}$. There were dramatic differences in the language area, with the infants in E$_1$ receiving far more live language directed to them than the infants in the other groups. Considering the central importance of this experience in our earlier analyses, this difference is worth noting. It should also be noted, however, that the verbal abilities and general educational level of the PC$_1$ families were substantially higher than those in the other groups.

Another potentially significant difference was found in the area of nontask experience, with the infants in group E$_1$ having the least "time on their hands" of all the children. In addition, time spent in exploration and mastery activities seemed to vary, with infants in group E$_1$ differing from the others.

All in all, the patterns of experience seemed to vary a fair amount across these groups of firstborns, especially in the case of the PC$_1$ and E$_1$ infants. We have already concluded that both E$_1$ and C$_{1,1}$ infants had patterns of experience that should have led to good development, and indeed, at 3 years of age those children had achieved impressive levels of intellectual and language skills. The elements of experience during the 11- to 16-month period that seem most important for good development are a good deal of social contact featuring language spoken to the baby *about what the infant is attending to at the moment*, the opportunity and encouragement to explore small objects and simple mechanisms, and the opportunity and encouragement to practice motor skills leading to mastery of the body. In general, the infants in the PC$_1$ group had experiences compatible with very good development in the intellectual and linguistic realms. We are less confident about how small differences in the patterns of social experiences affect the development of social skills. The loss of our social achievement data severely restricts our ability to deal with this topic. At the very least, we can say that substantial amounts of daily contact by an infant with his mother in the 11- to 16-month age range would seem to be more beneficial than only occasional interaction. Other factors conducive to healthy social development were dealt with in our adult assessment data. Those data indicated that the behavior of the mothers in the PC_1 group was not very different from that of the mothers in E_1 and $C_{1,1}$ groups, except in regard to language. In the case of language, the differences seen were consistent with the differences noted here in the patterns of experience.

In sum, we should expect high levels of achievement at 3 years of age from the infants in group PC_1 on the basis of both the data on their mothers' behavior with them and on their moment-to-moment experiences. Had these families been adequately matched with those in groups E_1 and $C_{1,1}$, we would have predicted better linguistic and intellectual achievement by infants in the latter groups. As it is, we expected the greater teaching resources of the PC_1 group to offset the greater efforts of the mothers in groups E_1 and $C_{1,1}$.

The Development of Competence in Children in the PC Group

Intellectual Development

Table 7-6 presents data on the intellectual development of the PC_1 children as compared with the other firstborn children in the study (E_1, $C_{1,1}$, and $C_{2,1}$). The PC_1 group did quite well, with a central tendency of 111.5 on the Binet test

Table 7-6
Intellectual Development Group Comparisons (with PC_1 S's),
Preschool Project Test of Abstract Abilities (12 to 24 Months),
and Stanford-Binet Test (36 Months)

Group		12 Months	14½ Months	24 Months	36 Months
PC_1	N		13	13	12
	Range		2-4	5-9.5	88-149
	Median		3	7	111.5
E_1	N	7	7	7	7
	Range	1-3	2-3	7-8	103-137
	Median	2	2	8	118
$C_{1,1}$	N	7	8	8	8
	Range	1-3	2-3	5-8	118-132
	Median	2	2.5	7	122
$C_{2,1}$	N	Not tested	Not tested	6	8
	Range			4-7	83-129
	Median			7	111.5

at 3 years of age. The E_1 and $C_{1,1}$ groups did somewhat better (118 and 122, respectively, differences not significant), however, once again reinforcing the notion that what you *actually do* in raising a baby is likely to be just as important as what you *can* do. In spite of a generally stronger socioeconomic background, substantially greater language skill, and much more frequent contact from the medical staff, the families in the PC_1 group did not achieve quite as good results with respect to their infants' performance on the Binet test at 3 years of age as did those in the E_1 and $C_{1,1}$ groups.

General Development

Table 7-7 presents data on the general development of the PC_1 children as compared with the other firstborn children in the study. The results are consistent with the data on the Binet test. Once again, the PC_1 children do better than the average but not quite as well as the E_1 and $C_{1,1}$ children. Once again, the differences do not reach the 0.05 level, but they indicate a strong trend.

Language Development

Table 7-8 presents data on the language development of the PC_1 children as compared with the other firstborn children in the study. Once again, the results are consistent with those already presented. (The reader is reminded that testing was done by specialists who were not aware of either the design of the study or

Table 7-7
General Development Group Comparisons (with PC_1 S's),
Performance on the Bayley Mental Development Scale

Group		4½ Months	12 Months	24 Months
PC_1	N	13	13	13
	Range	86-130	81-137	95-140
	Median	104	102	109
E_1	N	7	7	7
	Range	83-123	90-122	99-137
	Median	109	112	116
$C_{1,1}$	N	8	8	8
	Range	94-111	93-112	96-143
	Median	102.5	98	115
$C_{2,1}$	N	8	Not tested	8
	Range	89-107		75-132
	Median	103		107.5

Table 7-8
Language Ability Group Comparisons (with PC_1 S's)

Group		12 Months	14½ Months	24 Months	36 Months
PC_1	N	11	12	13	12
	Range	12-21	16-24	18-45	33-57
	Median	16	18	30	46.5
E_1	N	7	7	7	7
	Range	10-16	14-18	33-45	42-57
	Median	16	16	39	48
$C_{1,1}$	N	8	8	7	8
	Range	12-17	16-18	24-39	42-51
	Median	14	17	36	46.5
$C_{2,1}$	N	Not tested	Not tested	5	8
	Range			18-36	27-48
	Median			33	42

the group assignment of the families.) Once again, the PC_1 children seemed to be developing quite well but not quite as well as the E_1 children. The language abilities of the mothers of the PC_1 children were markedly superior to those of the mothers of the E_1 children (median values 85 versus 66, $p > 0.001$). Here, and also in the case of the $C_{2,1}$ children, we believe that the data of this study indicate something of real value with regard to childrearing practices. Bear in mind that the child under 3 years of age can learn only the basic features of his language. A very sophisticated vocabulary or other aspects of outstanding adult language are probably not as important for early language learning as they might be in the case of older children.

The Capacity to Sense Dissonance

Table 7-9 presents data on the capacity of the PC_1 children to notice small differences in visible patterns as compared with the abilities of the other firstborn children in the study. No differences of consequences were found between groups on this instrument. Earlier we had reported that the testers had found that the test lost its appeal to many of the brighter 2-year-olds. Given this observation, we would not place much stock in data gathered on children over 15 months of age with this instrument.

Table 7-9

Capacity to Sense Dissonance Group Comparisons (with PC_1 S's)

Group		12 Months	14½ Months	24 Months
PC_1	N	9	13	13
	Range	1-4	1-6	6-8
	Median	2	4	7
E_1	N	7	7	7
	Range	0-2	1-3	6-8
	Median	2	3	7
$C_{1,1}$	N	7	8	8
	Range	1-3	2-3	5-8
	Median	2	2	7
$C_{2,1}$	N	Not tested	Not tested	8
	Range			4-8
	Median			6

Note

1. Families paid for their own medical care, so all these visits and contacts were not included in the cost of the program.

Part III
Conclusions

8 Findings as They Relate to Child Development

The research of the Preschool Project has relevance for those concerned with child development, early education, and society. We shall discuss our findings in relation to each of these areas in turn.

Perhaps the most unusual features of our research are the study of child development and childrearing *in the homes of a wide variety of children*, a special focus on optimal early human development, and longitudinal research on the moment-to-moment processes of development. These special qualities have required continuous and substantial funding over many years and a willingness to cope with the requirements of large-scale field-based research. Partly as a result of the style of the research, we have found it comparatively easy to learn many basic and useful facts about young children. It does not take a great deal of ingenuity or sophisticated thinking to gather data on the evolution of interests, abilities, and experiences of infants and toddlers. Yet such information is of fundamental value in the construction of a science of human development. Remarkably, for the first years of a child's life, little of such data has ever been gathered before (Siegel 1967). The study of childrearing in the United States has conventionally been done at a distance or by proxy. Witness the Sears et al. (1957) study of the topic by interviewing mothers several years after the events, or the use of mothers by Church (1966) and Thomas et al. (1964) to gather data on their children to be forwarded to the professional for analysis.

Perhaps the most remarkable finding about early development from this latest work is the striking difference firstborn status makes. In our previous longitudinal work, only two of our subjects were firstborns. In selecting families to study, we used the achievement levels of older siblings as a major guide to childrearing effectiveness. The current study allowed us to compare children as a function of birth order for the first time. The finding that mothers spent twice as much time with firstborns as compared to later-borns went considerably beyond what we expected. The resultant differences in the patterns of experience followed logically, but the improved quality of language did not. It, too, surprised us. While we have by no means proven for all time anything about child development, our new information on the everyday differences in life between firstborns and later-borns helps fill a gap in the knowledge base.

The huge amounts of time spent by mothers of firstborn children usually involved considerably more language spoken by the mothers to the children, and the result seemed to be most advantageous for early language and cognitive development. Indeed, it seems to us that parents with a high school education can, without much difficulty and with few exceptions, raise children with remarkably high levels of such skill by their third birthday. What happens after that we cannot say, for such high levels of ability at 3 years of age may not relate as well to high levels of later academic ability as previous studies might suggest. Previous longitudinal work (Bloom 1964) indicated that very high scores on intelligence tests at 3 years of age predicted well to scores at school-entrance age and later. Those predictions, however, reflected the continued effects of the child's ordinary home environment as well as the child's level of ability acquired by the third birthday. Whether comparably high scores at 3 years, induced by the effects of participation in a research study involving parent training, will be accompanied by continued strong environmental support after the project support ends is not known. Even if the motivation remains very high, the resources of families with only average educational backgrounds may not be adequate to enable such families to keep up with those with greater educational backgrounds.

In any event, as far as the first few years of life are concerned, this study seems to indicate that experience plays a very substantial role in the rate and level of achievement of early linguistic and cognitive abilities.

This finding underlines once again the necessity of supplementing controlled studies of what subjects *can* do with field-based data on what they *do* in fact do. Numerous recent studies of visual capacities in newborns clearly indicate that they are capable of far more sophisticated visual function than previously thought. Such information, however, has to be combined with information from appropriate observational studies which indicate that the newborn sleeps more than 90 percent of the time and when awake is more likely to be either very drowsy or uncomfortable rather than actively exercising his visual skills in exploration of the environment (White 1971).

We seemed to have a powerful effect on the families we worked with regularly, whether or not we guided their childrearing efforts, but *only* in the case of first-time parents. We were unable to modify significantly either the childrearing of the other parents or the level of development of their children. What does this mean? Why has no one else reported this phenomenon in the literature? Is there something peculiar about our staff? Do other trainers actually effect greater changes in the behavior of adults of later-born children? How would we know? We cannot know unless the projects monitor the behavior of the adults in their programs. Very few do.

In the case of the untutored successful families, we found a strong association between the amount of close social contact a child had between 12 and 15 months of age and the development of competence. In the current study, the same finding appeared. However, instead of seeking attention or responding to requests, the social contact featured considerably greater quantities of talk by the parent to the infant, focused on whatever it was the infant was attending to at the moment.

In the case of the untutored successful families, we observed huge quantities of steady staring (*gain information, visual*). In the current study, this was partially replaced by steady staring with accompanying (and relevant) language from the parent (*gain information, auditory and visual*).

In many previous research studies, correlational analysis has linked socioeconomic status and, in particular, mother's educational level with the child's development of linguistic and intellectual abilities. By taking a closer look at the process we have seen that it is not so much what an adult *can* do, but what the adult *does* do that makes the difference (at least when the SES and maternal language ranges are broad but still narrower than they could be).

Only two other current students of infant development have ever reported such data, B. Caldwell (1968) and A. Clarke-Stewart (1973). Neither researcher did analyses on the basis of birth order.

The most conservative interpretation of our findings is that first-time parents have more time for their infants, have more open minds on the subject of childrearing, and are less set in their ways. If true, the ramifications for the rapidly burgeoning field of education for parenthood are substantial.

On the one hand, we have found that we cannot easily get all parents to rear their children the way we have repeatedly seen lead to excellent development. On the other hand, we had little difficulty in the case of first-time parents in the trained group, and indeed, our mere presence, along with our testing episodes (in front of the parents), seemed to lead first-time parents not being trained and supported by us to spend much more time with their infants to the great benefit of all.

The plain fact is that virtually all the firstborn children in this study tested (in language and intelligence) as considerably more able on their third birthdays than they otherwise would have.

When we began to receive the results of testing of the children at 3 years of age, we wondered about why the PC children did so well. We also were surprised at how well the monitored control (C_1) children did. Had we not gathered data on the behavior of the parents and on the experiences of the children (process analysis), we could not have asked and examined the following several important questions.

Just how did the mothers act in regard to their children? Did group affiliation determine their behavior? Did the E parents behave in a manner that reflected our influence? Did any of the other parents behave similarly? What kind of variability did they exhibit in their groups? Did some parents play a much more active role in their children's day than others? And so on.

Considerations of mothers' behavior aside, what kinds of experiences did the children have? Did the E children wind up with the patterns of experiences they needed if we were to have an adequate test of our hypotheses about the role of experience in development?

Put in other ways, how well did our curriculum take? Did any of the mothers in the PC or C_1 groups act in a manner consistent with our training in spite of the fact that we were not guiding them? Wherever the curriculum was implemented, was it accompanied by the desired patterns of experiences? Did the same patterns of experience at 11 to 16 months predict achievement at 3 years of age?

These kinds of questions can be approached *if the process of development is monitored.* In our view, such questions *must* be approached if the study of childrearing and early development is to make any real progress. The far more popular style of research featuring correlational analysis may be cheaper, but from a scientific standpoint, it is a feeble way to study causal processes. We never expected process analysis to be easy. We certainly have made mistakes. Indeed some of them have been quite serious. Yet we remain convinced that methodologically the field of child development research must take this route if it is ever to reach maturity. Considering the current styles in graduate training and the current situation with regard to research funding, we believe progress will be very slow.

The Preschool Project Receptive Language Test came through our work with high grades. Reliable scoring was comparatively easy to obtain. Training required to administer the test was not especially difficult or lengthy. Scores intercorrelated consistently and reasonably with the other tests, including the Bayley mental scale and the Binet. Most interestingly, as we expected, scores at 14½ months of age correlated well with language and intellectual achievement at 3 years of age. No other test procedure that we know of has this kind of predictive power so early. The test needs standard psychometric development but even now is valuable for research purposes.

Our social competence assessment procedures are not as useful at this point. The conceptual base remains sound. We have identified *what* there is to measure in the area of first social skill development. Yet, we have not determined to our satisfaction *how* to measure these abilities well. Anyone can construct a useful 3- or 5-point rating scale from our conceptualizations, but rating scales lack precision. Our checklist is a reasonably good start on a precise instrument, but reliability is questionable, training is difficult, and administration requires lengthy naturalistic observations. All in all, this is some distance from what is needed. On the other hand, what Walker (1973) pointed out a few years ago is still true: no one else has done as well, let alone better. The governmentally sponsored efforts of recent years (for example, Anderson and Messick 1974) border on the ludicrous, including within the scope of social competence not only interpersonal skills, but also language, intelligence, motor abilities, perceptual abilities, and over twenty other types of skills, thereby obliterating any definitional validity. Since we are most impressed by the remarkable social developments of the first years, we are particularly disappointed that we have not done better in this area.

9 Findings as They Relate to the Field of Early Education

Since the advent of Project Head Start in 1965, the field of early education has evolved with dramatic speed to a position of special importance. Before that time, the focus in educational thinking rarely included developments during the preschool years, except among the minority with special interests in the age range. Elsewhere (White 1975; *Experience and Environment*, Volume 2), we have discussed the remarkable shifts in thinking about early education brought about by the events of the past 13 years. To get to the heart of the matter, it appears that a first-rate educational experience during the first 3 years of life is required if a person is to develop to his or her full potential. While excellent early development does not guarantee lifelong excellent development, poor progress during the early years seems to be remarkably difficult to overcome (Bronfenbrenner 1974).

For professionals in education, the implications are powerful and clear. The field cannot continue to devote little attention to the first 3 years of life, let alone the first 6. Too much that is fundamental to educational success is at risk during these years. The questions then become technical in nature. Do we have the knowledge to help guide educational development during the preschool years? If not, how do we obtain it? Who educates children during the preschool years? If parents control the day-to-day learning opportunities of infants and toddlers, what do they need to be maximally effective? How do we combine the teaching needs of parents with our traditional attitudes toward the sanctity of the family and the home, etc.?

Several years ago, the superintendent of a local school system enlisted our aid in designing a cost-effectiveness study on this topic. It was named the Brookline Early Education Project (BEEP). It has worked with several hundred families for the past 5 years. Parents were offered preparation and ongoing assistance to help them educate their new children as well as possible. They received assurance that their children could not pass through the preschool years with any undetected educational handicaps. On the whole they valued the experience greatly.

The BEEP model is, in our minds, both feasible and quite likely to be emulated widely over the next few decades. For most families it could cost as little as $600 per year or as much as $1,400. For families with special needs, it could cost considerably more. But if such programs are needed to build a solid foundation for educational growth, they will gradually come to be seen as the first step in any country's educational system. Indeed, such a recommendation was unanimously endorsed by twenty countries at UNESCO meetings in January of 1976 (UNESCO 1976).

Another significant change that is accompanying the evolution of thinking in educational policy concerns teacher prestige. Until recently, teacher prestige (and salary) was directly linked to the age of the student. No teacher had lower prestige than the nursery school teacher. As the educational importance of the first few years of life grows, the prestige of professionals concerned with the age range grows with it. There is now a new profession coming into its own, the parent educator. Although there are now parent educators for parents of children of all ages, it is the educator of parents of infants and toddlers that has the highest priority task. (During the last 3 years, over 540 of such individuals from education, social work, medicine, and related fields have attended workshops offered by our staff.)

It should be noted that the students of these new professionals are not preschool children, but rather their parents. Interestingly, the field of teaching in early education is shifting from immediate work with children to a prime focus on young adults. Furthermore, the focus is on young adults who are not usually enrolled in any school. The tools and practices of adult education have to be used, for example, evening classes, televised materials, neighborhood resource centers, and home visits. If we want optimally prepared first-graders, these are the kinds of required activities.

Also required is a capacity for multidisciplinary function. Parent education is, after all, not a brand-new topic. Medical personnel, although not primarily trained for the task, have been performing parent education for years. It is no accident that the most important sources of guidance for parents over the last four decades have been two pediatricians, Drs. Arnold Gesell and Benjamin Spock. Any new initiatives by educators will be perceived as threatening by professionals already working with young parents, yet cooperation is necessary and also possible. BEEP has proven that such cooperation is possible.

Parent educators can do very little for families with the greatest needs. Families with multiple stresses such as serious health, employment, and economic needs are, in our opinion, beyond the capacity of educators. Many a recently initiated early education program has with the best of intentions blundered into family situations where multiple social services were needed and found themselves over their heads. Our suggestion is that any new programs take into consideration what is minimally required by a family before education for parenthood programs with modest budgets can be effective. At BEEP we used a social work mechanism to help us keep our primary identity as an educational project. When a family's needs went beyond the *directly* educational, we were able to help them find other special services.

10 Findings as They Relate to Society as a Whole

After 20 years of research on the origins of human competence, we are convinced that much that shapes the final human product takes place during the first years of life. We are also convinced that the traditional failure of society to offer training and assistance to new parents has several harmful consequences. Put simply, people could grow up to be more able and more secure if their first teachers did not have to be "self-taught" and unsupported. There are some who argue that society should not interfere with family life. In our experience, those voicing such concern over "interference" with family prerogatives, are rarely young couples expecting their first child.

We are also convinced that much of the anxiety, stress, and ill feeling experienced by families raising young children is avoidable. As a case in point, it does not take a genius to note that most families with children spaced less than 3 years apart have much more difficulty raising them than those with wider spacing or only one child. The normal stress on young mothers and their very young children because of the difficulty toddlers have in sharing the home cannot be conducive to family solidity.

Another important (and common) source of family stress and human underachievement is moderate hearing losses. Total deafness, while tragic, is easily noticed rather early in infancy. A moderate loss, however, given current educational and medical practice, can easily remain undetected and untreated until the child's elementary school years. The consequences for the child's development and everyday family life can be devastating. The hard-of-hearing infant seems unresponsive and defiant at times. He tends to develop social awkwardness. He becomes less interested and less able in language skills. In addition, the growth of higher mental abilities is jeopardized. All these consequences occur all too often, partly as a result of our previous lack of attention to the details of early educational development. It is one thing to respect the privacy of family life, it is another to neglect the basic needs of new children and their parents.

These issues are now becoming more visible thanks to the tremendous increase in attention to early education. It seems inevitable that we shall see more appropriate educational services for families raising young children, probably before the turn of the century. When every family is routinely offered support for preschool childrearing, this fundamental task will be performed with less stress, more pleasure, and better results for growing children, families, and society as a whole.

183

11 Epilogue

This book, the third in a series of reports on the research of the Preschool Project, signals the end of one type of activity and the beginning of another for the senior author. His original purpose in entering child development research some 20 years ago was to generate useful information about how to help each new child make the most of his potential. After two decades of continuous research on this issue, his efforts shall now be devoted to the application of research results. The Preschool Project has ended and the Center for Parent Education has begun.

The Center for Parent Education, a nonprofit service organization, has two purposes. The first purpose is to raise the level of consciousness of the public as to the special importance of educational development during the first 3 years of life. This goal will be pursued through the publication of books and magazine articles, the creation of radio and television messages, and through oral presentations and newspaper interviews.

The second goal of the center is to provide assistance to professionals helping families with respect to the education of their infants and toddlers. The center will offer workshops, consulting services to programs, evaluations of curricula, assessment techniques, and audiovisual materials for parent education, with job placement services and other support to the rapidly emerging field of education for parenthood. Over the last 3 years, more than 500 professionals from education, medicine, social work, and related areas have attended our workshops. Such volume is a tangible indication of the vigor of this long overdue expansion of professional interest in the full development of children. While progress in this field will probably face many obstacles, it seems to us to be well underway. What seems to be needed now is a conservative policy in the selection of information and programs for use, and continued development of knowledge through research.

We are basically optimistic about the future because parents (and grandparents) want the best for each new child, and now that their childrearing needs are more clearly understood and acknowledged, it seems inevitable that this society, at least, will respond appropriately.

Appendixes
Individual Subject Data

Appendix A
Experimental Firstborn Children (E$_1$)

Group E$_1$

Subject Number:	1
SES:	III
Sex:	Female
Mother's Education:	High School
Mother's Quick Word Test:	65
Father's Education:	High School
Father's Occupation:	Administrative Supervisor

Adult Assessment Scales Data: 11 to 16 Months

Subject Number: 1   Group: Experimental Firstborn

Interactions Initiated by the Child

Child's Behavior

Frequency of overtures per 30 minutes (median): 7
Purposes of overtures (frequency):

To please	0	To annoy	0
To gain approval	0	To direct	0
To procure a service	1	To compete	0
To gain attention	3.5	To ease discomfort	0
To maintain social contact	0		

Adult's Response (percent frequency)

1. Timing and direction
   of adult's response:
   a. Immediately   96.2
   b. Delayed   3.8
      Length of delay (seconds)   7.2
   c. No response   0
   d. Rejects   0

2. Perceptions of child's need:
   a. Accurately   100
   b. Partially   0
   c. Not at all   0

3. Level of difficulty of words:
   a. Appropriate   96.2
   b. Too complex   0
   c. Too simple   0
   d. Babytalk   0
   e. None   3.8

4. Provision of related ideas:
   a. Yes   96.2
   b. No   3.8

5. Complexity of language:
   a. Complex sentence, 3s   46.2
   b. Phrase/sentence, 3s   50
   c. One word   0
   d. None   3.8

6. Provision of encouragement,
   reinforcement of enthusiasm:
   a. Yes   100
   b. No   0
   c. Inappropriate   0

7. Teaching realistic limits:
   a. Yes   11.5
   b. No   0
   c. Inappropriate   88.5

8. Satisfaction of child's needs:
   a. Yes   100
   b. No   0
   c. Partial   0

Average duration of adult's response (seconds): 46.2.
Time spent by adult responding (percent): 16.7.

Adult Assessment Scales Data: 11 to 16 Months

Subject Number: 1   Group: Experimental Firstborn

Interactions Initiated by the Adult

Frequency per 30 minutes (median):   12

Purposes of adult (percent duration):
   Stimulate child   15.9
   Contol positive   5.9
   Control negative   0
   Routine caretaking   3.5

Emotional tone (percent frequency):
   Positive   95.9
   Negative   0.3
   Neutral   0

Average duration of adult-initiated interactions (seconds): 38.6.
Time spent by adult in adult-initiated interactions (percent): 25.7.
Total time spent by the adult in interactions with the child (percent): 42.4.

Task Data (Percent of Total Time): 11 to 16 Months

Subject Number: 1   Group: Experimental Firstborn

Social tasks:

All social tasks	4.5
To cooperate	1.4
To procure a service	0.7
To gain attention	1.3
To maintain social contact	1.7
To assert self	0.0

Nonsocial tasks:

To eat	7.4
To gain information (visual)	5.7
To gain information (visual and auditory)	28.1
Live language	20.2
Overheard language	0.0
Mechanical language	2.4
Nontask	5.0
To pass time	0.0
To procure an object	1.8
To gain pleasure	0.0
To ease discomfort	0.0
To explore	11.4
Mastery	8.1
Gross motor	3.9
Fine motor	2.8

Test Data

Subject Number: 1   Group: Experimental Firstborn

Test	Age (months)	Score	Group Median
Bayley Scales	4½	96	109
of Infant Development	12	122	112
Mental Index	24	123	116
Stanford-Binet	36	137	118
Preschool Project	12	18	16
Receptive Language Test	14½	18	16
(score in months)	24	42	39
	36	57	48
Preschool Project	12	1	2
Abstract Abilities Test	14½	3	2
(score in levels)	24	7	8
Preschool Project	12	0	2
Dissonance Test	14½	2	3
(score in levels)	24	7	7

Group E₁

Subject Number:	3
SES:	III
Sex:	Female
Mother's Education:	High School
Mother's Quick Word Test:	67
Father's Education:	Partial College
Father's Occupation:	X-Ray Technician

Adult Assessment Scales Data: 11 to 16 Months

Subject Number: 3   Group: Experimental Firstborn

Interactions Initiated by the Child

Child's Behavior

Frequency of overtures per 30 minutes (median): 5
Purposes of overtures (frequency):

To please	0	To annoy	0
To gain approval	0	To direct	0
To procure a service	1	To compete	0
To gain attention	1.5	To ease discomfort	0
To maintain social contact	0		

Adult's Response (percent frequency)

1. Timing and direction
   of adult's response
   a. Immediately   76.2
   b. Delayed   9.5
      Length of delay (seconds) 28.2
   c. No response   14.3
   d. Rejects   0

2. Perceptions of child's need:
   a. Accurately   100
   b. Partially   0
   c. Not at all   0

3. Level of difficulty of words:
   a. Appropriate   94.4
   b. Too complex   0
   c. Too simple   5.6
   d. Babytalk   0
   e. None   0

4. Provision of related ideas:
   a. Yes   77.8
   b. No   22.2

5. Complexity of language:
   a. Complex sentence, 3s 16.7
   b. Phrase/sentence, 3s   77.8
   c. One word   5.6
   d. None   0

6. Provision of encouragement,
   reinforcement of enthusiasm:
   a. Yes   83.3
   b. No   5.6
   c. Inappropriate   11.1

7. Teaching realistic limits:
   a. Yes   5.6
   b. No   0
   c. Inappropriate   94.4

8. Satisfaction of child's needs:
   a. Yes   80
   b. No   10
   c. Partial   10

Average duration of adult's response (seconds): 20.2.
Time spent by adult responding (percent): 5.9.

Adult Assessment Scales Data: 11 to 16 months

Subject Number: 3   Group: Experimental Firstborn

Interactions Initiated by the Adult

Frequency per 30 minutes (median):   3.5

Purposes of adult (percent duration):
    Stimulate child   6.0
    Contol positive   3.5
    Control negative   2.6
    Routine caretaking   1.0

Emotional tone (percent frequency):
    Positive   80
    Negative   20
    Neutral   0

Average duration of adult-initiated interactions (seconds): 32.8.
Time spent by adult in adult-initiated interactions (percent): 13.2.
Total time spent by the adult in interactions with the child (percent): 19.1.

Task Data (Percent of Total Time): 11 to 16 Months

Subject Number: 3   Group: Experimental Firstborn

Social tasks:
All social tasks	16.6
To cooperate	3.2
To procure a service	0.3
To gain attention	3.2
To maintain social contact	3.5
To assert self	0.4

Nonsocial tasks:
To eat	0.0
To gain information (visual)	8.5
To gain information (visual and auditory)	5.3
Live language	4.9
Overheard language	0.0
Mechanical language	0.0
Nontask	14.7
To pass time	0.0
To procure an object	1.8
To gain pleasure	0.0
To ease discomfort	0.6
To explore	8.6
Mastery	32.4
Gross motor	9.7
Fine motor	11.3

Test Data

Subject Number: 3   Group: Experimental Firstborn

Test	Age (months)	Score	Group Median
Bayley Scales	4½	110	109
of Infant Development	12	90	112
Mental Index	24	99	116
Stanford-Binet	36	120	118
Preschool Project	12	14	16
Receptive Language Test	14½	14[a]	16
(score in months)	24	39	39
	36	42	48
Preschool Project	12	2	2
Abstract Abilities Test	14½	3	2
(score in levels)	24	7	8
Preschool Project	12	1	2
Dissonance Test	14½	1	3
(score in levels)	24	b	7

[a]Questionable validity.
[b]No valid score.

Group E₁

Subject Number:	6
SES:	II
Sex:	Male
Mother's Education:	High School, plus
Mother's Quick Word Test:	65
Father's Education:	College Graduate
Father's Occupation:	Teacher

Adult Assessment Scales Data: 11 to 16 Months

Subject Number: 6   Group: Experimental Firstborn

Interactions Initiated by the Child

Child's Behavior

Frequency of overtures per 30 minutes (median): 4
Purposes of overtures (frequency):

To please	0	To annoy	0
To gain approval	0	To direct	0
To procure a service	1.5	To compete	0
To gain attention	2.0	To ease discomfort	0
To maintain social contact	0		

Adult's Response (percent frequency)

1. Timing and direction
   of adult's response
   a. Immediately   100
   b. Delayed   0
      Length of delay (seconds)   0
   c. No response   0
   d. Rejects   0

2. Perceptions of child's need:
   a. Accurately   100
   b. Partially   0
   c. Not at all   0

3. Level of difficulty of words:
   a. Appropriate   100
   b. Too complex   0
   c. Too simple   0
   d. Babytalk   0
   e. None   0

4. Provision of related ideas:
   a. Yes   70.6
   b. No   29.4

5. Complexity of language:
   a. Complex sentence, 3s   41.2
   b. Phrase/sentence, 3s   58.8
   c. One word   0
   d. None   0

6. Provision of encouragement,
   reinforcement of enthusiasm:
   a. Yes   76.5
   b. No   0
   c. Inappropriate   23.5

7. Teaching realistic limits:
   a. Yes   29.4
   b. No   0
   c. Inappropriate   70.6

8. Satisfaction of child's needs:
   a. Yes   70.6
   b. No   29.4
   c. Partial   0

Average duration of adult's response (seconds): 25.4.
Time spent by adult responding (percent): 6.0.

Adult Assessment Scales Data: 11 to 16 Months

Subject Number: 6   Group: Experimental Firstborn

Interactions Initiated by the Adult

Frequency per 30 minutes (median):   23

Purposes of adult (percent duration):
    Stimulate child   29.9
    Contol positive   6.7
    Control negative   0.1
    Routine caretaking   0.4

Emotional tone (percent frequency):
    Positive   99.6
    Negative   0
    Neutral   0.4

Average duration of adult-initiated interactions (seconds): 33.0.
Time spent by adult in adult-initiated interactions (percent): 37.1.
Total time spent by the adult in interactions with the child (percent): 43.1.

Task Data (Percent of Total Time): 11 to 16 Months

Subject Number: 6   Group: Experimental Firstborn

Social tasks:
All social tasks	4.7
To cooperate	4.2
To procure a service	0.0
To gain attention	0.0
To maintain social contact	0.0
To assert self	0.0

Nonsocial tasks:
To eat	0.0
To gain information (visual)	1.1
To gain information (visual and auditory)	43.8
Live language	29.0
Overheard language	0.0
Mechanical language	17.7
Nontask	6.3
To pass time	0.3
To procure an object	2.2
To gain pleasure	0.6
To ease discomfort	0.0
To explore	7.1
Mastery	20.6
Gross motor	0.3
Fine motor	12.5

Test Data

Subject Number: 6   Group: Experimental Firstborn

Test	Age (months)	Score	Group Median
Bayley Scales	4½	104	109
of Infant Development	12	109	112
Mental Index	24	137	116
Stanford-Binet	36	108	118
Preschool Project	12	16	16
Receptive Language Test	14½	18	16
(score in months)	24	45	39
	36	54	48
Preschool Project	12	1	2
Abstract Abilities Test	14½	2	2
(score in levels)	24	8	8
Preschool Project	12	2	2
Dissonance Test	14½	3	3
(score in levels)	24	a	7

[a]No valid score.

Group E₁

Subject Number:	8
SES:	III
Sex:	Male
Mother's Education:	High School, plus
Mother's Quick Word Test:	73
Father's Education:	Partial College
Father's Occupation:	Mechanic

Adult Assessment Scales Data: 11 to 16 Months

Subject Number: 8   Group: Experimental Firstborn

Interactions Initiated by the Child

Child's Behavior

Frequency of overtures per 30 minutes (median): 13.5
Purposes of overtures (frequency):

To please	0	To annoy	0
To gain approval	0	To direct	0
To procure a service	1	To compete	0
To gain attention	1.5	To ease discomfort	0.5
To maintain social contact	0		

Adult's Response (percent frequency)

1. Timing and direction
   of adult's response:
   a. Immediately   100
   b. Delayed   0
      Length of delay (seconds)   0
   c. No response   0
   d. Rejects   0

2. Perceptions of child's need:
   a. Accurately   100
   b. Partially   0
   c. Not at all   0

3. Level of difficulty of words:
   a. Appropriate   89.5
   b. Too complex   0
   c. Too simple   5.3
   d. Babytalk   0
   e. None   5.3

4. Provision of related ideas:
   a. Yes   78.9
   b. No   21.1

5. Complexity of language:
   a. Complex sentence, 3s   44.4
   b. Phrase/sentence, 3s   50
   c. One word   0
   d. None   5.6

6. Provision of encouragement,
   reinforcement of enthusiasm:
   a. Yes   84.2
   b. No   5.3
   c. Inappropriate   10.5

7. Teaching realistic limits:
   a. Yes   16.7
   b. No   5.6
   c. Inappropriate   77.8

8. Satisfaction of child's needs:
   a. Yes   88.2
   b. No   5.9
   c. Partial   5.9

Average duration of adult's response (seconds): 41.7.
Time spent by adult responding (percent): 11.0.

Adult Assessment Scales Data: 11 to 16 Months

Subject Number: 8   Group: Experimental Firstborn

Interactions Initiated by the Adult

Frequency per 30 minutes (median):   5

Purposes of adult (percent duration):
  Stimulate child   6.7
  Contol positive   19.7
  Control negative   1.8
  Routine caretaking   0.6

Emotional tone (percent frequency):
  Positive   85.5
  Negative   12.3
  Neutral   1.0

Average duration of adult-initiated interactions (seconds): 37.6.
Time spent by adult in adult-initiated interactions (percent): 28.7.
Total time spent by the adult in interactions with the child (percent): 39.7.

Task Data (Percent of Total Time): 11 to 16 Months

Subject Number: 8   Group: Experimental Firstborn

Social tasks:

All social tasks	8.0
To cooperate	2.2
To procure a service	0.0
To gain attention	0.6
To maintain social contact	5.0
To assert self	0.0

Nonsocial tasks:

To eat	2.4
To gain information (visual)	3.4
To gain information (visual and auditory)	22.4
Live language	22.4
Overheard language	0.0
Mechanical language	0.0
Nontask	9.6
To pass time	3.4
To procure an object	2.6
To gain pleasure	6.0
To ease discomfort	1.7
To explore	16.8
Mastery	14.7
Gross motor	3.3
Fine motor	9.7

Test Data

Subject Number: 8   Group: Experimental Firstborn

Test	Age (months)	Score	Group Median
Bayley Scales	4½	109	109
of Infant Development	12	115	112
Mental Index	24	113	116
Stanford-Binet	36	108	118
Preschool Project	12	16	16
Receptive Language Test	14½	16	16
(score in months)	24	33	39
	36	48	48
Preschool Project	12	2	2
Abstract Abilities Test	14½	2	2
(score in levels)	24	7	8
Preschool Project	12	2	2
Dissonance Test	14½	3	3
(score in levels)	24	a	7

[a]No valid score.

Group E₁

Subject Number:	10
SES:	IV
Sex:	Male
Mother's Education:	High School
Mother's Quick Word Test:	66
Father's Education:	Partial High School
Father's Occupation:	Painter

Adult Assessment Scales Data: 11 to 16 Months

Subject Number: 10   Group: Experimental Firstborn

Interactions Initiated by the Child

Child's Behavior

Frequency of overtures per 30 minutes (median): 6.5
Purposes of overtures (frequency):

To please	0	To annoy	0
To gain approval	0	To direct	0
To procure a service	2.5	To compete	0
To gain attention	1.5	To ease discomfort	0
To maintain social contact	0		

Adult's Response (percent frequency)

1. Timing and direction
   of adult's response:
   a. Immediately — 100
   b. Delayed — 0
      Length of delay (seconds) — 0
   c. No response — 0
   d. Rejects — 0

2. Perceptions of child's need:
   a. Accurately — 100
   b. Partially — 0
   c. Not at all — 0

3. Level of difficulty of words:
   a. Appropriate — 82.6
   b. Too complex — 0
   c. Too simple — 17.4
   d. Babytalk — 0
   e. None — 0

4. Provision of related ideas:
   a. Yes — 65.2
   b. No — 34.8

5. Complexity of language:
   a. Complex sentence, 3s — 17.4
   b. Phrase/sentence, 3s — 78.3
   c. One word — 48.3
   d. None — 0

6. Provision of encouragement,
   reinforcement of enthusiasm:
   a. Yes — 91.3
   b. No — 4.3
   c. Inappropriate — 4.3

7. Teaching realistic limits:
   a. Yes — 17.4
   b. No — 0
   c. Inappropriate — 82.6

8. Satisfaction of child's needs:
   a. Yes — 82.6
   b. No — 4.3
   c. Partial — 13.0

Average duration of adult's response (seconds): 37.3.
Time spent by adult responding (percent): 11.9.

Adult Assessment Scales Data: 11 to 16 Months

Subject Number: 10   Group: Experimental Firstborn

Interactions Initiated by the Adult

Frequency per 30 minutes (median):   18

Purposes of adult (percent duration):
    Stimulate child   28.3
    Contol positive   3.9
    Control negative   0.8
    Routine caretaking   2.6

Emotional tone (percent frequency):
    Positive   93.2
    Negative   2.1
    Neutral   4.7

Average duration of adult-initiated interactions (seconds): 37.1.
Time spent by adult in adult-initiated interactions (percent): 35.6.
Total time spent by the adult in interactions with the child (percent): 47.5.

Task Data (Percent of Total Time): 11 to 16 Months

Subject Number: 10   Group: Experimental Firstborn

Social tasks:
All social tasks	9.1
To cooperate	4.2
To procure a service	1.4
To gain attention	2.3
To maintain social contact	1.3
To assert self	0.0

Nonsocial tasks:
To eat	2.7
To gain information (visual)	7.9
To gain information (visual and auditory)	11.0
Live language	10.6
Overheard language	0.0
Mechanical language	0.0
Nontask	5.7
To pass time	0.0
To procure an object	5.2
To gain pleasure	3.5
To ease discomfort	0.0
To explore	14.5
Mastery	23.1
Gross motor	13.4
Fine motor	10.7

Test Data

Subject Number: 10   Group: Experimental Firstborn

Test	Age (months)	Score	Group Median
Bayley Scales	4½	109	109
of Infant Development	12	100	112
Mental Index	24	116	116
Stanford-Binet	36	137	118
Preschool Project	12	10[a]	16
Receptive Language Test	14½	16	16
(score in months)	24	36	39
	36	54	48
Preschool Project	12	2	2
Abstract Abilities Test	14½	3	2
(score in levels)	24	8	8
Preschool Project	12	2	2
Dissonance Test	14½	2	3
(score in levels)	24	7	7

[a]Questionable validity.

Group E₁

Subject Number: 11
SES: III
Sex: Female
Mother's Education: High School, plus
Mother's Quick Word Test: 60
Father's Education: Partial College
Father's Occupation: Accountant

Adult Assessment Scales Data: 11 to 16 Months

Subject Number: 11   Group: Experimental Firstborn

Interactions Initiated by the Child

Child's Behavior

Frequency of overtures per 30 minutes (median): 5
Purposes of overtures (frequency):

To please	0	To annoy	0.5
To gain approval	0	To direct	0
To procure a service	1	To compete	0
To gain attention	0.5	To ease discomfort	0
To maintain social contact	0.5		

Adult's Response (percent frequency)

1. Timing and direction
   of adult's response:
   a. Immediately   95.7
   b. Delayed   14.3
      Length of delay (seconds)   7.2
   c. No response   0
   d. Rejects   0

2. Perceptions of child's need:
   a. Accurately   100
   b. Partially   0
   c. Not at all   0

3. Level of difficulty of words:
   a. Appropriate   91.3
   b. Too complex   0
   c. Too simple   0
   d. Babytalk   0
   e. None   8.7

4. Provision of related ideas:
   a. Yes   69.6
   b. No   30.4

5. Complexity of language:
   a. Complex sentence, 3s   69.6
   b. Phrase/sentence, 3s   21.7
   c. One word   0
   d. None   8.7

6. Provision of encouragement,
   reinforcement of enthusiasm:
   a. Yes   87.0
   b. No   8.7
   c. Inappropriate   4.3

7. Teaching realistic limits:
   a. Yes   26.1
   b. No   0
   c. Inappropriate   73.9

8. Satisfaction of child's needs:
   a. Yes   100
   b. No   0
   c. Partial   0

Average duration of adult's response (seconds): 47.0.
Time spent by adult responding (percent): 15.3.

Adult Assessment Scales Data: 11 to 16 Months

Subject Number: 11   Group: Experimental Firstborn

Interactions Initiated by the Adult

Frequency per 30 minutes (median):   17.5

Purposes of adult (percent duration):
    Stimulate child   25.5
    Contol positive   7.2
    Control negative   2.2
    Routine caretaking   11.7

Emotional tone (percent frequency):
    Positive   94.2
    Negative   4.8
    Neutral   1.0

Average duration of adult-initiated interactions (seconds): 53.4.
Time spent by adult in adult-initiated interactions (percent): 46.7.
Total time spent by the adult in interactions with the child (percent): 61.9.

Task Data (Percent of Total Time): 11 to 16 Months

Subject Number: 11   Group: Experimental Firstborn

Social tasks:
All social tasks	25.6
To cooperate	3.2
To procure a service	1.4
To gain attention	1.4
To maintain social contact	5.3
To assert self	0.2

Nonsocial tasks:
To eat	0.0
To gain information (visual)	6.4
To gain information (visual and auditory)	32.7
Live language	32.7
Overheard language	0.0
Mechanical language	0.0
Nontask	3.6
To pass time	0.0
To procure an object	3.8
To gain pleasure	0.0
To ease discomfort	0.0
To explore	8.2
Mastery	14.3
Gross motor	9.5
Fine motor	2.7

Test Data

Subject Number: 11   Group: Experimental Firstborn

Test	Age (months)	Score	Group Median
Bayley Scales	4½	123	109
of Infant Development	12	115	112
Mental Index	24	123	116
Stanford-Binet	36	118	118
Preschool Project	12	12	16
Receptive Language Test	14½	18	16
(score in months)	24	39	39
	36	42	48
Preschool Project	12	3	2
Abstract Abilities Test	14½	2	2
(score in levels)	24	8	8
Preschool Project	12	0	2
Dissonance Test	14½	3	3
(score in levels)	24	8	7

Group E₁

Subject Number:	12
SES:	III
Sex:	Male
Mother's Education:	High School
Mother's Quick Word Test:	67
Father's Education:	High School
Father's Occupation:	Mechanic

Adult Assessment Scales Data: 11 to 16 Months

Subject Number: 12   Group: Experimental Firstborn

Interactions Initiated by the Child

Child's Behavior

Frequency of overtures per 30 minutes (median): 11.5
Purposes of overtures (frequency):

To please	0	To annoy	0
To gain approval	0	To direct	0
To procure a service	3.5	To compete	0
To gain attention	6.5	To ease discomfort	0.5
To maintain social contact	0		

Adult's Response (percent frequency)

1. Timing and direction
   of adult's response:
   a. Immediately   93.6
   b. Delayed   6.4
      Length of delay (seconds) 86.4
   c. No response   0
   d. Rejects   0

2. Perceptions of child's need:
   a. Accurately   97.9
   b. Partially   2.1
   c. Not at all   0

3. Level of difficulty of words:
   a. Appropriate   48.9
   b. Too complex   0
   c. Too simple   34.0
   d. Babytalk   0
   e. None   17.0

4. Provision of related ideas:
   a. Yes   38.3
   b. No   61.7

5. Complexity of language:
   a. Complex sentence, 3s   0
   b. Phrase/sentence, 3s   70.2
   c. One word   12.8
   d. None   17.0

6. Provision of encouragement,
   reinforcement of enthusiasm:
   a. Yes   83.0
   b. No   2.1
   c. Inappropriate   14.9

7. Teaching realistic limits:
   a. Yes   8.5
   b. No   2.1
   c. Inappropriate   89.4

8. Satisfaction of child's needs:
   a. Yes   93.6
   b. No   2.1
   c. Partial   4.3

Average duration of adult's response (seconds): 32.4.
Time spent by adult responding (percent): 20.3.

Adult Assessment Scales Data: 11 to 16 Months

Subject Number: 12   Group: Experimental Firstborn

Interactions Initiated by the Adult

Frequency per 30 minutes (median):   3

Purposes of adult (percent duration):
Stimulate child   2.8
Contol positive   2.0
Control negative   0.0
Routine caretaking   3.7

Emotional tone (percent frequency):
Positive   87
Negative   0
Neutral   13

Average duration of adult-initiated interactions (seconds): 26.6.
Time spent by adult in adult-initiated interactions (percent): 8.5.
Total time spent by the adult in interactions with the child (percent): 28.9.

Task Data (Percent of Total Time): 11 to 16 Months

Subject Number: 12   Group: Experimental Firstborn

Social tasks:
All social tasks	12.9
To cooperate	0.6
To procure a service	0.7
To gain attention	1.8
To maintain social contact	2.8
To assert self	0.0

Nonsocial tasks:
To eat	14.2
To gain information (visual)	6.0
To gain information (visual and auditory)	12.3
Live language	4.9
Overheard language	0.0
Mechanical language	1.0
Nontask	10.7
To pass time	3.8
To procure an object	1.4
To gain pleasure	0.0
To ease discomfort	0.3
To explore	6.1
Mastery	11.7
Gross motor	0.6
Fine motor	14.5

Test Data

Subject Number: 12   Group: Experimental Firstborn

Test	Age (months)	Score	Group Median
Bayley Scales	4½	83[a]	109
of Infant Development	12	112	112
Mental Index	24	114	116
Stanford-Binet	36	103	118
Preschool Project	12	16	16
Receptive Language Test	14½	16	16
(score in months)	24	36	39
	36	45	48
Preschool Project	12	2	2
Abstract Abilities Test	14½	2	2
(score in levels)	24	8	8
Preschool Project	12	2	2
Dissonance Test	14½	3	3
(score in levels)	24	6	7

[a]Questionable validity.

Appendix B
Experimental Later-Born
Children (E$_2$)

Group E$_2$

Subject Number:	2
SES:	III
Sex:	Female
Mother's Education:	High School, plus
Mother's Quick Word Test:	70
Father's Education:	High School
Father's Occupation:	Service Representative
Sibling Gap:	25 months

Adult Assessment Scales Data: 11 to 16 Months

Subject Number: 2   Group: Experimental Firstborn

Interactions Initiated by the Child

Child's Behavior

Frequency of overtures per 30 minutes (median): 8
Purposes of overtures (frequency):
To please	0	To annoy	0
To gain approval	0	To direct	0
To procure a service	1.5	To compete	0
To gain attention	5.0	To ease discomfort	0.5
To maintain social contact	0		

Adult's Response (percent frequency)

1. Timing and direction
   of adult's response:
   a. Immediately   82.9
   b. Delayed   5.7
      Length of delay (seconds) 14.4
   c. No response   11.4
   d. Rejects   0

2. Perceptions of child's need:
   a. Accurately   100
   b. Partially   0
   c. Not at all   0

3. Level of difficulty of words:
   a. Appropriate   45.2
   b. Too complex   0
   c. Too simple   29.0
   d. Babytalk   0
   e. None   25.8

4. Provision of related ideas:
   a. Yes   29
   b. No   71

5. Complexity of language:
   a. Complex sentence, 3s   25.8
   b. Phrase/sentence, 3s   38.7
   c. One word   9.7
   d. None   25.8

6. Provision of encouragement,
   reinforcement of enthusiasm:
   a. Yes   83.3
   b. No   6.7
   c. Inappropriate   10.0

7. Teaching realistic limits:
   a. Yes   10
   b. No   0
   c. Inappropriate   90

8. Satisfaction of child's needs:
   a. Yes   90.3
   b. No   6.5
   c. Partial   3.2

Average duration of adult's response (seconds): 18.9.
Time spent by adult responding (percent): 9.2.

Adult Assessment Scales Data: 11 to 16 Months

Subject Number: 2   Group: Experimental Later-Born

Interactions Initiated by the Adult

Frequency per 30 minutes (median):   4.5

Purposes of adult (percent duration):
Stimulate child   2.7
Contol positive   1.9
Control negative   0.3
Routine caretaking   1.7

Emotional tone (percent frequency):
Positive   73.4
Negative   1.1
Neutral   25.5

Average duration of adult-initiated interactions (seconds): 23.4.
Time spent by adult in adult-initiated interactions (percent): 6.5.
Total time spent by the adult in interactions with the child (percent): 15.7.

Task Data (Percent of Total Time): 11 to 16 Months

Subject Number: 2   Group: Experimental Later-Born

Social tasks:
All social tasks	8.8
To cooperate	0.0
To procure a service	1.0
To gain attention	2.1
To maintain social contact	4.7
To assert self	0.2

Nonsocial tasks:
To eat	0.0
To gain information (visual)	4.8
To gain information (visual and auditory)	10.7
Live language	3.2
Overheard language	2.4
Mechanical language	0.0
Nontask	26.0
To pass time	0.0
To procure an object	3.2
To gain pleasure	0.0
To ease discomfort	0.0
To explore	15.9
Mastery	10.3
Gross motor	4.2
Fine motor	0.4

Test Data

Subject Number: 2 Group: Experimental Later-Born

Test	Age (months)	Score	Group Median
Bayley Scales	4½	93	106
of Infant Development	12	117	106
Mental Index	24	114	112
Stanford-Binet	36	113	98
Preschool Project	12	10[a]	14
Receptive Language Test	14½	12[a]	16
(score in months)	24	33	30
	36	45	39
Preschool Project	12	<1	2
Abstract Abilities Test	14½	b	3
(score in levels)	24	7	55
Preschool Project	12	2	2
Dissonance Test	14½	2	2
(score in levels)	24	7	5

[a]Questionable validity.
[b]No valid score.

Group E$_2$

Subject Number:	4
SES:	III
Sex:	Male
Mother's Education:	High School
Mother's Quick Word Test:	73
Father's Education:	High School
Father's Occupation:	Electronic Assembler
Sibling Gap:	51 months

Adult Assessment Scales Data: 11 to 16 Months

Subject Number: 4   Group: Experimental Later-Born

Interactions Initiated by the Child

Child's Behavior

Frequency of overtures per 30 minutes (median): 4
Purposes of overtures (frequency):

To please	0	To annoy	0
To gain approval	0	To direct	0
To procure a service	2.0	To compete	0
To gain attention	0.5	To ease discomfort	0.5
To maintain social contact	0.0		

Adult's Response (percent frequency)

1. Timing and direction
   of adult's response:
   a. Immediately   75
   b. Delayed   25
      Length of delay (seconds) 79.2
   c. No response   0
   d. Rejects   0

2. Perceptions of child's need:
   a. Accurately   93.7
   b. Partially   6.2
   c. Not at all   0

3. Level of difficulty of words:
   a. Appropriate   25
   b. Too complex   0
   c. Too simple   68.7
   d. Babytalk   0
   e. None   6.2

4. Provision of related ideas:
   a. Yes   25
   b. No   75

5. Complexity of language:
   a. Complex sentence, 3s   6.2
   b. Phrase/sentence, 3s   50.0
   c. One word   31.2
   d. None   12.5

6. Provision of encouragement,
   reinforcement of enthusiasm:
   a. Yes   75
   b. No   12.5
   c. Inappropriate   12.5

7. Teaching realistic limits:
   a. Yes   12.5
   b. No   0
   c. Inappropriate   87.5

8. Satisfaction of child's needs:
   a. Yes   86.7
   b. No   0
   c. Partial   13.3

Average duration of adult's response (seconds): 39.2.
Time spent by adult responding (percent): 8.7.

Adult Assessment Scales Data: 11 to 16 Months

Subject Number: 4   Group: Experimental Later-Born

Interactions Initiated by the Adult

Frequency per 30 minutes (median):   2

Purposes of adult (percent duration):
Stimulate child	0.0
Contol positive	1.2
Control negative	0.2
Routine caretaking	5.1

Emotional tone (percent frequency):
Positive	90.0
Negative	6.3
Neutral	1.1

Average duration of adult-initiated interactions (seconds): 43.2.
Time spent by adult in adult-initiated interactions (percent): 6.6.
Total time spent by the adult in interactions with the child (percent): 15.3.

Task Data (Percent of Total Time): 11 to 16 Months

Subject Number: 4   Group: Experimental Later-Born

Social tasks:
All social tasks	16.5
To cooperate	0.9
To procure a service	1.0
To gain attention	2.5
To maintain social contact	7.4
To assert self	1.6

Nonsocial tasks:
To eat	5.7
To gain information (visual)	8.6
To gain information (visual and auditory)	18.4
Live language	8.2
Overheard language	6.3
Mechanical language	0.0
Nontask	7.2
To pass time	1.9
To procure an object	0.7
To gain pleasure	0.0
To ease discomfort	9.6
To explore	16.1
Mastery	10.5
Gross motor	0.5
Fine motor	10.4

Test Data

Subject Number: 4   Group: Experimental Later-Born

Test	Age (months)	Score	Group Median
Bayley Scales	4½	145	106
of Infant Development	12	117	106
Mental Index	24	123	112
Stanford-Binet	36	115	98
Preschool Project	12	16	14
Receptive Language Test	14½	16	16
(score in months)	24	36	30
	36	45	39
Preschool Project	12	1	2
Abstract Abilities Test	14½	4	3
(score in levels)	24	5	55
Preschool Project	12	a	2
Dissonance Test	14½	1	2
(score in levels)	24	6	5

[a]No valid score.

Group E$_2$

Subject Number:	5
SES:	III
Sex:	Female
Mother's Education:	High School
Mother's Quick Word Test:	67
Father's Education:	High School
Father's Occupation:	Wallpaper Hanger
Sibling Gap:	30 months

Adult Assessment Scales Data: 11 to 16 Months

Subject Number: 5   Group: Experimental Later-Born

Interactions Initiated by the Child

Child's Behavior

Frequency of overtures per 30 minutes (median): 4.5
Purposes of overtures (frequency):

To please	0	To annoy	0
To gain approval	0	To direct	0
To procure a service	1.0	To compete	0
To gain attention	2.0	To ease discomfort	0.5
To maintain social contact	0.5		

Adult's Response (percent frequency)

1. Timing and direction
   of adult's response:
   a. Immediately   78.9
   b. Delayed   15.8
      Length of delay (seconds) 21.6
   c. No response   5.3
   d. Rejects   0

2. Perceptions of child's need:
   a. Accurately   83.3
   b. Partially   11.1
   c. Not at all   5.6

3. Level of difficulty of words:
   a. Appropriate   33.3
   b. Too complex   0
   c. Too simple   50
   d. Babytalk   5.6
   e. None   11.1

4. Provision of related ideas:
   a. Yes   33.3
   b. No   66.7

5. Complexity of language:
   a. Complex sentence, 3s   0
   b. Phrase/sentence, 3s   55.6
   c. One word   27.8
   d. None   16.7

6. Provision of encouragement,
   reinforcement of enthusiasm:
   a. Yes   44.4
   b. No   38.9
   c. Inappropriate   6.7

7. Teaching realistic limits:
   a. Yes   33.3
   b. No   11.1
   c. Inappropriate   55.6

8. Satisfaction of child's needs:
   a. Yes   72.2
   b. No   22.2
   c. Partial   5.6

Average duration of adult's response (seconds): 32.6.
Time spent by adult responding (percent): 8.6.

Adult Assessment Scales Data: 11 to 16 Months

Subject Number: 5   Group: Experimental Later-Born

Interactions Initiated by the Adult

Frequency per 30 minutes (median):   8

Purposes of adult (percent duration):
    Stimulate child   3.1
    Contol positive   1.9
    Control negative   1.2
    Routine caretaking   3.9

Emotional tone (percent frequency):
    Positive   70.5
    Negative   6.8
    Neutral   22.6

Average duration of adult-initiated interactions (seconds): 22.5.
Time spent by adult in adult-initiated interactions (percent): 10.1.
Total time spent by the adult in interactions with the child (percent): 18.7.

Task Data (Percent of Total Time): 11 to 16 Months

Subject Number: 5   Group: Experimental Later-Born

Social tasks:

All social tasks	9.4
To cooperate	4.3
To procure a service	0.3
To gain attention	2.0
To maintain social contact	1.6
To assert self	0.0

Nonsocial tasks:

To eat	11.7
To gain information (visual)	1.1
To gain information (visual and auditory)	3.5
Live language	1.1
Overheard language	2.4
Mechanical language	0.0
Nontask	19.6
To pass time	1.6
To procure an object	3.6
To gain pleasure	0.0
To ease discomfort	0.4
To explore	6.3
Mastery	13.5
Gross motor	8.3
Fine motor	5.2

Test Data

Subject Number: 5   Group: Experimental Later-Born

Test	Age (months)	Score	Group Median
Bayley Scales	4½	106	106
of Infant Development	12	106	106
Mental Index	24	88	112
Stanford-Binet	36	88	98
Preschool Project	12	12	14
Receptive Language Test	14½	12	16
(score in months)	24	24	30
	36	36	39
Preschool Project	12	1	2
Abstract Abilities Test	14½	3	3
(score in levels)	24	4	5.5
Preschool Project	12	1[a]	2
Dissonance Test	14½	2	2
(score in levels)	24	5	5

[a]Questionable validity.

Group E₂

Subject Number:	7
SES:	III
Sex:	Female
Mother's Education:	High School, plus
Mother's Quick Word Test:	78
Father's Education:	High School, plus
Father's Occupation:	Sales Representative
Sibling Gap:	48 months (78 months)

Adult Assessment Scales Data: 11 to 16 Months

Subject Number: 7   Group: Experimental Later-Born

Interactions Initiated by the Child

Child's Behavior

Frequency of overtures per 30 minutes (median): 4.5
Purposes of overtures (frequency):

To please	0	To annoy	0
To gain approval	0	To direct	0
To procure a service	0.5	To compete	0
To gain attention	2.5	To ease discomfort	0
To maintain social contact	0.5		

Adult's Response (percent frequency)

1. Timing and direction
   of adult's response:
   a. Immediately   90
   b. Delayed   10
      Length of delay (seconds) 21.6
   c. No response   0
   d. Rejects   0

2. Perceptions of child's need:
   a. Accurately   100
   b. Partially   0
   c. Not at all   0

3. Level of difficulty of words:
   a. Appropriate   40
   b. Too complex   0
   c. Too simple   45
   d. Babytalk   5
   e. None   10

4. Provision of related ideas:
   a. Yes   50
   b. No   50

5. Complexity of language:
   a. Complex sentence, 3s   0
   b. Phrase/sentence, 3s   80
   c. One word   10
   d. None   10

6. Provision of encouragement,
   reinforcement of enthusiasm:
   a. Yes   80
   b. No   10
   c. Inappropriate   10

7. Teaching realistic limits:
   a. Yes   0
   b. No   5
   c. Inappropriate   95

8. Satisfaction of child's needs:
   a. Yes   100
   b. No   0
   c. Partial   0

Average duration of adult's response (seconds): 37.8.
Time spent by adult responding (percent): 10.5.

Adult Assessment Scales Data: 11 to 16 Months

Subject Number: 7   Group: Experimental Later-Born

Interactions Initiated by the Adult

Frequency per 30 minutes (median):   5.5

Purposes of adult (percent duration):
    Stimulate child   3.7
    Contol positive   2.2
    Control negative   0.8
    Routine caretaking   0.0

Emotional tone (percent frequency):
    Positive   66.7
    Negative   1.0
    Neutral   22.9

Average duration of adult-initiated interactions (seconds): 21.0.
Time spent by adult in adult-initiated interactions (percent): 6.7.
Total time spent by the adult in interactions with the child (percent): 17.2.

Task Data (Percent of Total Time): 11 to 16 Months

Subject Number: 7   Group: Experimental Later Born

Social tasks:

All social tasks	16.5
To cooperate	1.7
To procure a service	0.2
To gain attention	0.9
To maintain social contact	11.9
To assert self	0.9

Nonsocial tasks:

To eat	1.4
To gain information (visual)	2.8
To gain information (visual and auditory)	5.4
Live language	4.5
Overheard language	1.8
Mechanical language	0.0
Nontask	23.2
To pass time	0.0
To procure an object	2.3
To gain pleasure	0.0
To ease discomfort	0.0
To explore	17.7
Mastery	11.0
Gross motor	8.9
Fine motor	0.0

Test Data

Subject Number: 7   Group: Experimental Later-Born

Test	Age (months)	Score	Group Median
Bayley Scales	4½	111	106
of Infant Development	12	93	106
Mental Index	24	89	112
Stanford-Binet	36	95	98
Preschool Project	12	14	14
Receptive Language Test	14½	16	16
(score in months)	24	30	30
	36	39	39
Preschool Project	12	2	2
Abstract Abilities Test	14	3	3
(score in levels)	24	4	5.5
Preschool Project	12	1	2
Dissonance Test	14½	2	2
(score in levels)	24	4	5

Group E$_2$

Subject Number:	9
SES:	III
Sex:	Male
Mother's Education:	High School
Mother's Quick Word Test:	71
Father's Education:	Partial College
Father's Occupation:	Salesman
Sibling Gap:	95 months (107 months)

Adult Assessment Scales Data: 11 to 16 Months

Subject Number: 9   Group: Experimental Later-Born

Interactions Initiated by the Child

Child's Behavior

Frequency of overtures per 30 minutes (median): 3
Purposes of overtures (frequency):

To please	0	To annoy	0
To gain approval	0	To direct	0
To procure a service	0	To compete	0
To gain attention	2.0	To ease discomfort	0
To maintain social contact	0		

Adult's Response (percent frequency)

1. Timing and direction
   of adult's response:
   a. Immediately   83.3
   b. Delayed   11.1
      Length of delay (seconds) 100.8
   c. No response   5.6
   d. Rejects   0

2. Perceptions of child's need:
   a. Accurately   88.2
   b. Partially   5.9
   c. Not at all   5.9

3. Level of difficulty of words:
   a. Appropriate   88.2
   b. Too complex   0
   c. Too simple   11.8
   d. Babytalk   0
   e. None   0

4. Provision of related ideas:
   a. Yes   94.1
   b. No   5.9

5. Complexity of language:
   a. Complex sentence, 3s   0
   b. Phrase/sentence, 3s   94.1
   c. One word   5.9
   d. None   0

6. Provision of encouragement,
   reinforcement of enthusiasm:
   a. Yes   94.1
   b. No   5.9
   c. Inappropriate   0

7. Teaching realistic limits:
   a. Yes   5.9
   b. No   5.9
   c. Inappropriate   88.0

8. Satisfaction of child's needs:
   a. Yes   94.1
   b. No   5.9
   c. Partial   00.0

Average duration of adult's response (seconds): 22.0.
Time spent by adult responding (percent): 5.5.

Adult Assessment Scales Data: 11 to 16 Months

Subject Number: 9   Group: Experimental Later-Born

Interactions Initiated by the Adult

Frequency per 30 minutes (median):   7

Purposes of adult (percent duration):
Stimulate child   5.1
Contol positive   3.2
Control negative   0.1
Routine caretaking   1.2

Emotional tone (percent frequency):
Positive   95.8
Negative   2.8
Neutral   0.0

Average duration of adult-initiated interactions (seconds): 25.4.
Time spent by adult in adult-initiated interactions (percent): 9.9.
Total time spent by the adult in interactions with the child (percent): 15.3.

Task Data (Percent of Total Time): 11 to 16 Months

Subject Number: 9   Group: Experimental Later-Born

Social tasks:
All social tasks	21.1
To cooperate	3.6
To procure a service	0.9
To gain attention	2.4
To maintain social contact	7.5
To assert self	0.0

Nonsocial tasks:
To eat	7.1
To gain information (visual)	5.4
To gain information (visual and auditory)	16.3
Live language	13.2
Overheard language	0.0
Mechanical language	1.0
Nontask	9.9
To pass time	9.0
To procure an object	1.1
To gain pleasure	0.0
To ease discomfort	0.2
To explore	16.1
Mastery	11.9
Gross motor	1.4
Fine motor	10.6

Test Data

Subject Number: 9   Group: Experimental Later-Born

Test	Age (months)	Score	Group Median
Bayley Scales	4½	100	106
of Infant Development	12	117	106
Mental Index	24	112	112
Stanford-Binet	36	118	98
Preschool Project	12	16	14
Receptive Language Test	14½	16	16
(score in months)	24	27	30
	36	39	39
Preschool Project	12	2	2
Abstract Abilities Test	14½	2	3
(score in levels)	24	6	5.5
Preschool Project	12	3	2
Dissonance Test	14½	3	2
(score in levels)	24	5	5

Group E$_2$

Subject Number:	13
SES:	IV
Sex:	Female
Mother's Education:	High School
Mother's Quick Word Test:	67
Father's Education:	High School
Father's Occupation:	Truck Driver
Sibling Gap:	53 months

Adult Assessment Scales Data: 11 to 16 Months

Subject Number: 13   Group: Experimental Later-Born

Interactions Initiated by the Child

Child's Behavior

Frequency of overtures per 30 minutes (median): 6.5
Purposes of overtures (frequency):

To please	0	To annoy	0
To gain approval	0	To direct	0
To procure a service	1.0	To compete	0
To gain attention	2.5	To ease discomfort	0.5
To maintain social contact	2.0		

Adult's Response (percent frequency)

1. Timing and direction
   of adult's response:
   a. Immediately   83.3
   b. Delayed   16.7
      Length of delay (seconds)   122.4
   c. No response   0
   d. Rejects   0

2. Perceptions of child's need:
   a. Accurately   91.7
   b. Partially   8.3
   c. Not at all   0

3. Level of difficulty of words:
   a. Appropriate   87.5
   b. Too complex   0
   c. Too simple   8.3
   d. Babytalk   0
   e. None   4.2

4. Provision of related ideas:
   a. Yes   79.2
   b. No   20.8

5. Complexity of language:
   a. Complex sentence, 3s   21.7
   b. Phrase/sentence, 3s   73.9
   c. One word   4.3
   d. None   0

6. Provision of encouragement,
   reinforcement of enthusiasm:
   a. Yes   91.3
   b. No   0
   c. Inappropriate   8.7

7. Teaching realistic limits:
   a. Yes   21.7
   b. No   0
   c. Inappropriate   78.3

8. Satisfaction of child's needs:
   a. Yes   91.3
   b. No   0
   c. Partial   8.7

Average duration of adult's response (seconds): 51.6.
Time spent by adult responding (percent): 17.2.

Adult Assessment Scales Data: 11 to 16 Months

Subject Number: 13   Group: Experimental Later-Born

Interactions Initiated by the Adult

Frequency per 30 minutes (median):

Purposes of adult (percent duration):
    Stimulate child   5.1
    Contol positive   1.0
    Control negative   0.0
    Routine caretaking   0.4

Emotional tone (percent frequency):
    Positive   90.3
    Negative   0.0
    Neutral   9.7

Average duration of adult-initiated interactions (seconds): 26.0.
Time spent by adult in adult-initiated interactions (percent): 6.5.
Total time spent by the adult in interactions with the child (percent): 23.6.

Task Data (Percent of Total Time): 11 to 16 Months

Subject Number: 13   Group: Experimental Later-Born

Social tasks:

All social tasks	20.6
To cooperate	1.4
To procure a service	1.1
To gain attention	3.1
To maintain social contact	7.4
To assert self	1.2

Nonsocial tasks:

To eat	3.1
To gain information (visual)	23.6
To gain information (visual and auditory)	8.7
Live language	5.6
Overheard language	3.8
Mechanical language	0.0
Nontask	6.4
To pass time	0.0
To procure an object	5.2
To gain pleasure	0.0
To ease discomfort	1.1
To explore	16.8
Mastery	18.1
Gross motor	0.6
Fine motor	17.5

Test Data

Subject Number: 13   Group: Experimental Later-Born

Test	Age (months)	Score	Group Median
Bayley Scales	4½	94	106
of Infant Development	12	98	106
Mental Index	24	112	112
Stanford-Binet	36	93	98
Preschool Project	12	14	14
Receptive Language Test	14½	18	16
(score in months)	24	36	30
	36	45	39
Preschool Project	12	2	2
Abstract Abilities Test	14½	3	3
(score in levels)	24	6	5.5
Preschool Project	12	2	2
Dissonance Test	14½	2	2
(score in levels)	24	6	5

Group E$_2$

Subject Number:	14
SES:	II
Sex:	Male
Mother's Education:	High School, plus
Mother's Quick Word Test:	74
Father's Education:	College Graduate
Father's Occupation:	Accountant
Sibling Gap:	47 months

Adult Assessment Scales Data: 11 to 16 Months

Subject Number: 14   Group: Experimental Later-Born

Interactions Initiated by the Child

Child's Behavior

Frequency of overtures per 30 minutes (median): 6
Purposes of overtures (frequency):

To please	0	To annoy	0
To gain approval	0	To direct	0
To procure a service	1.0	To compete	0
To gain attention	1.0	To ease discomfort	0
To maintain social contact	1.0		

Adult's Response (percent frequency)

1. Timing and direction
   of adult's response:
   a. Immediately   55.6
   b. Delayed   14.8
      Length of delay (seconds) 115.2
   c. No response   11.1
   d. Rejects   18.5

2. Perceptions of child's need:
   a. Accurately   71.4
   b. Partially   23.8
   c. Not at all   4.8

3. Level of difficulty of words:
   a. Appropriate   14.3
   b. Too complex   0
   c. Too simple   71.4
   d. Babytalk   0
   e. None   14.3

4. Provision of related ideas:
   a. Yes   19
   b. No   81

5. Complexity of language:
   a. Complex sentence, 3s   0
   b. Phrase/sentence, 3s   47.6
   c. One word   38.1
   d. None   14.3

6. Provision of encouragement,
   reinforcement of enthusiasm:
   a. Yes   61.6
   b. No   22.2
   c. Inappropriate   16.7

7. Teaching realistic limits:
   a. Yes   11.8
   b. No   11.8
   c. Inappropriate   76.5

8. Satisfaction of child's needs:
   a. Yes   60
   b. No   25
   c. Partial   15

Average duration of adult's response (seconds): 21.9.
Time spent by adult responding (percent): 8.2.

Adult Assessment Scales Data: 11 to 16 Months

Subject Number: 14   Group: Experimental Later-Born

Interactions Initiated by the Adult

Frequency per 30 minutes (median):   4

Purposes of adult (percent duration):
    Stimulate child   1.1
    Contol positive   2.5
    Control negative   0.0
    Routine caretaking   0.8

Emotional tone (percent frequency):
    Positive   81.2
    Negative   0.0
    Neutral   18.7

Average duration of adult-initiated interactions (seconds): 19.8.
Time spent by adult in adult-initiated interactions (percent): 4.4.
Total time spent by the adult in interactions with the child (percent): 12.6.

Task Data (Percent of Total Time): 11 to 16 Months

Subject Number: 14   Group: Experimental Later-Born

As a result of problems in the subject's family, observers were unable to record enough data to calculate values for the 11- to 16-month time period.

Test Data

Subject Number: 14   Group: Experimental Later-Born

Test	Age (months)	Score	Group Median
Bayley Scales	4½	110	106
of Infant Development	12	91	106
Mental Index	24	83	112
Stanford-Binet	36	98	98
Preschool Project	12	16	14
Receptive Language Test	14½	a	16
(score in months)	24	27	30
	36	39	39
Preschool Project	12	2	2
Abstract Abilities Test	14½	a	3
(score in levels)	24	a	5.5
Preschool Project	12	3.5	2
Dissonance Test	14½	a	2
(score in levels)	24	5	5

[a]No valid scores.

Appendix C
Monitored Control
Firstborn Children ($C_{1,1}$)

Group $C_{1,1}$

Subject Number:	16
SES:	III
Sex:	Female
Mother's Education:	High School, plus
Mother's Quick Word Test:	83
Father's Education:	Partial High School
Father's Occupation:	Painter

Adult Assessment Scales Data: 11 to 16 Months

Subject Number: 16   Group: Monitored Control Firstborn

Interactions Initiated by the Child

Child's Behavior

Frequency of overtures per 30 minutes (median): 4.5
Purposes of overtures (frequency):

To please	0	To annoy	0
To gain approval	0	To direct	0
To procure a service	0.5	To compete	0
To gain attention	3.0	To ease discomfort	0
To maintain social contact	0		

Adult's Response (percent frequency)

1. Timing and direction
   of adult's response:
   a. Immediately   73.7
   b. Delayed   10.5
      Length of delay (seconds) 28.8
   c. No response   15.8
   d. Rejects   0

2. Perceptions of child's need:
   a. Accurately   93.7
   b. Partially   6.2
   c. Not at all   0

3. Level of difficulty of words:
   a. Appropriate   18.7
   b. Too complex   0
   c. Too simple   75.0
   d. Babytalk   0
   e. None   6.2

4. Provision of related ideas:
   a. Yes   62.5
   b. No   37.5

5. Complexity of language:
   a. Complex sentence, 3s   0
   b. Phrase/sentence, 3s   87.5
   c. One word   6.2
   d. None   6.2

6. Provision of encouragement,
   reinforcement of enthusiasm:
   a. Yes   93.7
   b. No   6.2
   c. Inappropriate   0

7. Teaching realistic limits:
   a. Yes   18.7
   b. No   6.2
   c. Inappropriate   75.0

8. Satisfaction of child's needs:
   a. Yes   93.7
   b. No   6.2
   c. Partial   0

Average duration of adult's response (seconds): 26.2.
Time spent by adult responding (percent): 14.9.

Adult Assessment Scales Data: 11 to 16 Months

Subject Number: 16   Group: Monitored Control Firstborn

Interactions Initiated by the Adult

Frequency per 30 minutes (median):   9.5

Purposes of adult (percent duration):
   Stimulate child   4.7
   Contol positive   12.6
   Control negative   1.9
   Routine caretaking   7.4

Emotional tone (percent frequency):
   Positive   81.7
   Negative   5.9
   Neutral   10.6

Average duration of adult-initiated interactions (seconds): 41.2.
Time spent by adult in adult-initiated interactions (percent): 26.9.
Total time spent by the adult in interactions with the child (percent): 41.8.

Task Data (Percent of Total Time): 11 to 16 Months

Subject Number: 16   Group: Monitored Control Firstborn

Social tasks:
All social tasks	18.0
To cooperate	0.6
To procure a service	0.0
To gain attention	3.1
To maintain social contact	9.8
To assert self	0.0

Nonsocial tasks:
To eat	10.0
To gain information (visual)	4.2
To gain information (visual and auditory)	20.5
Live language	17.8
Overheard language	1.0
Mechanical language	0.0
Nontask	0.0
To pass time	23.0
To procure an object	0.4
To gain pleasure	0.0
To ease discomfort	0.0
To explore	6.1
Mastery	4.3
Gross motor	0.0
Fine motor	4.3

Test Data

Subject Number: 16   Group: Monitored Control Firstborn

Test	Age (months)	Score	Group Median
Bayley Scales	4½	107	102.5
of Infant Development	12	93	98
Mental Index	24	96	115
Stanford-Binet	36	118	122
Preschool Project	12	12	14
Receptive Language Test	14½	16	17
(score in months)	24	39	36
	36	45	46.5
Preschool Project	12	1[a]	2
Abstract Abilities Test	14½	2	2.5
(score in levels)	24	5	7
Preschool Project	12	[b]	2
Dissonance Test	14½	2	2
(score in levels)	24	7	7

[a]Questionable validity.
[b]Invalid score.

Group $C_{1,1}$

Subject Number:	18
SES:	IV
Sex:	Female
Mother's Education:	High School
Mother's Quick Word Test:	65
Father's Education:	High School
Father's Occupation:	Newspaper Handler

Adult Assessment Scales Data: 11 to 16 Months

Subject Number: 18   Group: Monitored Control Firstborn

Interactions Initiated by the Child

Child's Behavior

Frequency of overtures per 30 minutes (median): 4
Purposes of overtures (frequency):

To please	0	To annoy	0
To gain approval	0	To direct	0
To procure a service	2.5	To compete	0
To gain attention	1.0	To ease discomfort	0
To maintain social contact	0		

Adult's Response (percent frequency)

1. Timing and direction
   of adult's response:
   a. Immediately   88.9
   b. Delayed   11.1
      Length of delay (seconds)   7.2
   c. No response   0
   d. Rejects   0

2. Perceptions of child's need:
   a. Accurately   94.4
   b. Partially   5.6
   c. Not at all   0

3. Level of difficulty of words:
   a. Appropriate   44.4
   b. Too complex   0
   c. Too simple   55.6
   d. Babytalk   0
   e. None   0

4. Provision of related ideas:
   a. Yes   27.8
   b. No   72.2

5. Complexity of language:
   a. Complex sentence, 3s   22.2
   b. Phrase/sentence, 3s   77.8
   c. One word   0
   d. None   0

6. Provision of encouragement,
   reinforcement of enthusiasm:
   a. Yes   83.3
   b. No   0
   c. Inappropriate   16.7

7. Teaching realistic limits:
   a. Yes   5.7
   b. No   1.1
   c. Inappropriate   83.3

8. Satisfaction of child's needs:
   a. Yes   77.8
   b. No   16.7
   c. Partial   5.6

Average duration of adult's response (seconds): 24.8.
Time spent by adult responding (percent): 6.2.

Adult Assessment Scales Data: 11 to 16 Months

Subject Number: 18   Group: Monitored Control Firstborn

Interactions Initiated by the Adult

Frequency per 30 minutes (median):   6

Purposes of adult (percent duration):
  Stimulate child   5.3
  Contol positive   2.2
  Control negative   0.1
  Routine caretaking   1.0

Emotional tone (percent frequency):
  Positive   89.7
  Negative   0.0
  Neutral   7.9

Average duration of adult-initiated interactions (seconds): 25.1.
Time spent by adult in adult-initiated interactions (percent): 8.7.
Total time spent by the adult in interactions with the child (percent): 15.0.

Task Data (Percent of Total Time): 11 to 16 Months

Subject Number: 18   Group: Monitored Control Firstborn

Social tasks:

All social tasks	10.9
To cooperate	1.1
To procure a service	0.6
To gain attention	2.3
To maintain social contact	4.7
To assert self	0.9

Nonsocial tasks:

To eat	2.2
To gain information (visual)	11.1
To gain information (visual and auditory)	24.2
Live language	6.1
Overheard language	10.0
Mechanical language	1.1
Nontask	20.3
To pass time	7.0
To procure an object	0.0
To gain pleasure	0.8
To ease discomfort	0.0
To explore	12.5
Mastery	6.4
Gross motor	0.9
Fine motor	5.6

Test Data

Subject Number: 18   Group: Monitored Control Firstborn

Test	Age (months)	Score	Group Median
Bayley Scales	4½	97	102.5
of Infant Development	12	112	98
Mental Index	24	102	115
Stanford-Binet	₁36	118	122
Preschool Project	12	14	14
Receptive Language Test	14½	16	17
(score in months)	24	a	36
	36	42	46.5
Preschool Project	12	3	2
Abstract Abilities Test	14½	2	2.5
(score in levels)	24	6	7
Preschool Project	12	2	2
Dissonance Test	14½	2	2
(score in levels)	24	8	7

[a]No valid score.

Group $C_{1,1}$

Subject Number:	19
SES:	II
Sex:	Female
Mother's Education:	High School
Mother's Quick Word Test:	64
Father's Education:	College Graduate
Father's Occupation:	Fund Administrator

Adult Assessment Scales Data: 11 to16 Months

Subject Number: 19   Group: Monitored Control Firstborn

Interactions Initiated by the Child

Child's Behavior

Frequency of overtures per 30 minutes (median): 8
Purposes of overtures (frequency):

To please	0	To annoy	0
To gain approval	0	To direct	0
To procure a service	2.0	To compete	0
To gain attention	2.5	To ease discomfort	0.5
To maintain social contact	0		

Adult's Response (percent frequency)

1. Timing and direction
   of adult's response:
   a. Immediately   90.3
   b. Delayed   6.5
      Length of delay (seconds)   21.6
   c. No response   3.2
   d. Rejects   0

2. Perceptions of child's need:
   a. Accurately   100
   b. Partially   0
   c. Not at all   0

3. Level of difficulty of words:
   a. Appropriate   63.3
   b. Too complex   0
   c. Too simple   30
   d. Babytalk   0
   e. None   6.7

4. Provision of related ideas:
   a. Yes   56.7
   b. No   43.3

5. Complexity of language:
   a. Complex sentence, 3s 10
   b. Phrase/sentence, 3s   73.3
   c. One word   10
   d. None   6.7

6. Provision of encouragement,
   reinforcement of enthusiasm:
   a. Yes   90
   b. No   6.7
   c. Inappropriate   3.3

7. Teaching realistic limits:
   a. Yes   10
   b. No   0
   c. Inappropriate   90

8. Satisfaction of child's needs:
   a. Yes   96.7
   b. No   0
   c. Partial   3.3

Average duration of adult's response (seconds): 41.1.
Time spent by adult responding (percent): 17.7.

Adult Assessment Scales Data: 11 to 16 Months

Subject Number: 19   Group: Monitored Control Firstborn

Interactions Initiated by the Adult

Frequency per 30 minutes (median):   8.5

Purposes of adult (percent duration):
    Stimulate child   8.9
    Contol positive   0.7
    Control negative   1.0
    Routine caretaking   2.2

Emotional tone (percent frequency):
    Positive   77.7
    Negative   2.7
    Neutral   19.6

Average duration of adult-initiated interactions (seconds): 27.9.
Time spent by adult in adult-initiated interactions (percent): 12.8.
Total time spent by the adult in interactions with the child (percent): 30.5.

Task Data (Percent of Total Time): 11 to 16 Months

Subject Number: 19   Group: Monitored Control Firstborn

Social tasks:
All social tasks	6.7
To cooperate	0.2
To procure a service	1.2
To gain attention	1.3
To maintain social contact	2.3
To assert self	0.0

Nonsocial tasks:
To eat	0.0
To gain information (visual)	7.8
To gain information (visual and auditory)	10.7
Live language	10.0
Overheard language	0.0
Mechanical language	0.7
Nontask	11.6
To pass time	0.0
To procure an object	2.5
To gain pleasure	0.0
To ease discomfort	0.8
To explore	16.9
Mastery	30.6
Gross motor	3.1
Fine motor	26.8

Test Data

Subject Number: 19   Group: Monitored Control Firstborn

Test	Age (months)	Score	Group Median
Bayley Scales	4½	105	102.5
of Infant Development	12	103	98
Mental Index	24	119	115
Stanford-Binet	36	122	122
Preschool Project	12	16	14
Receptive Language Test	14½	18	17
(score in months)	24	36	36
	36	51	46.5
Preschool Project	12	2	2
Abstract Abilities Test	14½	3	2.5
(score in levels)	24	7	7
Preschool Project	12	3	2
Dissonance Test	14½	2	2
(score in levels)	24	7	7

Group $C_{1,1}$

Subject Number:	20
SES:	III
Sex:	Female
Mother's Education:	High School, plus
Mother's Quick Word Test:	73
Father's Education:	Partial College
Father's Occupation:	Computer Programmer

Adult Assessment Scales Data: 11 to 16 Months

Subject Number: 20   Group: Monitored Control Firstborn

Interactions Initiated by the Child

Child's Behavior

Frequency of overtures per 30 minutes (median): 10.5
Purposes of overtures (frequency):

To please	0	To annoy	0
To gain approval	0	To direct	0
To procure a service	0.5	To compete	0
To gain attention	4.5	To ease discomfort	0.5
To maintain social contact	0.5		

Adult's Response (percent frequency)

1. Timing and direction
   of adult's response:
   a. Immediately   86.5
   b. Delayed   8.1
      Length of delay (seconds) 36.0
   c. No response   5.4
   d. Rejects   0

2. Perceptions of child's need:
   a. Accurately   97.1
   b. Partially   2.9
   c. Not at all   0

3. Level of difficulty of words:
   a. Appropriate   91.4
   b. Too complex   0
   c. Too simple   8.6
   d. Babytalk   0
   e. None   0

4. Provision of related ideas:
   a. Yes   77.1
   b. No   22.9

5. Complexity of language:
   a. Complex sentence, 3s   5.4
   b. Phrase/sentence, 3s   37.1
   c. One word   5.7
   d. None   0

6. Provision of encouragement,
   reinforcement of enthusiasm:
   a. Yes   57.1
   b. No   22.9
   c. Inappropriate   20

7. Teaching realistic limits:
   a. Yes   37.1
   b. No   0
   c. Inappropriate   62.9

8. Satisfaction of child's needs:
   a. Yes   80
   b. No   5.7
   c. Partial   14.3

Average duration of adult's response (seconds): 43.4.
Time spent by adult responding (percent): 22.3.

Adult Assessment Scales Data: 11 to 16 Months

Subject Number: 20   Group: Monitored Control Firstborn

Interactions Initiated by the Adult

Frequency per 30 minutes (median):   5

Purposes of adult (percent duration):
  Stimulate child   9.1
  Contol positive   2.1
  Control negative   1.7
  Routine caretaking   3.3

Emotional tone (percent frequency):
  Positive   85.0
  Negative   1.3
  Neutral   13.7

Average duration of adult-initiated interactions (seconds): 38.9.
Time spent by adult in adult-initiated interactions (percent): 16.2.
Total time spent by the adult in interactions with the child (percent): 38.5.

Task Data (Percent of Total Time): 11 to 16 Months

Subject Number: 20   Group: Monitored Control Firstborn

Social tasks:
All social tasks	12.1
To cooperate	1.1
To procure a service	0.6
To gain attention	2.5
To maintain social contact	4.8
To assert self	0.0

Nonsocial tasks:
To eat	7.8
To gain information (visual)	10.0
To gain information (visual and auditory)	8.5
Live language	8.5
Overheard language	0.0
Mechanical language	0.0
Nontask	23.2
To pass time	0.6
To procure an object	1.6
To gain pleasure	0.0
To ease discomfort	0.0
To explore	10.7
Mastery	9.1
Gross motor	0.6
Fine motor	8.5

Test Data

Subject Number: 20   Group: Monitored Control Firstborn

Test	Age (months)	Score	Group Median
Bayley Scales	4½	111	102.5
of Infant Development	12	112	98
Mental Index	24	114	115
Stanford-Binet	36	125	122
Preschool Project	12	16	14
Receptive Language Test	14½	18	17
(score in months)	24	36	36
	36	51	46.5
Preschool Project	12	a	2
Abstract Abilities Test	14½	2	2.5
(score in levels)	24	8	7
Preschool Project	12	2	2
Dissonance Test	14½	3	2
(score in levels)	24	7	7

[a]No valid score.

Group $C_{1,1}$

Subject Number:	22
SES:	III
Sex:	Male
Mother's Education:	High School, plus
Mother's Quick Word Test:	89
Father's Education:	High School
Father's Occupation:	Chemical Worker

Adult Assessment Scales Data: 11 to 16 Months

Subject Number: 22   Group: Monitored Control Firstborn

Interactions Initiated by the Child

Child's Behavior

Frequency of overtures per 30 minutes (median): 4
Purposes of overtures (frequency):

To please	0	To annoy	0
To gain approval	0	To direct	0
To procure a service	2.0	To compete	0
To gain attention	3.5	To ease discomfort	0
To maintain social contact	1.5		

Adult's Response (percent frequency)

1. Timing and direction
   of adult's response:
   a. Immediately   83.3
   b. Delayed   16.7
      Length of delay (seconds) 28.8
   c. No response   0
   d. Rejects   0

2. Perceptions of child's need:
   a. Accurately   100
   b. Partially   0
   c. Not at all   0

3. Level of difficulty of words:
   a. Appropriate   88.9
   b. Too complex   0
   c. Too simple   11.1
   d. Babytalk   0
   e. None   0

4. Provision of related ideas:
   a. Yes   72.2
   b. No   27.8

5. Complexity of language:
   a. Complex sentence, 3s   5.6
   b. Phrase/sentence, 3s   83.3
   c. One word   11.1
   d. None   0

6. Provision of encouragement,
   reinforcement of enthusiasm:
   a. Yes   77.8
   b. No   11.1
   c. Inappropriate   11.1

7. Teaching realistic limits:
   a. Yes   22.2
   b. No   0
   c. Inappropriate   77.8

8. Satisfaction of child's needs:
   a. Yes   83.3
   b. No   11.1
   c. Partial   5.6

Average duration of adult's response (seconds): 29.2.
Time spent by adult responding (percent): 7.3.

Adult Assessment Scales Data: 11 to 16 Months

Subject Number: 22   Group: Monitored Control Firstborn

Interactions Initiated by the Adult

Frequency per 30 minutes (median):   3

Purposes of adult (percent duration):
  Stimulate child   7.2
  Contol positive   5.2
  Control negative   3.1
  Routine caretaking   1.7

Emotional tone (percent frequency):
  Positive   79.8
  Negative   17.7
  Neutral   2.4

Average duration of adult-initiated interactions (seconds): 35.4.
Time spent by adult in adult-initiated interactions (percent): 17.2.
Total time spent by the adult in interactions with the child (percent): 24.5.

Task Data (Percent of Total Time): 11 to 16 Months

Subject Number: 22   Group: Monitored Control Firstborn

Social tasks:
All social tasks	9.9
To cooperate	2.7
To procure a service	1.0
To gain attention	1.3
To maintain social contact	2.8
To assert self	0.0

Nonsocial tasks:
To eat	0.3
To gain information (visual)	5.3
To gain information (visual and auditory)	13.8
Live language	10.4
Overheard language	0.0
Mechanical language	1.0
Nontask	29.1
To pass time	1.7
To procure an object	0.3
To gain pleasure	0.5
To ease discomfort	0.3
To explore	18.1
Mastery	12.7
Gross motor	0.9
Fine motor	6.4

Test Data

Subject Number: 22   Group: Monitored Control Firstborn

Test	Age (months)	Score	Group Median
Bayley Scales	4½	98	102.5
of Infant Development	12	98	98
Mental Index	24	143	115
Stanford-Binet	36	132	122
Preschool Project	12	17	14
Receptive Language Test	14½	18	17
(score in months)	24	36	36
	36	48	46.5
Preschool Project	12	3	2
Abstract Abilities Test	14½	2	2.5
(score in levels)	24	6	7
Preschool Project	12	2	2
Dissonance Test	14½	3	2
(score in levels)	24	7	7

Group C$_{1,1}$

Subject Number:	25
SES:	II
Sex:	Female
Mother's Education:	High School
Mother's Quick Word Test:	80
Father's Education:	College Graduate
Father's Occupation:	Insurance Supervisor

Adult Assessment Scales Data: 11 to 16 Months

Subject Number: 25   Group: Monitored Control Firstborn

Interactions Initiated by the Child

Child's Behavior

Frequency of overtures per 30 minutes (median): 4.5
Purposes of overtures (frequency):

To please	0	To annoy	0
To gain approval	0	To direct	0
To procure a service	1.0	To compete	0
To gain attention	0.5	To ease discomfort	0.5
To maintain social contact	0		

Adult's Response (percent frequency)

1. Timing and direction
   of adult's response:
   a. Immediately   75
   b. Delayed   20.8
      Length of delay (seconds) 108
   c. No response   0
   d. Rejects   4.2

2. Perceptions of child's need:
   a. Accurately   95.8
   b. Partially   4.2
   c. Not at all   0

3. Level of difficulty of words:
   a. Appropriate   37.5
   b. Too complex   0
   c. Too simple   54.2
   d. Babytalk   0
   e. None   8.3

4. Provision of related ideas:
   a. Yes   41.7
   b. No   58.3

5. Complexity of language:
   a. Complex sentence, 3s   4.5
   b. Phrase/sentence, 3s   59.1
   c. One word   27.3
   d. None   9.1

6. Provision of encouragement
   reinforcement of enthusiasm:
   a. Yes   66.7
   b. No   16.7
   c. Inappropriate   16.7

7. Teaching realistic limits:
   a. Yes   0
   b. No   4.2
   c. Inappropriate   95.8

8. Satisfaction of child's needs:
   a. Yes   87.5
   b. No   4.2
   c. Partial   8.3

Average duration of adult's response (seconds): 24.3.
Time spent by adult responding (percent): 8.1.

Adult Assessment Scales Data: 11 to 16 Months

Subject Number: 25   Group: Monitored Control Firstborn

Interactions Initiated by the Adult

Frequency per 30 minutes (median):   12.5

Purposes of adult (percent duration):
    Stimulate child   7.3
    Contol positive   5.2
    Control negative   3.1
    Routine caretaking   1.7

Emotional tone (percent frequency):
    Positive   79.8
    Negative   17.7
    Neutral   2.4

Average duration of adult-initiated interactions (seconds): 25.2.
Time spent by adult in adult-initiated interactions (percent): 16.8.
Total time spent by the adult in interactions with the child (percent): 24.9.

Task Data (Percent of Total Time): 11 to 16 Months

Subject Number: 25   Group: Monitored Control Firstborn

Social tasks:
All social tasks	5.3
To cooperate	0.6
To procure a service	0.0
To gain attention	1.0
To maintain social contact	0.0
To assert self	1.9

Nonsocial tasks:
To eat	9.8
To gain information (visual)	3.3
To gain information (visual and auditory)	19.3
Live language	1.8
Overheard language	0.0
Mechanical language	17.6
Nontask	11.8
To pass time	0.9
To procure an object	3.5
To gain pleasure	0.0
To ease discomfort	1.1
To explore	15.3
Mastery	10.6
Gross motor	3.1
Fine motor	7.5

Test Data

Subject Number: 25   Group: Monitored Control Firstborn

Test	Age (months)	Score	Group Median
Bayley Scales	4½	111	102.5
of Infant Development	12	98	98
Mental Index	24	116	115
Stanford-Binet	36	122	122
Preschool Project	12	14	14
Receptive Language Test	14½	16	17
(score in months)	24	24	36
	36	42	46.5
Preschool Project	12	2	2
Abstract Abilities Test	14½	3	2.5
(score in levels)	24	7	7
Preschool Project	12	2	2
Dissonance Test	14½	2	2
(score in levels)	24	5	7

[a]No valid score.

Group C$_{1,1}$

Subject Number:	28
SES:	III
Sex:	Male
Mother's Education:	High School
Mother's Quick Word Test:	56
Father's Education:	High School
Father's Occupation:	Mechanic

Adult Assessment Scales Data: 11 to 16 Months

Subject Number: 28   Group: Monitored Control Firstborn

Interactions Initiated by the Child

Child's Behavior

Frequency of overtures per 30 minutes (median): 8.5
Purposes of overtures (frequency):

To please	0	To annoy	0
To gain approval	0	To direct	0
To procure a service	2.0	To compete	0
To gain attention	2.5	To ease discomfort	0.5
To maintain social contact	1.5		

Adult's Response (percent frequency)

1. Timing and direction
   of adult's response:
   a. Immediately   92.6
   b. Delayed   7.4
      Length of delay (seconds) 7.2
   c. No response   0
   d. Rejects   0

2. Perceptions of child's need:
   a. Accurately   100
   b. Partially   0
   c. Not at all   0

3. Level of difficulty of words:
   a. Appropriate   74.1
   b. Too complex   0
   c. Too simple   18.5
   d. Babytalk   0
   e. None   7.4

4. Provision of related ideas:
   a. Yes   63
   b. No   37

5. Complexity of language:
   a. Complex sentence, 3s   51.9
   b. Phrase/sentence, 3s   40.7
   c. One word   0
   d. None   7.4

6. Provision of encouragement,
   reinforcement of enthusiasm:
   a. Yes   85.2
   b. No   3.7
   c. Inappropriate   11.1

7. Teaching realistic limits:
   a. Yes   7.7
   b. No   19.2
   c. Inappropriate   73.1

8. Satisfaction of child's needs:
   a. Yes   96.3
   b. No   0
   c. Partial   3.7

Average duration of adult's response (seconds): 45.9.
Time spent by adult responding (percent): 17.2.

Adult Assessment Scales Data: 11 to 16 Months

Subject Number: 28 Group: Monitored Control Firstborn

Interactions Initiated by the Adult

Frequency per 30 minutes (median): 9

Purposes of adult (percent duration):
Stimulate child	16.7
Contol positive	5.9
Control negative	0.1
Routine caretaking	1.2

Emotional tone (percent frequency):
Positive	99.4
Negative	0.3
Neutral	0.3

Average duration of adult-initiated interactions (seconds): 45.5.
Time spent by adult in adult-initiated interactions (percent): 24.0.
Total time spent by the adult in interactions with the child (percent): 41.2.

Task Data (Percent of Total Time): 11 to 16 Months

Subject Number: 28   Group: Monitored Control Firstborn

Social tasks:

All social tasks	11.0
To cooperate	3.0
To procure a service	2.1
To gain attention	0.9
To maintain social contact	3.2
To assert self	0.0

Nonsocial tasks:

To eat	8.2
To gain information (visual)	19.3
To gain information (visual and auditory)	7.1
Live language	7.1
Overheard language	0.0
Mechanical language	0.0
Nontask	8.2
To pass time	0.6
To procure an object	1.1
To gain pleasure	0.0
To ease discomfort	1.5
To explore	19.3
Mastery	13.8
Gross motor	8.2
Fine motor	2.7

Test Data

Subject Number: 28   Group: Monitored Control Firstborn

Test	Age (months)	Score	Group Median
Bayley Scales	4½	94	102.5
of Infant Development	12	98	98
Mental Index	24	132	115
Stanford-Binet	36	120	122
Preschool Project	12	12	14
Receptive Language Test	14½	18	17
(score in months)	24	36	36
	36	51	46.5
Preschool Project	12	2	2
Abstract Abilities Test	14½	3	2.5
(score in levels)	24	8	7
Preschool Project	12	1	2
Dissonance Test	14½	2	2
(score in levels)	24	7	7

Group $C_{1,1}$

Subject Number:	27
SES:	III
Sex:	Female
Mother's Education:	High School
Mother's Quick Word Test:	72
Father's Education:	Partial College
Father's Occupation:	Elevator Mechanic

Adult Assessment Scales Data: 11 to 16 Months

Subject Number: 27   Group: Monitored Control Firstborn

Interactions Initiated by the Child

Child's Behavior

Frequency of overtures per 30 minutes (median): 8
Purposes of overtures (frequency):

To please	0	To annoy	0
To gain approval	0	To direct	0
To procure a service	3.5	To compete	0
To gain attention	2.5	To ease discomfort	0
To maintain social contact	1.0		

Adult's Response (percent frequency)

1. Timing and direction
   of adult's response:
   a. Immediately   80.6
   b. Delayed   5.6
       Length of delay (seconds)   28.8
   c. No response   2.8
   d. Rejects   11.1

2. Perceptions of child's need:
   a. Accurately   88.6
   b. Partially   11.4
   c. Not at all   0

3. Level of difficulty of words:
   a. Appropriate   74.3
   b. Too complex   0
   c. Too simple   14.3
   d. Babytalk   0
   e. None   11.4

4. Provision of related ideas:
   a. Yes   68.6
   b. No   31.4

5. Complexity of language:
   a. Complex sentence, 3s   54.3
   b. Phrase/sentence, 3s   34.3
   c. One word   0
   d. None   11.4

6. Provision of encouragement,
   reinforcement of enthusiasm:
   a. Yes   70.6
   b. No   26.5
   c. Inappropriate   2.9

7. Teaching realistic limits:
   a. Yes   47.1
   b. No   5.9
   c. Inappropriate   47.1

8. Satisfaction of child's needs:
   a. Yes   66.7
   b. No   24.2
   c. Partial   9.1

Average duration of adult's response (seconds): 32.8.
Time spent by adult responding (percent): 16.4.

Adult Assessment Scales Data: 11 to 16 Months

Subject Number: 27   Group: Monitored Control Firstborn

Interactions Initiated by the Adult

Frequency per 30 minutes (median):   8.5

Purposes of adult (percent duration):
    Stimulate child   29.2
    Contol positive   3.7
    Control negative   1.8
    Routine caretaking   0.6

Emotional tone (percent frequency):
    Positive   92.7
    Negative   4.1
    Neutral   3.2

Average duration of adult-initiated interactions (seconds): 57.6.
Time spent by adult in adult-initiated interactions (percent): 35.2.
Total time spent by the adult in interactions with the child (percent): 51.6.

Task Data (Percent of Total Time): 11 to 16 Months

Subject Number: 27   Group: Monitored Control Firstborn

Social tasks:
All social tasks	17.7
To cooperate	1.4
To procure a service	2.4
To gain attention	3.8
To maintain social contact	0.9
To assert self	2.3

Nonsocial tasks:
To eat	11.4
To gain information (visual)	9.4
To gain information (visual and auditory)	18.9
Live language	18.9
Overheard language	0.0
Mechanical language	0.0
Nontask	8.0
To pass time	0.0
To procure an object	1.1
To gain pleasure	1.7
To ease discomfort	0.4
To explore	13.5
Mastery	2.5
Gross motor	0.0
Fine motor	2.0

Test Data

Subject Number: 27   Group: Monitored Control Firstborn

Test	Age (months)	Score	Group Median
Bayley Scales	4½	100	102.5
of Infant Development	12	98	98
Mental Index	24	109	115
Stanford-Binet	36	125	122
Preschool Project	12	14	14
Receptive Language Test	14½	16	17
(score in months)	24	33	36
	36	45	46.5
Preschool Project	12	2	2
Abstract Abilities Test	14½	3	2.5
(score in levels)	24	7	7
Preschool Project	12	2	2
Dissonance Test	14½	2	2
(score in levels)	24	7	7

Appendix D
Monitored Control
Later-Born
Children ($C_{1,2}$)

Group $C_{1,2}$

Subject Number:	15
SES:	III
Sex:	Male
Mother's Education:	High School, plus
Mother's Quick Word Test:	68
Father's Education:	College Graduate
Father's Occupation:	Insurance Appraiser
Sibling Gap:	41 months (59 months)

Adult Assessment Scales Data: 11 to 16 Months

Subject Number: 15   Group: Monitored Control Later-Born

Interactions Initiated by the Child

Child's Behavior

Frequency of overtures per 30 minutes (median): 4.5
Purposes of overtures (frequency):

To please	0	To annoy	0
To gain approval	0	To direct	0
To procure a service	0	To compete	0
To gain attention	3.0	To ease discomfort	0.5
To maintain social contact	0		

Adult's Response (percent frequency)

1. Timing and direction
   of adult's response:
   a. Immediately   56.5
   b. Delayed   17.4
      Length of delay (seconds) 64.8
   c. No response   26.1
   d. Rejects   0

2. Perceptions of child's need:
   a. Accurately   88.2
   b. Partially   5.9
   c. Not at all   5.9

3. Level of difficulty of words:
   a. Appropriate   11.8
   b. Too complex   0
   c. Too simple   64.7
   d. Babytalk   5.9
   e. None   17.6

4. Provision of related ideas:
   a. Yes   5.9
   b. No   94.1

5. Complexity of language:
   a. Complex sentence, 3s   0
   b. Phrase/sentence, 3s   35.3
   c. One word   47.1
   d. None   17.6

6. Provision of encouragement,
   reinforcement of enthusiasm:
   a. Yes   81.2
   b. No   12.5
   c. Inappropriate   6.2

7. Teaching realistic limits:
   a. Yes   6.2
   b. No   0
   c. Inappropriate   93.7

8. Satisfaction of child's needs:
   a. Yes   87.5
   b. No   6.2
   c. Partial   6.2

Average duration of adult's response (seconds): 11.3.
Time spent by adult responding (percent): 3.6.

Adult Assessment Scales Data: 11 to 16 Months

Subject Number: 15   Group: Monitored Control Later-Born

Interactions Initiated by the Adult

Frequency per 30 minutes (median):   8

Purposes of adult (percent duration):
  Stimulate child   2.9
  Contol positive   0.6
  Control negative   1.5
  Routine caretaking   1.0

Emotional tone (percent frequency):
  Positive   69.0
  Negative   21.8
  Neutral   9.2

Average duration of adult-initiated interactions (seconds): 13.1.
Time spent by adult in adult-initiated interactions (percent): 6.0.
Total time spent by the adult in interactions with the child (percent): 9.6.

Task Data (Percent of Total Time): 11 to 16 Months

Subject Number: 15   Group: Monitored Control Later-Born

Social tasks:

All social tasks	3.4
To cooperate	0.9
To procure a service	0.0
To gain attention	1.6
To maintain social contact	0.0
To assert self	0.0

Nonsocial tasks:

To eat	2.4
To gain information (visual)	8.8
To gain information (visual and auditory)	10.5
Live language	3.8
Overheard language	5.1
Mechanical language	0.0
Nontask	29.6
To pass time	2.0
To procure an object	1.3
To gain pleasure	0.0
To ease discomfort	0.0
To explore	10.3
Mastery	10.7
Gross motor	7.0
Fine motor	5.3

Test Data

Subject Number: 15   Group: Monitored Control Later-Born

Test	Age (months)	Score	Group Median
Bayley Scales	4½	110	106
of Infant Development	12	126	109
Mental Index	24	106	106
Stanford-Binet	36	118	99
Preschool Project	12	12	12
Receptive Language Test	14½	14	16
(score in months)	24	36	30
	36	48	42
Preschool Project	12	2	2
Abstract Abilities Test	14½	2	2
(score in levels)	24	7	6.5
Preschool Project	12	2	2
Dissonance Test	14½	2	2
(score in levels)	24	6	6.5

Group $C_{1,2}$

Subject Number:	17
SES:	IV
Sex:	Male
Mother's Education:	High School
Mother's Quick Word Test:	67
Father's Education:	High School
Father's Occupation:	Shipper/Receiver
Sibling Gap:	43 months

Adult Assessment Scales Data: 11 to 16 Months

Subject Number: 17   Group: Monitored Control Later-Born

Interactions Initiated by the Child

Child's Behavior

Frequency of overtures per 30 minutes (median): 7.5
Purposes of overtures (frequency):

To please	0	To annoy	0
To gain approval	0	To direct	0
To procure a service	3.5	To compete	0
To gain attention	1.5	To ease discomfort	0
To maintain social contact	0.5		

Adult's Response (percent frequency)

1. Timing and direction
   of adult's response:
   a. Immediately   87.1
   b. Delayed   9.7
      Length of delay (seconds)   43.2
   c. No response   3.2
   d. Rejects   0

2. Perceptions of child's need:
   a. Accurately   83.3
   b. Partially   16.7
   c. Not at all   0

3. Level of difficulty of words:
   a. Appropriate   36.7
   b. Too complex   0
   c. Too simple   63.3
   d. Babytalk   0
   e. None   0

4. Provision of related ideas:
   a. Yes   40
   b. No   60

5. Complexity of language:
   a. Complex sentence, 3s   0
   b. Phrase/sentence, 3s   60
   c. One word   40
   d. None   0

6. Provision of encouragement,
   reinforcement of enthusiasm:
   a. Yes   63.3
   b. No   36.7
   c. Inappropriate   0

7. Teaching realistic limits:
   a. Yes   23.3
   b. No   0
   c. Inappropriate   76.7

8. Satisfaction of child's needs:
   a. Yes   71
   b. No   19.4
   c. Partial   9.7

Average duration of adult's response (seconds): 36.7.
Time spent by adult responding (percent): 15.8.

Adult Assessment Scales Data: 11 to 16 Months

Subject Number: 17   Group: Monitored Control Later-Born

Interactions Initiated by the Adult

Frequency per 30 minutes (median):   11

Purposes of adult (percent duration):
   Stimulate child   5.4
   Contol positive   4.0
   Control negative   1.6
   Routine caretaking   4.1

Emotional tone (percent frequency):
   Positive   71.4
   Negative   11.9
   Neutral   16.6

Average duration of adult-initiated interactions (seconds): 24.2.
Time spent by adult in adult-initiated interactions (percent): 15.1.
Total time spent by the adult in interactions with the child (percent): 30.9.

Task Data (Percent of Total Time): 11 to 16 Months

Subject Number: 17   Group: Monitored Control Later-Born

Social tasks:
All social tasks	18.8
To cooperate	2.1
To procure a service	0.6
To gain attention	1.7
To maintain social contact	8.5
To assert self	0.3

Nonsocial tasks:
To eat	16.3
To gain information (visual)	4.9
To gain information (visual and auditory)	10.9
Live language	10.9
Overheard language	0.0
Mechanical language	0.0
Nontask	22.1
To pass time	0.0
To procure an object	0.9
To gain pleasure	0.6
To ease discomfort	0.0
To explore	5.2
Mastery	9.5
Gross motor	3.8
Fine motor	5.6

Test Data

Subject Number: 17   Group: Monitored Control Later-Born

Test	Age (months)	Score	Group Median
Bayley Scales	4½	113	106
of Infant Development	12	106	109
Mental Index	24	106	106
Stanford-Binet	36	98	99
Preschool Project	12	14	12
Receptive Language Test	14½	16	16
(score in months)	24	30	30
	36	42	42
Preschool Project	12	1[a]	2
Abstract Abilities Test	14½	2	2
(score in levels)	24	6	6.5
Preschool Project	12	2	2
Dissonance Test	14½	2	2
(score in levels)	24	5	6.5

[a]Questionable validity.

Group $C_{1,2}$

Subject Number:	21
SES:	III
Sex:	Female
Mother's Education:	High School
Mother's Quick Word Test:	78
Father's Education:	Partial College
Father's Occupation:	Steam Engineer
Sibling Gap:	63 months

Adult Assessment Scales Data: 11 to 16 Months

Subject Number: 21   Group: Monitored Control Later-Born

Interactions Initiated by the Child

Child's Behavior

Frequency of overtures per 30 minutes (median): 5.5
Purposes of overtures (frequency):

To please	0	To annoy	0
To gain approval	0	To direct	0
To procure a service	2.0	To compete	0
To gain attention	1.5	To ease discomfort	0
To maintain social contact	0.5		

Adult's Response (percent frequency)

1. Timing and direction
   of adult's response:
   a. Immediately   75
   b. Delayed   25
      Length of delay (seconds) 36
   c. No response   0
   d. Rejects   0

2. Perceptions of child's need:
   a. Accurately   80
   b. Partially   20
   c. Not at all   0

3. Level of difficulty of words:
   a. Appropriate   25
   b. Too complex   0
   c. Too simple   75
   d. Babytalk   0
   e. None   0

4. Provision of related ideas:
   a. Yes   25
   b. No   75

5. Complexity of language:
   a. Complex sentence, 3s   0
   b. Phrase/sentence, 3s   85
   c. One word   15
   d. None   0

6. Provision of encouragement,
   reinforcement of enthusiasm:
   a. Yes   85
   b. No   15
   c. Inappropriate   0

7. Teaching realistic limits:
   a. Yes   5
   b. No   20
   c. Inappropriate   75

8. Satisfaction of child's needs:
   a. Yes   85
   b. No   5
   c. Partial   10

Average duration of adult's response (seconds): 40.1.
Time spent by adult responding (percent): 11.7.

Adult Assessment Scales Data: 311

Subject Number: 21   Group: Monitored Control Later-Born

Interactions Initiated by the Adult

Frequency per 30 minutes (median):   5

Purposes of adult (percent duration):
Stimulate child   7.3
Contol positive   0.0
Control negative   1.1
Routine caretaking   2.1

Emotional tone (percent frequency):
Positive   71.5
Negative   4.6
Neutral   12.6

Average duration of adult-initiated interactions (seconds): 37.8.
Time spent by adult in adult-initiated interactions (percent): 10.5.
Total time spent by the adult in interactions with the child (percent): 22.2.

Task Data (Percent of Total Time): 11 to 16 Months

Subject Number: 21   Group: Monitored Control Later-Born

Social tasks:
All social tasks	9.3
To cooperate	4.0
To procure a service	0.3
To gain attention	1.0
To maintain social contact	2.9
To assert self	0.3

Nonsocial tasks:
To eat	14.6
To gain information (visual)	12.1
To gain information (visual and auditory)	11.2
Live language	4.6
Overheard language	0.7
Mechanical language	1.7
Nontask	28.8
To pass time	1.8
To procure an object	0.6
To gain pleasure	0.0
To ease discomfort	0.0
To explore	10.0
Mastery	1.5
Gross motor	0.3
Fine motor	0.6

Test Data

Subject Number: 21   Group: Monitored Control Later-Born

Test	Age (months)	Score	Group Median
Bayley Scales	4½	106	106
of Infant Development	12	112	109
Mental Index	24	102	106
Stanford-Binet	36	86	99
Preschool Project	12	16	12
Receptive Language Test	14½	16	16
(score in months)	24	24	30
	36	39	42
Preschool Project	12	2	2
Abstract Abilities Test	14½	2	2
(score in levels)	24	5	6.5
Preschool Project	12	2	2
Dissonance Test	14½	2	2
(score in levels)	24	7	6.5

Group $C_{1,2}$

Subject Number:	23
SES:	III
Sex:	Female
Mother's Education:	High School
Mother's Quick Word Test:	72
Father's Education:	Partial College
Father's Occupation:	Electronics Technician
Sibling Gap:	62 months

Adult Assessment Scales Data: 11 to 16 Months

Subject Number: 23   Group: Monitored Control Later-Born

Interactions Initiated by the Child

Child's Behavior

Frequency of overtures per 30 minutes (median): 10
Purposes of overtures (frequency):

To please	0	To annoy	0
To gain approval	0	To direct	0
To procure a service	2.5	To compete	0
To gain attention	3.0	To ease discomfort	0
To maintain social contact	2.5		

Adult's Response (percent frequency)

1. Timing and direction
   of adult's response:
   a. Immediately   78.4
   b. Delayed   13.5
      Length of delay (seconds)   72
   c. No response   5.4
   d. Rejects   2.7

2. Perceptions of child's need:
   a. Accurately   100
   b. Partially   0
   c. Not at all   0

3. Level of difficulty of words:
   a. Appropriate   51.4
   b. Too complex   0
   c. Too simple   31.4
   d. Babytalk   0
   e. None   17.1

4. Provision of related ideas:
   a. Yes   34.3
   b. No   65.7

5. Complexity of language:
   a. Complex sentence, 3s   20
   b. Phrase/sentence, 3s   60
   c. One word   2.9
   d. None   17.1

6. Provision of encouragement,
   reinforcement of enthusiasm:
   a. Yes   74.3
   b. No   20
   c. Inappropriate   5.7

7. Teaching realistic limits:
   a. Yes   22.9
   b. No   22.9
   c. Inappropriate   54.3

8. Satisfaction of child's needs:
   a. Yes   75
   b. No   13.9
   c. Partial   11.1

Average duration of adult's response (seconds): 53.3.
Time spent by adult responding (percent): 29.6.

Adult Assessment Scales Data: 11 to 16 Months

Subject Number: 23   Group: Monitored Control Later-Born

Interactions Initiated by the Adult

Frequency per 30 minutes (median):   10.5

Purposes of adult (percent duration):
Stimulate child   10.7
Contol positive   1.0
Control negative   2.0
Routine caretaking   0.7

Emotional tone (percent frequency):
Positive   83.7
Negative   9.6
Neutral   6.7

Average duration of adult-initiated interactions (seconds): 24.7.
Time spent by adult in adult-initiated interactions (percent): 14.4.
Total time spent by the adult in interactions with the child (percent): 44.0.

Task Data (Percent of Total Time): 11 to 16 Months

Subject Number: 23   Group: Monitored Control Later-Born

Social tasks:
All social tasks	27.9
To cooperate	8.3
To procure a service	1.4
To gain attention	2.5
To maintain social contact	5.8
To assert self	3.3

Nonsocial tasks:
To eat	11.6
To gain information (visual)	8.1
To gain information (visual and auditory)	4.1
Live language	0.8
Overheard language	3.0
Mechanical language	0.0
Nontask	12.2
To pass time	2.7
To procure an object	3.6
To gain pleasure	0.0
To ease discomfort	2.1
To explore	5.2
Mastery	2.7
Gross motor	2.7
Fine motor	0.0

Test Data

Subject Number: 23   Group: Monitored Control Later-Born

Test	Age (months)	Score	Group Median
Bayley Scales	4½	104	106
of Infant Development	12	81	109
Mental Index	24	102	106
Stanford-Binet	36	105	99
Preschool Project	12	10	12
Receptive Language Test	14½	16	16
(score in months)	24	30	30
	36	36	42
Preschool Project	12	2	2
Abstract Abilities Test	14½	3	2
(score in levels)	24	4	6.5
Preschool Project	12	1	2
Dissonance Test	14½	1	2
(score in levels)	24	4	6.5

Group C$_{1,2}$

Subject Number:	26
SES:	III
Sex:	Male
Mother's Education:	High School, plus
Mother's Quick Word Test:	68
Father's Education:	Partial College
Father's Occupation:	Insurance Underwriter
Sibling Gap:	25 months

Adult Assessment Scales Data: 11 to 16 Months

Subject Number: 26   Group: Monitored Control Later-Born

Interactions Initiated by the Child

Child's Behavior

Frequency of overtures per 30 minutes (median): 3.5
Purposes of overtures (frequency):

To please	0	To annoy	0
To gain approval	0	To direct	0
To procure a service	0.5	To compete	0
To gain attention	3.5	To ease discomfort	0
To maintain social contact	0		

Adult's Response (percent frequency)

1. Timing and direction
   of adult's response:
   a. Immediately   55.6
   b. Delayed   22.2
      Length of delay (seconds) 122.4
   c. No response   22.2
   d. Rejects   0

2. Perceptions of child's need:
   a. Accurately   84.6
   b. Partially   7.7
   c. Not at all   7.7

3. Level of difficulty of words:
   a. Appropriate   28.6
   b. Too complex   0
   c. Too simple   21.4
   d. Babytalk   14.3
   e. None   35.7

4. Provision of related ideas:
   a. Yes   7.1
   b. No   92.9

5. Complexity of language:
   a. Complex sentence, 3s   14.3
   b. Phrase/sentence, 3s   50
   c. One word   0
   d. None   35.7

6. Provision of encouragement,
   reinforcement of enthusiasm:
   a. Yes   100
   b. No   0
   c. Inappropriate   0

7. Teaching realistic limits:
   a. Yes   0
   b. No   14.3
   c. Inappropriate   85.7

8. Satisfaction of child's needs:
   a. Yes   92.9
   b. No   0
   c. Partial   7.1

Average duration of adult's response (seconds): 16.8.
Time spent by adult responding (percent): 4.2.

Adult Assessment Scales Data: 11 to 16 Months

Subject Number: 26   Group: Monitored Control Later-Born

Interactions Initiated by the Adult

Frequency per 30 minutes (median):   4

Purposes of adult (percent duration):
   Stimulate child   4.2
   Contol positive   1.4
   Control negative   0.3
   Routine caretaking   0.3

Emotional tone (percent frequency):
   Positive   84.4
   Negative   1.1
   Neutral   14.4

Average duration of adult-initiated interactions (seconds): 22.3.
Time spent by adult in adult-initiated interactions (percent): 6.2.
Total time spent by the adult in interactions with the child (percent): 10.4.

Task Data (Percent of Total Time): 11 to 16 Months

Subject Number: 26   Group: Monitored Control Later-Born

Social tasks:
All social tasks	6.0
To cooperate	1.3
To procure a service	0.0
To gain attention	2.3
To maintain social contact	2.5
To assert self	0.0

Nonsocial tasks:
To eat	0.9
To gain information (visual)	7.1
To gain information (visual and auditory)	7.1
Live language	1.3
Overheard language	3.6
Mechanical language	0.4
Nontask	2.0
To pass time	20.7
To procure an object	0.0
To gain pleasure	0.0
To ease discomfort	3.5
To explore	16.8
Mastery	4.8
Gross motor	0.3
Fine motor	4.8

Test Data

Subject Number: 26   Group: Monitored Control Later-Born

Test	Age (months)	Score	Group Median
Bayley Scales	4½	102	106
of Infant Development	12	89	109
Mental Index	24	119	106
Stanford-Binet	36	100	99
Preschool Project	12	12	12
Receptive Language Test	14½	12	16
(score in months)	24	33	30
	36	45	42
Preschool Project	12	2	2
Abstract Abilities Test	14½	2	2
(score in levels)	24	7	6.5
Preschool Project	12	a	2
Dissonance Test	14½	1	2
(score in levels)	24	8	6.5

[a]Invalid score.

Group C$_{1,2}$

Subject Number:	29
SES:	IV
Sex:	Female
Mother's Education:	High School
Mother's Quick Word Test:	51
Father's Education:	Partial College
Father's Occupation:	Truck Driver
Sibling Gap:	30 months

Adult Assessment Scales Data: 11 to 16 Months

Subject Number: 29   Group: Monitored Control Later-Born

Interactions Initiated by the Child

Child's Behavior

Frequency of overtures per 30 minutes (median): 6
Purposes of overtures (frequency):

To please	0	To annoy	0
To gain approval	0	To direct	0
To procure a service	0.5	To compete	0
To gain attention	2.5	To ease discomfort	0
To maintain social contact	2.5		

Adult's Response (percent frequency)

1. Timing and direction
   of adult's response:
   a. Immediately   41.7
   b. Delayed   33.3
      Length of delay (seconds)   158.4
   c. No response   25
   d. Rejects   0

2. Perceptions of child's need:
   a. Accurately   83.3
   b. Partially   5.6
   c. Not at all   11.1

3. Level of difficulty of words:
   a. Appropriate   66.7
   b. Too complex   0
   c. Too simple   22.2
   d. Babytalk   0
   e. None   11.1

4. Provision of related ideas:
   a. Yes   44.4
   b. No   55.6

5. Complexity of language:
   a. Complex sentence, 3s   11.1
   b. Phrase/sentence, 3s   77.8
   c. One word   0
   d. None   11.1

6. Provision of encouragement,
   reinforcement of enthusiasm:
   a. Yes   66.7
   b. No   5.6
   c. Inappropriate   27.8

7. Teaching realistic limits:
   a. Yes   22.2
   b. No   0
   c. Inappropriate   77.8

8. Satisfaction of child's needs:
   a. Yes   83.3
   b. No   11.1
   c. Partial   5.6

Average duration of adult's response (seconds): 27.7.
Time spent by adult responding (percent): 9.2.

Adult Assessment Scales Data: 11 to 16 Months

Subject Number: 29   Group: Monitored Control Later-Born

Interactions Initiated by the Adult

Frequency per 30 minutes (median):   6

Purposes of adult (percent duration):
    Stimulate child   1.2
    Contol positive   0.3
    Control negative   4.2
    Routine caretaking   4.6

Emotional tone (percent frequency):
    Positive   42.6
    Negative   38.5
    Neutral   18.9

Average duration of adult-initiated interactions (seconds): 33.7.
Time spent by adult in adult-initiated interactions (percent): 10.3.
Total time spent by the adult in interactions with the child (percent): 19.4.

Task Data (Percent of Total Time): 11 to 16 Months

Subject Number: 29   Group: Monitored Control Later-Born

Social tasks:
All social tasks	11.0
To cooperate	2.0
To procure a service	0.0
To gain attention	2.8
To maintain social contact	2.0
To assert self	0.7

Nonsocial tasks:
To eat	1.1
To gain information (visual)	7.2
To gain information (visual and auditory)	8.1
Live language	1.8
Overheard language	4.3
Mechanical language	0.0
Nontask	20.3
To pass time	2.8
To procure an object	2.5
To gain pleasure	2.0
To ease discomfort	1.7
To explore	10.8
Mastery	5.5
Gross motor	3.6
Fine motor	0.4

Test Data

Subject Number: 29   Group: Monitored Control Later-Born

Test	Age (months)	Score	Group Median
Bayley Scales	4½	106	106
of Infant Development	12	117	109
Mental Index	24	116	106
Stanford-Binet	36	88	99
Preschool Project	12	12	12
Receptive Language Test	14½	16	16
(score in months)	24	a	30
	36	42	42
Preschool Project	12	1[b]	2
Abstract Abilities Test	14½	3	2
(score in levels)	24	7	6.5
Preschool Project	12	2	2
Dissonance Test	14½	2	2
(score in levels)	24	7	6.5

[a]Invalid score.
[b]Questionable validity.

Appendix E
Pretest and Posttest
Control Firstborn
Children ($C_{2,1}$)

Group $C_{2,1}$

Subject Number:	30
SES:	IV
Sex:	Female
Mother's Education:	High School
Mother's Quick Word Test:	68
Father's Education:	High School
Father's Occupation:	Shipper

Test Data

Subject Number: 30   Group: Pretest and Posttest Control Firstborn

Test	Age (months)	Score	Group Median
Bayley Scales	4½	89	103
of Infant Development	12	—	—
Mental Index	24	100	107.5
Stanford-Binet	36	115	111.5
Preschool Project	12	—	—
Receptive Language Test	14½	—	—
(score in months)	24	33	33
	36	36	42
Preschool Project	12	—	—
Abstract Abilities Test	14½	—	—
(score in levels)	24	4	7
Preschool Project	12	—	—
Dissonance Test	14½	—	—
(score in levels)	24	5	6

Group $C_{2,1}$

Subject Number:	31
SES:	II
Sex:	Female
Mother's Education:	High School, plus
Mother's Quick Word Test:	61
Father's Education:	College Graduate
Father's Occupation:	Accountant

Test Data

Subject Number: 31   Group: Pretest and Posttest Control Firstborn

Test	Age (months)	Score	Group Median
Bayley Scales	4½	104	103
of Infant Development	12	—	—
Mental Index	24	132	107.5
Stanford-Binet	36	110	111.5
Preschool Project	12	—	—
Receptive Language Test	14½	—	—
(score in months)	24	33	33
	36	42	42
Preschool Project	12	—	—
Abstract Abilities Test	14½	—	—
(score in levels)	24	4	7
Preschool Project	12	—	—
Dissonance Test	14½	—	—
(score in levels)	24	5	6

Group C$_{2,1}$

Subject Number:	32
SES:	III
Sex:	Male
Mother's Education:	High School
Mother's Quick Word Test:	66
Father's Education:	High School
Father's Occupation:	Truck Driver

Test Data

Subject Number: 32   Group: Pretest and Posttest Control Firstborn

Test	Age (months)	Score	Group Median
Bayley Scales	4½	104	103
of Infant Development	12	—	—
Mental Index	24	112	107.5
Stanford-Binet	36	98	111.5
Preschool Project	12	—	—
Receptive Language Test	14½	—	—
(score in months)	24	a	33
	36	45	42
Preschool Project	12	—	—
Abstract Abilities Test	14½	—	—
(score in levels)	24	5	7
Preschool Project	12	—	—
Dissonance Test	14½	—	—
(score in levels)	24	7	6

[a]No valid score.

Group C$_{2,1}$

Subject Number:	35
SES:	III
Sex:	Female
Mother's Education:	High School
Mother's Quick Word Test:	63
Father's Education:	High School
Father's Occupation:	Mailman

Test Data

Subject Number: 35   Group: Pretest and Posttest Control Firstborn

Test	Age (months)	Score	Group Median
Bayley Scales	4½	107	103
of Infant Development	12	—	—
Mental Index	24	109	107.5
Stanford-Binet	36	93	111.5
Preschool Project	12	—	—
Receptive Language Test	14½	—	—
(score in months)	24	a	33
	36	42	42
Preschool Project	12	—	—
Abstract Abilities Test	14½	—	—
(score in levels)	24	7	7
Preschool Project	12	—	—
Dissonance Test	14½	—	—
(score in levels)	24	4	6

[a]No valid score.

Group C$_{2,1}$

Subject Number:	37
SES:	III
Sex:	Female
Mother's Education:	High School, plus
Mother's Quick Word Test:	70
Father's Education:	High School
Father's Occupation:	Bookkeeper

Test Data

Subject Number: 37   Group: Pretest and Posttest Control Firstborn

Test	Age (months)	Score	Group Median
Bayley Scales	4½	107	103
of Infant Development	12	—	—
Mental Index	24	119	107.5
Stanford-Binet	36	118	111.5
Preschool Project	12	—	—
Receptive Language Test	14½	—	—
(score in months)	24	36	33
	36	51	42
Preschool Project	12	—	—
Abstract Abilities Test	14½	—	—
(score in levels)	24	7	7
Preschool Project	12	—	—
Dissonance Test	14½	—	—
(score in levels)	24	8	6

Group $C_{2,1}$

Subject Number:	39
SES:	IV
Sex:	Male
Mother's Education:	High School
Mother's Quick Word Test:	57
Father's Education:	High School
Father's Occupation:	Laborer

Test Data

Subject Number: 39   Group: Pretest and Posttest Control Firstborn

Test	Age (months)	Score	Group Median
Bayley Scales	4½	91	103
of Infant Development	12	—	—
Mental Index	24	106	107.5
Stanford-Binet	36	113	111.5
Preschool Project	12	—	—
Receptive Language Test	14½	—	—
(score in months)	24	27	33
	36	42	42
Preschool Project	12	—	—
Abstract Abilities Test	14½	—	—
(score in levels)	24	a	7
Preschool Project	12	—	—
Dissonance Test	14½	—	—
(score in levels)	24	7	6

[a]No valid score.

Group C$_{2,1}$

Subject Number:	41
SES:	II
Sex:	Male
Mother's Education:	High School, plus
Mother's Quick Word Test:	70
Father's Education:	College Graduate
Father's Occupation:	Programmer

Test Data

Subject Number: 41   Group: Pretest and Posttest Control Firstborn

Test	Age (months)	Score	Group Median
Bayley Scales	4½	99	103
of Infant Development	12	—	—
Mental Index	24	91	107.5
Stanford-Binet	36	129	111.5
Preschool Project	12	—	—
Receptive Language Test	14½	—	—
(score in months)	24	a	33
	36	48	42
Preschool Project	12	—	—
Abstract Abilities Test	14½	—	—
(score in levels)	24	a	7
Preschool Project	12	—	—
Dissonance Test	14½	—	—
(score in levels)	24	7	6

[a]No valid score.

Group $C_{2,1}$

Subject Number: 43
SES: IV
Sex: Female
Mother's Education: High School, plus
Mother's Quick Word Test: 68
Father's Education: High School
Father's Occupation: Cloth Spreader

Test Data

Subject Number: 43   Group: Pretest and Posttest Control Firstborn

Test	Age (months)	Score	Group Median
Bayley Scales	4½	102	103
of Infant Development	12	—	—
Mental Index	24	75	107.5
Stanford-Binet	36	83	111.5
Preschool Project	12	—	—
Receptive Language Test	14½	—	—
(score in months)	24	18	33
	36	27	42
Preschool Project	12	—	—
Abstract Abilities Test	14½	—	—
(score in levels)	24	7	7
Preschool Project	12	—	—
Dissonance Test	14½	—	—
(score in levels)	24	5	6

Appendix F
Pretest and Posttest Control Later-Born Children ($C_{2,2}$)

Group $C_{2,2}$

Subject Number:	33
SES:	III
Sex:	Female
Mother's Education:	High School
Mother's Quick Word Test:	62
Father's Education:	Partial College
Father's Occupation:	Car Salesman
Sibling Gap:	43 months (80 months)

Test Data

Subject Number: 33   Group: Pretest and Posttest Control Later-Born

Test	Age (months)	Score	Group Median
Bayley Scales	4½	107	107
of Infant Development	12	—	—
Mental Index	24	116	112
Stanford-Binet	36	108	113
Preschool Project	12	—	—
Receptive Language Test	14½	—	—
(score in months)	24	a	30
	36	45	45
Preschool Project	12	—	—
Abstract Abilities Test	14½	—	—
(score in levels)	24	6	5.5
Preschool Project	12	—	—
Dissonance Test	14½	—	—
(score in levels)	24	7	7

[a]No valid score.

Group $C_{2,2}$

Subject Number:	34
SES:	III
Sex:	Male
Mother's Education:	High School
Mother's Quick Word Test:	57
Father's Education:	Partial College
Father's Occupation:	Fireman
Sibling Gap:	31 months

Test Data

Subject Number: 34   Group: Pretest and Posttest Control Later-Born

Test	Age (months)	Score	Group Median
Bayley Scales	4½	107	107
of Infant Development	12	—	—
Mental Index	24	112	112
Stanford-Binet	36	113	113
Preschool Project	12	—	—
Receptive Language Test	14½	—	—
(score in months)	24	30	30
	36	45	45
Preschool Project	12	—	—
Abstract Abilities Test	14½	—	—
(score in levels)	24	4	5.5
Preschool Project	12	—	—
Dissonance Test	14½	—	—
(score in levels)	24	5	7

Group C$_{2,2}$

Subject Number:	36
SES:	III
Sex:	Male
Mother's Education:	High School
Mother's Quick Word Test:	74
Father's Education:	Partial College
Father's Occupation:	Student
Sibling Gap:	34 months

Test Data

Subject Number: 36   Group: Pretest and Posttest Control Later-Born

Test	Age (months)	Score	Group Median
Bayley Scales	4½	94	107
of Infant Development	12	—	—
Mental Index	24	83	112
Stanford-Binet	36	120	113
Preschool Project	12	—	—
Receptive Language Test	14½	—	—
(score in months)	24	24	30
	36	45	45
Preschool Project	12	—	—
Abstract Abilities Test	14½	—	—
(score in levels)	24	5	5.5
Preschool Project	12	—	—
Dissonance Test	14½	—	—
(score in levels)	24	7	7

Group $C_{2,2}$

Subject Number:	38
SES:	III
Sex:	Male
Mother's Education:	High School
Mother's Quick Word Test:	74
Father's Education:	Partial College
Father's Occupation:	Engineer Aide
Sibling Gap:	33 months

Test Data

Subject Number: 38   Group: Pretest and Posttest Control Later-Born

Test	Age (months)	Score	Group Median
Bayley Scales	4½	102	107
of Infant Development	12	—	—
Mental Index	24	112	112
Stanford-Binet	36	98	113
Preschool Project	12	—	—
Receptive Language Test	14½	—	—
(score in months)	24	a	30
	36	48	45
Preschool Project	12	—	—
Abstract Abilities Test	14½	—	—
(score in levels)	24	7	5.5
Preschool Project	12	—	—
Dissonance Test	14½	—	—
(score in levels)	24	7	7

[a]No valid score.

Group $C_{2,2}$

Subject Number:	40
SES:	II
Sex:	Female
Mother's Education:	High School, plus
Mother's Quick Word Test:	85
Father's Education:	Graduate Training
Father's Occupation:	Systems Analyst
Sibling Gap:	29 months (51 months)

Test Data

Subject Number: 40   Group: Pretest and Posttest Control Later-Born

Test	Age (months)	Score	Group Median
Bayley Scales	4½	109	107
of Infant Development	12	—	—
Mental Index	24	132	112
Stanford-Binet	36	125	113
Preschool Project	12	—	—
Receptive Language Test	14½	—	—
(score in months)	24	30	30
	36	48	45
Preschool Project	12	—	—
Abstract Abilities Test	14½	—	—
(score in levels)	24	8.5	5.5
Preschool Project	12	—	—
Dissonance Test	14½	—	—
(score in levels)	24	7	7

Group $C_{2,2}$

Subject Number:	42
SES:	III
Sex:	Male
Mother's Education:	High School
Mother's Quick Word Test:	74
Father's Education:	High School
Father's Occupation:	Postal Employee
Sibling Gap:	52 months

Test Data

Subject Number: 42   Group: Pretest and Posttest Control Later-Born

Test	Age (months)	Score	Group Median
Bayley Scales	4½	100	107
of Infant Development	12	—	—
Mental Index	24	127	112
Stanford-Binet	36	113	113
Preschool Project	12	—	—
Receptive Language Test	14½	—	—
(score in months)	24	33	30
	36	45	45
Preschool Project	12	—	—
Abstract Abilities Test	14½	—	—
(score in levels)	24	a	5.5
Preschool Project	12	—	—
Dissonance Test	14½	—	—
(score in levels)	24	7	7

[a]No valid score.

Group C$_{2,2}$

Subject Number:	44
SES:	IV
Sex:	Male
Mother's Education:	High School, plus
Mother's Quick Word Test:	68
Father's Education:	High School
Father's Occupation:	Unemployed
Sibling Gap:	41 months

Test Data

Subject Number: 44   Group: Pretest and Posttest Control Later-Born

Test	Age (months)	Score	Group Median
Bayley Scales	4½	123	107
of Infant Development	12	—	—
Mental Index	24	94	112
Stanford-Binet	36	90	113
Preschool Project	12	—	—
Receptive Language Test	14½	—	—
(score in months)	24	a	30
	36	33	45
Preschool Project	12	—	—
Abstract Abilities Test	14½	—	—
(score in levels)	24	4	5.5
Preschool Project	12	—	—
Dissonance Test	14½	—	—
(score in levels)	24	7	7

[a]No valid score.

Appendix G
Pediatric Control
Firstborn
Children (PC₁)

Group PC₁

Subject Number:	45
SES:	II
Sex:	Female
Mother's Education:	High School, plus
Mother's Quick Word Test:	87
Father's Education:	High School, plus
Father's Occupation:	Systems Coordinator

Adult Assessment Scales Data: 11 to 16 Months

Subject Number: 45   Group: Pediatric Firstborn

Interactions Initiated by the Child

Child's Behavior

Frequency of overtures per 30 minutes (median): 9
Purposes of overtures (frequency):

To please	0	To annoy	0
To gain approval	0	To direct	0.5
To procure a service	1	To compete	0
To gain attention	2	To ease discomfort	0
To maintain social contact	2		

Adult's Response (percent frequency)

1. Timing and direction
   of adult's response:
   a. Immediately   82.9
   b. Delayed   5.7
      Length of delay (seconds) 28.8
   c. No response   11.4
   d. Rejects   0.0

2. Perceptions of child's need:
   a. Accurately   100.0
   b. Partially   0.0
   c. Not at all   0.0

3. Level of difficulty of words:
   a. Appropriate   92.9
   b. Too complex   0.0
   c. Too simple   3.6
   d. Babytalk   0.0
   e. None   3.6

4. Provision of related ideas:
   a. Yes   67.9
   b. No   32.1

5. Complexity of language:
   a. Complex sentence, 3s   39.3
   b. Phrase/sentence, 3s   39.3
   c. One word   14.3
   d. None   7.1

6. Provision of encouragement,
   reinforcement of enthusiasm:
   a. Yes   89.3
   b. No   10.7
   c. Inappropriate   0.0

7. Teaching realistic limits:
   a. Yes   21.4
   b. No   7.1
   c. Inappropriate   71.4

8. Satisfaction of child's needs:
   a. Yes   92.9
   b. No   7.1
   c. Partial   0.0

Average duration of adult's response (seconds): 37.2.
Time spent by adult responding (percent): 18.6.

Adult Assessment Scales Data: 11 to 16 Months

Subject Number: 45   Group: Pediatric Firstborn

Interactions Initiated by the Adult

Frequency per 30 minutes (median):   13

Purposes of adult (percent duration):
  Stimulate child   21.8
  Contol positive   4.5
  Control negative   0.3
  Routine caretaking   3.5

Emotional tone (percent frequency):
  Positive   91.9
  Negative   1.6
  Neutral   6.5

Average duration of adult-initiated interactions (seconds): 41.7.
Time spent by adult in adult-initiated interactions (percent): 30.1.
Total time spent by the adult in interactions with the child (percent): 48.7.

Task Data (Percent of Total Time): 11 to 16 Months

Subject Number: 45   Group: Pediatric Control Group Firstborn

Social tasks:
All social tasks	20.5
To cooperate	3.9
To procure a service	0.0
To gain attention	1.0
To maintain social contact	14.8
To assert self	0.0

Nonsocial tasks:
To eat	1.4
To gain information (visual)	15.3
To gain information (visual and auditory)	13.0
Live language	13.0
Overheard language	0.0
Mechanical language	0.0
Nontask	5.0
To pass time	2.0
To procure an object	0.0
To gain pleasure	1.6
To ease discomfort	0.0
To explore	4.6
Mastery	7.3
Gross motor	2.5
Fine motor	4.8

Test Data

Subject Number: 45   Group: Pediatric Control Group Firstborn

Test	Age (months)	Score	Group Median
Bayley Scales	4½	109	104
of Infant Development	12	96	102
Mental Index	24	90	109
Stanford-Binet	36	100	111.5
Preschool Project	12	14	16
Receptive Language Test	14½	18	18
(score in months)	24	30	30
	36	45	46.5
Preschool Project	12	2	2
Abstract Abilities Test	14½	2	3
(score in levels)	24	6	7
Preschool Project	12	2	2
Dissonance Test	14½	1	4
(score in levels)	24	6	7

Group PC$_1$

Subject Number:	46
SES:	III
Sex:	Female
Mother's Education:	High School, plus
Mother's Quick Word Test:	83
Father's Education:	High School
Father's Occupation:	Cabinetmaker

Adult Assessment Scales Data: 11 to 16 Months

Subject Number: 46   Group: Pediatric Firstborn

Interactions Initiated by the Child

Child's Behavior

Frequency of overtures per 30 minutes (median): 8.5
Purposes of overtures (frequency):

To please	0	To annoy	2.5
To gain approval	0	To direct	0
To procure a service	5.0	To compete	0
To gain attention	1.0	To ease discomfort	0
To maintain social contact	0		

Adult's Response (percent frequency)

1. Timing and direction
   of adult's response:
   a. Immediately   94.9
   b. Delayed   2.6
      Length of delay (seconds) 7.2
   c. No response   2.6
   d. Rejects   0.0

2. Perceptions of child's need:
   a. Accurately   100.0
   b. Partially   0.0
   c. Not at all   0.0

3. Level of difficulty of words:
   a. Appropriate   92.1
   b. Too complex   0.0
   c. Too simple   2.6
   d. Babytalk   0.0
   e. None   5.3

4. Provision of related ideas:
   a. Yes   81.6
   b. No   18.4

5. Complexity of language:
   a. Complex sentence, 3s   31.6
   b. Phrase/sentence, 3s   60.5
   c. One word   2.6
   d. None   5.3

6. Provision of encouragement,
   reinforcement of enthusiasm:
   a. Yes   94.7
   b. No   0.0
   c. Inappropriate   5.3

7. Teaching realistic limits:
   a. Yes   21.1
   b. No   0.0
   c. Inappropriate   78.9

8. Satisfaction of child's needs:
   a. Yes   94.7
   b. No   0.0
   c. Partial   5.3

Average duration of adult's response (seconds): 62.9.
Time spent by adult responding (percent): 29.7.

Adult Assessment Scales Data: 11 to 16 Months

Subject Number: 46   Group: Pediatric Firstborn

Interactions Initiated by the Adult

Frequency per 30 minutes (median):   14.5

Purposes of adult (percent duration):
  Stimulate child   17.5
  Contol positive   16.5
  Control negative   0.5
  Routine caretaking   1.3

Emotional tone (percent frequency):
  Positive   93.4
  Negative   1.6
  Neutral   5.0

Average duration of adult-initiated interactions (seconds): 44.4.
Time spent by adult in adult-initiated interactions (percent): 35.8.
Total time spent by the adult in interactions with the child (percent): 65.4.

Task Data (Percent of Total Time): 11 to 16 Months

Subject Number: 46   Group: Pediatric Control Group Firstborn

Social tasks:
All social tasks	12.3
To cooperate	3.1
To procure a service	3.4
To gain attention	0.7
To maintain social contact	0.0
To assert self	1.7

Nonsocial tasks:
To eat	1.8
To gain information (visual)	8.0
To gain information (visual and auditory)	43.1
Live language	41.0
Overheard language	0.0
Mechanical language	0.0
Nontask	5.6
To pass time	5.3
To procure an object	1.1
To gain pleasure	0.0
To ease discomfort	0.3
To explore	7.2
Mastery	1.4
Gross motor	0.0
Fine motor	0.7

Test Data

Subject Number: 46   Group: Pediatric Control Group Firstborn

Test	Age (months)	Score	Group Median
Bayley Scales	4½	99	104
of Infant Development	12	137	102
Mental Index	24	140	109
Stanford-Binet	36	149	111.5
Preschool Project	12	21	16
Receptive Language Test	14½	24	18
(score in months)	24	45	30
	36	57	46.5
Preschool Project	12	2	2
Abstract Abilities Test	14½	4	3
(score in levels)	24	9.5	7
Preschool Project	12	2	2
Dissonance Test	14½	3.5	4
(score in levels)	24	8	7

Group PC$_1$

Subject Number:	47
SES:	II
Sex:	Male
Mother's Education:	High School, plus
Mother's Quick Word Test:	69
Father's Education:	Graduate Training
Father's Occupation:	Guidance Counsellor

Adult Assessment Scales Data: 11 to 16 Months

Subject Number: 47   Group: Pediatric Firstborn

Interactions Initiated by the Child

Child's Behavior

Frequency of overtures per 30 minutes (median): 6.5
Purposes of overtures (frequency):

To please	0	To annoy	0
To gain approval	0	To direct	0
To procure a service	0.5	To compete	0
To gain attention	2	To ease discomfort	0.5
To maintain social contact	1.5		

Adult's Response (percent frequency)

1. Timing and direction
   of adult's response:
   a. Immediately   65.4
   b. Delayed   34.6
      Length of delay (seconds) 144
   c. No response   0.0
   d. Rejects   0.0

2. Perceptions of child's need:
   a. Accurately   76.9
   b. Partially   23.1
   c. Not at all   0.0

3. Level of difficulty of words:
   a. Appropriate   38.5
   b. Too complex   0.0
   c. Too simple   42.3
   d. Babytalk   0.0
   e. None   19.2

4. Provision of related ideas:
   a. Yes   38.5
   b. No   61.5

5. Complexity of language:
   a. Complex sentence, 3s   15.4
   b. Phrase/sentence, 3s   42.3
   c. One word   23.1
   d. None   19.2

6. Provision of encouragement,
   reinforcement of enthusiasm:
   a. Yes   30.8
   b. No   38.5
   c. Inappropriate   30.8

7. Teaching realistic limits:
   a. Yes   23.1
   b. No   15.4
   c. Inappropriate   61.5

8. Satisfaction of child's needs:
   a. Yes   84.0
   b. No   12.0
   c. Partial   4.0

Average duration of adult's response (seconds): 31.8.
Time spent by adult responding (percent): 11.5.

Adult Assessment Scales Data: 11 to 16 Months

Subject Number: 47   Group: Pediatric Firstborn

Interactions Initiated by the Adult

Frequency per 30 minutes (median):   10.5

Purposes of adult (percent duration):
Stimulate child   9.6
Contol positive   1.0
Control negative   1.3
Routine caretaking   1.6

Emotional tone (percent frequency):
Positive   72.8
Negative   11.8
Neutral   15.4

Average duration of adult-initiated interactions (seconds): 23.1.
Time spent by adult in adult-initiated interactions (percent): 13.5.
Total time spent by the adult in interactions with the child (percent): 25.1.

Task Data (Percent of Total Time): 11 to 16 Months

Subject Number: 47   Group: Pediatric Control Group Firstborn

Social tasks:
All social tasks	21.0
To cooperate	3.3
To procure a service	0.4
To gain attention	3.2
To maintain social contact	15.2
To assert self	0.7

Nonsocial tasks:
To eat	0.0
To gain information (visual)	5.0
To gain information (visual and auditory)	10.0
Live language	6.5
Overheard language	0.7
Mechanical language	1.0
Nontask	14.5
To pass time	1.8
To procure an object	0.0
To gain pleasure	0.0
To ease discomfort	0.9
To explore	15.0
Mastery	12.1
Gross motor	2.3
Fine motor	7.5

Test Data

Subject Number: 47   Group: Pediatric Control Group Firstborn

Test	Age (months)	Score	Group Median
Bayley Scales	4½	86	104
of Infant Development	12	109	102
Mental Index	24	107	109
Stanford-Binet	36	96	111.5
Preschool Project	12	a	16
Receptive Language Test	14½	16	18
(score in months)	24	33	30
	36	39	46.5
Preschool Project	12	2	2
Abstract Abilities Test	14½	3	3
(score in levels)	24	7	7
Preschool Project	12	a	2
Dissonance Test	14½	3	4
(score in levels)	24	6	7

[a]No valid score.

Group PC₁

Subject Number:	48
SES:	II
Sex:	Male
Mother's Education:	High School, plus
Mother's Quick Word Test:	86
Father's Education:	College Graduate
Father's Occupation:	Probation Officer

Adult Assessment Scales Data: 11 to 16 Months

Subject Number: 48   Group: Pediatric Firstborn

Interactions Initiated by the Child

Child's Behavior

Frequency of overtures per 30 minutes (median): 5
Purposes of overtures (frequency):

To please	0	To annoy	0
To gain approval	0	To direct	0
To procure a service	0	To compete	0
To gain attention	3	To ease discomfort	0.5
To maintain social contact	0		

Adult's Response (percent frequency)

1. Timing and direction
   of adult's response:
   a. Immediately 84.2
   b. Delayed 10.5
      Length of delay (seconds) 14.4
   c. No response 5.3
   d. Rejects 0.0

2. Perceptions of child's need:
   a. Accurately 100.0
   b. Partially 0.0
   c. Not at all 0.0

3. Level of difficulty of words:
   a. Appropriate 55.6
   b. Too complex 0.0
   c. Too simple 27.8
   d. Babytalk 5.6
   e. None 11.1

4. Provision of related ideas:
   a. Yes 50.0
   b. No 50.0

5. Complexity of language:
   a. Complex sentence, 3s 33.3
   b. Phrase/sentence, 3s 44.4
   c. One word 11.1
   d. None 11.1

6. Provision of encouragement,
   reinforcement of enthusiasm:
   a. Yes 72.2
   b. No 5.6
   c. Inappropriate 22.2

7. Teaching realistic limits:
   a. Yes 22.2
   b. No 0.0
   c. Inappropriate 77.8

8. Satisfaction of child's needs:
   a. Yes 94.4
   b. No 5.6
   c. Partial 0.0

Average duration of adult's response (seconds): 24.1.
Time spent by adult responding (percent): 6.7.

Adult Assessment Scales Data: 11 to 16 Months

Subject Number: 48   Group: Pediatric Firstborn

Interactions Initiated by the Adult

Frequency per 30 minutes (median):   4

Purposes of adult (percent duration):
   Stimulate child   4.7
   Contol positive   0.5
   Control negative   0.3
   Routine caretaking   0.0

Emotional tone (percent frequency):
   Positive   73.4
   Negative   5.1
   Neutral   21.5

Average duration of adult-initiated interactions (seconds): 24.7.
Time spent by adult in adult-initiated interactions (percent): 5.5.
Total time spent by the adult in interactions with the child (percent): 12.2.

Task Data (Percent of Total Time): 11 to 16 Months

Subject Number: 48   Group: Pediatric Control Group Firstborn

Social tasks:

All social tasks	11.5
To cooperate	1.4
To procure a service	0.0
To gain attention	3.2
To maintain social contact	5.3
To assert self	0.0

Nonsocial tasks:

To eat	0.0
To gain information (visual)	4.0
To gain information (visual and auditory)	1.2
Live language	0.9
Overheard language	0.0
Mechanical language	0.0
Nontask	13.0
To pass time	0.0
To procure an object	2.5
To gain pleasure	0.0
To ease discomfort	0.2
To explore	11.3
Mastery	28.8
Gross motor	6.8
Fine motor	13.5

Test Data

Subject Number: 48   Group: Pediatric Control Group Firstborn

Test	Age (months)	Score	Group Median
Bayley Scales	4½	126	104
of Infant Development	12	112	102
Mental Index	24	100	109
Stanford-Binet	36	108	111.5
Preschool Project	12	a	16
Receptive Language Test	14½	18	18
(score in months)	24	27	30
	36	45	46.5
Preschool Project	12	a	2
Abstract Abilities Test	14½	3	3
(score in levels)	24	6	7
Preschool Project	12	a	2
Dissonance Test	14½	3.5	4
(score in levels)	24	7	7

[a]No valid score.

Group PC$_1$

Subject Number: 51
SES: III
Sex: Male
Mother's Education: High School
Mother's Quick Word Test: 80
Father's Education: High School, plus
Father's Occupation: Payroll Clerk

Adult Assessment Scales Data: 11 to 16 Months

Subject Number: 51   Group: Pediatric Firstborn

Interactions Initiated by the Child

Child's Behavior

Frequency of overtures per 30 minutes (median): 2.5
Purposes of overtures (frequency):

To please	0	To annoy	0
To gain approval	0	To direct	0.5
To procure a service	2	To compete	0
To gain attention	0	To ease discomfort	0
To maintain social contact	0		

Adult's Response (percent frequency)

1. Timing and direction
   of adult's response:
   a. Immediately   90.0
   b. Delayed   0.0
      Length of delay (seconds)   0
   c. No response   10.0
   d. Rejects   0.0

2. Perceptions of child's need:
   a. Accurately   100.0
   b. Partially   0.0
   c. Not at all   0.0

3. Level of difficulty of words:
   a. Appropriate   66.7
   b. Too complex   0.0
   c. Too simple   22.2
   d. Babytalk   0.0
   e. None   11.1

4. Provision of related ideas:
   a. Yes   55.6
   b. No   44.4

5. Complexity of language:
   a. Complex sentence, 3s   33.3
   b. Phrase/sentence, 3s   44.4
   c. One word   11.1
   d. None   11.1

6. Provision of encouragement,
   reinforcement of enthusiasm:
   a. Yes   77.8
   b. No   22.2
   c. Inappropriate   0.0

7. Teaching realistic limits:
   a. Yes   22.2
   b. No   0.0
   c. Inappropriate   77.8

8. Satisfaction of child's needs:
   a. Yes   88.9
   b. No   0.0
   c. Partial   11.1

Average duration of adult's response (seconds): 50.1.
Time spent by adult responding (percent): 6.2.

Adult Assessment Scales Data: 11 to 16 Months

Subject Number: 51   Group: Pediatric Firstborn

Interactions Initiated by the Adult

Frequency per 30 minutes (median):   21

Purposes of adult (percent duration):
    Stimulate child   25.1
    Contol positive   16.7
    Control negative   4.7
    Routine caretaking   3.7

Emotional tone (percent frequency):
    Positive   68.6
    Negative   30.7
    Neutral   0.7

Average duration of adult-initiated interactions (seconds): 42.9.
Time spent by adult in adult-initiated interactions (percent): 50.1.
Total time spent by the adult in interactions with the child (percent): 56.4.

Task Data (Percent of Total Time): 11 to 16 Months

Subject Number: 51   Group: Pediatric Control Group Firstborn

Social tasks:
All social tasks	16.3
To cooperate	13.2
To procure a service	0.0
To gain attention	0.0
To maintain social contact	0.3
To assert self	0.8

Nonsocial tasks:
To eat	1.4
To gain information (visual)	7.8
To gain information (visual and auditory)	25.0
Live language	10.4
Overheard language	0.0
Mechanical language	12.7
Nontask	14.7
To pass time	2.5
To procure an object	0.8
To gain pleasure	5.0
To ease discomfort	0.0
To explore	8.9
Mastery	11.1
Gross motor	6.3
Fine motor	4.4

Test Data

Subject Number: 51   Group: Pediatric Control Group Firstborn

Test	Age (months)	Score	Group Median
Bayley Scales	4½	104	104
of Infant Development	12	115	102
Mental Index	24	123	109
Stanford-Binet	36	105	111.5
Preschool Project	12	16	16
Receptive Language Test	14½	18	18
(score in months)	24	36	30
	36	48	46.5
Preschool Project	12	3	2
Abstract Abilities Test	14½	4	3
(score in levels)	24	8	7
Preschool Project	12	2	2
Dissonance Test	14½	3.5	4
(score in levels)	24	7	7

Group PC₁

Subject Number:	52
SES:	III
Sex:	Male
Mother's Education:	High School, plus
Mother's Quick Word Test:	78
Father's Education:	College Graduate
Father's Occupation:	Accountant

Adult Assessment Scales Data: 11 to 16 Months

Subject Number: 52   Group: Pediatric Firstborn

Interactions Initiated by the Child

Child's Behavior

Frequency of overtures per 30 minutes (median): 6
Purposes of overtures (frequency):

To please	0	To annoy	0.5
To gain approval	0	To direct	0
To procure a service	1.5	To compete	0
To gain attention	2.0	To ease discomfort	1.0
To maintain social contact	1.0		

Adult's Response (percent frequency)

1. Timing and direction
   of adult's response:
   a. Immediately   74.1
   b. Delayed   14.8
      Length of delay (seconds)   57.6
   c. No response   11.1
   d. Rejects   0.0

2. Perceptions of child's need:
   a. Accurately   79.2
   b. Partially   20.8
   c. Not at all   0.0

3. Level of difficulty of words:
   a. Appropriate   50.0
   b. Too complex   0.0
   c. Too simple   41.7
   d. Babytalk   0.0
   e. None   8.3

4. Provision of related ideas:
   a. Yes   25.0
   b. No   75.0

5. Complexity of language:
   a. Complex sentence, 3s   20.8
   b. Phrase/sentence, 3s   58.3
   c. One word   12.5
   d. None   8.3

6. Provision of encouragement,
   reinforcement of enthusiasm:
   a. Yes   60.9
   b. No   17.4
   c. Inappropriate   21.7

7. Teaching realistic limits:
   a. Yes   13.0
   b. No   8.7
   c. Inappropriate   78.3

8. Satisfaction of child's needs:
   a. Yes   82.6
   b. No   4.3
   c. Partial   13.0

Average duration of adult's response (seconds): 11.8.
Time spent by adult responding (percent): 16.9.

Adult Assessment Scales Data: 11 to 16 Months

Subject Number: 52   Group: Pediatric Firstborn

Interactions Initiated by the Adult

Frequency per 30 minutes (median):   6

Purposes of adult (percent duration):
    Stimulate child   0.6
    Contol positive   1.7
    Control negative   0.0
    Routine caretaking   9.5

Emotional tone (percent frequency):
    Positive   77.1
    Negative   0.0
    Neutral   22.9

Average duration of adult-initiated interactions (seconds): 35.4.
Time spent by adult in adult-initiated interactions (percent): 11.8.
Total time spent by the adult in interactions with the child (percent): 28.7.

Task Data (Percent of Total Time): 11 to 16 Months

Subject Number: 52   Group: Pediatric Control Group Firstborn

Social tasks:
All social tasks	20.6
To cooperate	3.5
To procure a service	1.1
To gain attention	2.7
To maintain social contact	5.2
To assert self	2.1

Nonsocial tasks:
To eat	6.1
To gain information (visual)	18.2
To gain information (visual and auditory)	5.9
Live language	5.6
Overheard language	0.3
Mechanical language	0.0
Nontask	10.3
To pass time	8.6
To procure an object	3.1
To gain pleasure	0.0
To ease discomfort	0.2
To explore	9.3
Mastery	6.7
Gross motor	2.6
Fine motor	4.1

Test Data

Subject Number: 52   Group: Pediatric Control Group Firstborn

Test	Age (months)	Score	Group Median
Bayley Scales	4½	94	104
of Infant Development	12	103	102
Mental Index	24	109	109
Stanford-Binet	36	103	111.5
Preschool Project	12	16	16
Receptive Language Test	14½	18	18
(score in months)	24	27	30
	36	42	46.5
Preschool Project	12	3	2
Abstract Abilities Test	14½	4	3
(score in levels)	24	7	7
Preschool Project	12	3	2
Dissonance Test	14½	4	4
(score in levels)	24	7	7

Group PC₁

Subject Number:	53
SES:	III
Sex:	Male
Mother's Education:	High School, plus
Mother's Quick Word Test:	75
Father's Education:	High School, plus
Father's Occupation:	Photographer

Adult Assessment Scales Data: 11 to 16 Months

Subject Number: 53   Group: Pediatric Firstborn

Interactions Initiated by the Child

Child's Behavior

Frequency of overtures per 30 minutes (median): 10
Purposes of overtures (frequency):

To please	0	To annoy	0.5
To gain approval	0	To direct	0
To procure a service	3.5	To compete	0
To gain attention	3	To ease discomfort	0.5
To maintain social contact	0		

Adult's Response (percent frequency)

1. Timing and direction
   of adult's response:
   a. Immediately   84.6
   b. Delayed   12.8
      Length of delay (seconds) 108
   c. No response   0.0
   d. Rejects   2.6

2. Perceptions of child's need:
   a. Accurately   100.0
   b. Partially   0.0
   c. Not at all   0.0

3. Level of difficulty of words:
   a. Appropriate   76.9
   b. Too complex   0.0
   c. Too simple   10.3
   d. Babytalk   0.0
   e. None   12.8

4. Provision of related ideas:
   a. Yes   47.4
   b. No   52.6

5. Complexity of language:
   a. Complex sentence, 3s   25.6
   b. Phrase/sentence, 3s   56.4
   c. One word   5.1
   d. None   12.8

6. Provision of encouragement,
   reinforcement of enthusiasm:
   a. Yes   64.1
   b. No   17.9
   c. Inappropriate   17.9

7. Teaching realistic limits:
   a. Yes   23.1
   b. No   5.1
   c. Inappropriate   71.8

8. Satisfaction of child's needs:
   a. Yes   79.5
   b. No   15.4
   c. Partial   5.1

Average duration of adult's response (seconds): 28.1.
Time spent by adult responding (percent): 20.1.

Adult Assessment Scales Data: 11 to 16 Months

Subject Number: 53   Group: Pediatric Firstborn

Interactions Initiated by the Adult

Frequency per 30 minutes (median):   9.5

Purposes of adult (percent duration):
Stimulate child   17.3
Contol positive   7.2
Control negative   1.0
Routine caretaking   2.6

Emotional tone (percent frequency):
Positive   93.6
Negative   4.2
Neutral   2.2

Average duration of adult-initiated interactions (seconds): 53.2.
Time spent by adult in adult-initiated interactions (percent): 28.1.
Total time spent by the adult in interactions with the child (percent): 48.2.

Task Data (Percent of Total Time): 11 to 16 Months

Subject Number: 53   Group: Pediatric Control Group Firstborn

Social tasks:
All social tasks	12.0
To cooperate	0.7
To procure a service	2.0
To gain attention	1.7
To maintain social contact	5.6
To assert self	0.0

Nonsocial tasks:
To eat	4.7
To gain information (visual)	32.2
To gain information (visual and auditory)	7.8
Live language	7.8
Overheard language	0.0
Mechanical language	0.0
Nontask	10.5
To pass time	0.0
To procure an object	1.4
To gain pleasure	0.0
To ease discomfort	0.0
To explore	3.1
Mastery	25.3
Gross motor	5.8
Fine motor	12.1

Test Data

Subject Number: 53   Group: Pediatric Control Group Firstborn

Test	Age (months)	Score	Group Median
Bayley Scales	4½	91	104
of Infant Development	12	98	102
Mental Index	24	127	109
Stanford-Binet	36	115	111.5
Preschool Project	12	16	16
Receptive Language Test	14½	18	18
(score in months)	24	39	30
	36	51	46.5
Preschool Project	12	2	2
Abstract Abilities Test	14½	4	3
(score in levels)	24	8	7
Preschool Project	12	3	2
Dissonance Test	14½	3	4
(score in levels)	24	8	7

Group PC$_1$

Subject Number:	54
SES:	II
Sex:	Male
Mother's Education:	High School, plus
Mother's Quick Word Test:	85
Father's Education:	Graduate Training
Father's Occupation:	Student

Adult Assessment Scales Data: 11 to 16 Months

Subject Number: 54   Group: Pediatric Firstborn

Interactions Initiated by the Child

Child's Behavior

Frequency of overtures per 30 minutes (median): 7.5
Purposes of overtures (frequency):

To please	0	To annoy	0
To gain approval	0.5	To direct	0.5
To procure a service	2	To compete	0
To gain attention	5	To ease discomfort	1
To maintain social contact	0		

Adult's Response (percent frequency)

1. Timing and direction
   of adult's response:
   a. Immediately   96.6
   b. Delayed   0.0
      Length of delay (seconds) 0.0
   c. No response   3.4
   d. Rejects   0.0

2. Perceptions of child's need:
   a. Accurately   92.9
   b. Partially   7.1
   c. Not at all   0.0

3. Level of difficulty of words:
   a. Appropriate   92.9
   b. Too complex   0.0
   c. Too simple   7.1
   d. Babytalk   0.0
   e. None   0.0

4. Provision of related ideas:
   a. Yes   53.6
   b. No   46.4

5. Complexity of language:
   a. Complex sentence, 3s   78.6
   b. Phrase/sentence, 3s   17.9
   c. One word   3.6
   d. None   0.0

6. Provision of encouragement,
   reinforcement of enthusiasm:
   a. Yes   53.6
   b. No   3.6
   c. Inappropriate   42.9

7. Teaching realistic limits:
   a. Yes   21.4
   b. No   0.0
   c. Inappropriate   78.6

8. Satisfaction of child's needs:
   a. Yes   100.0
   b. No   0.0
   c. Partial   0.0

Average duration of adult's response (seconds): 47.2.
Time spent by adult responding (percent): 11.7.

Adult Assessment Scales Data: 11 to 16 Months

Subject Number: 54   Group: Pediatric Firstborn

Interactions Initiated by the Adult

Frequency per 30 minutes (median):   13.5

Purposes of adult (percent duration):
    Stimulate child   35.6
    Contol positive   6.4
    Control negative   0.1
    Routine caretaking   5.1

Emotional tone (percent frequency):
    Positive   98.2
    Negative   1.0
    Neutral   0.7

Average duration of adult-initiated interactions (seconds): 62.9.
Time spent by adult in adult-initiated interactions (percent): 47.2.
Total time spent by the adult in interactions with the child (percent): 59.0.

Task Data (Percent of Total Time): 11 to 16 Months

Subject Number: 54   Group: Pediatric Control Group Firstborn

Social tasks:
All social tasks	13.0
To cooperate	1.7
To procure a service	0.0
To gain attention	1.8
To maintain social contact	5.9
To assert self	1.0

Nonsocial tasks:
To eat	0.0
To gain information (visual)	13.0
To gain information (visual and auditory)	13.7
Live language	13.7
Overheard language	0.0
Mechanical language	0.0
Nontask	4.0
To pass time	0.6
To procure an object	6.6
To gain pleasure	2.6
To ease discomfort	0.3
To explore	17.2
Mastery	17.9
Gross motor	3.3
Fine motor	12.5

Test Data

Subject Number: 54   Group: Pediatric Control Group Firstborn

Test	Age (months)	Score	Group Median
Bayley Scales	4½	130	104
of Infant Development	12	100	102
Mental Index	24	119	109
Stanford-Binet	36	154	111.5
Preschool Project	12	14	16
Receptive Language Test	14½	18	18
(score in months)	24	36	30
	36	57	46.5
Preschool Project	12	3	2
Abstract Abilities Test	14½	4	3
(score in levels)	24	8	7
Preschool Project	12	a	2
Dissonance Test	14½	4	4
(score in levels)	24	8	7

[a]No valid score.

Group PC$_1$

Subject Number:	55
SES:	III
Sex:	Female
Mother's Education:	Less than High School
Mother's Quick Word Test:	76
Father's Education:	High School, plus
Father's Occupation:	Foreman

Adult Assessment Scales Data: 11 to 16 Months

Subject Number: 55   Group: Pediatric Firstborn

Interactions Initiated by the Child

Child's Behavior

Frequency of overtures per 30 minutes (median): 5
Purposes of overtures (frequency):

To please	0	To annoy	0
To gain approval	0	To direct	0
To procure a service	4	To compete	0
To gain attention	0	To ease discomfort	0
To maintain social contact	1		

Adult's Response (percent frequency)

1. Timing and direction
   of adult's response:
   a. . . . No
   b. . . . Data
   . . . Available
   c. . . .
   d. . . .

2. Perceptions of child's need:
   a. . . . No
   b. . . . Data
   c. . . . Available

3. Level of difficulty of words:
   a. . . . No
   b. . . . Data
   c. . . . Available
   d. . . .
   e. . . .

4. Provision of related ideas:
   a. . . . No Data
   b. . . . Available

5. Complexity of language:
   a. . . . No
   b. . . . Data
   c. . . . Available
   d. . . .

6. Provision of encouragement,
   reinforcement of enthusiasm:
   a. . . . No
   b. . . . Data
   c. . . . Available

7. Teaching realistic limits:
   a. . . . No
   b. . . . Data
   c. . . . Available

8. Satisfaction of child's needs:
   a. . . . No
   b. . . . Data
   c. . . . Available

Average duration of adult's response (seconds): No Data.
Time spent by adult responding (percent): No Data.

Adult Assessment Scales Data: 11 to 16 Months

Subject Number: 55   Group: Pediatric Firstborn

Interactions Initiated by the Adult

Frequency per 30 minutes (median):   9.5

Purposes of adult (percent duration):
  Stimulate child
  Contol positive
  Control negative   No Data Available
  Routine caretaking

Emotional tone (percent frequency):
  Positive
  Negative   No Data Available
  Neutral

Average duration of adult-initiated interactions (seconds): No Data.
Time spent by adult in adult-initiated interactions (percent): No Data.
Total time spent by the adult in interactions with the child (percent): No Data.

Task Data (Percent of Total Time): 11 to 16 Months

Subject Number: 55   Group: Pediatric Control Group Firstborn

Social tasks:

All social tasks	16.6
To cooperate	6.4
To procure a service	0.0
To gain attention	0.4
To maintain social contact	5.2
To assert self	1.1

Nonsocial tasks:

To eat	0.6
To gain information (visual)	5.3
To gain information (visual and auditory)	34.3
Live language	33.5
Overheard language	0.9
Mechanical language	0.0
Nontask	6.1
To pass time	1.7
To procure an object	2.1
To gain pleasure	0.0
To ease discomfort	0.0
To explore	2.8
Mastery	1.7
Gross motor	1.7
Fine motor	0.0

Test Data

Subject Number: 55   Group: Pediatric Control Group Firstborn

Test	Age (months)	Score	Group Median
Bayley Scales	4½	111	104
of Infant Development	12	98	102
Mental Index	24	114	109
Stanford-Binet	36	126	111.5
Preschool Project	12	16	16
Receptive Language Test	14½	18	18
(score in months)	24	33	30
	36	48	46.5
Preschool Project	12	2	2
Abstract Abilities Test	14½	3	3
(score in levels)	24	7	7
Preschool Project	12	a	2
Dissonance Test	14½	4	4
(score in levels)	24	8	7

[a]No valid score.

Group PC$_1$

Subject Number:	56
SES:	III
Sex:	Male
Mother's Education:	High School, plus
Mother's Quick Word Test:	85
Father's Education:	College Graduate
Father's Occupation:	Sheet Metal Engineer

Adult Assessment Scales Data: 11 to 16 Months

Subject Number: 56   Group: Pediatric Firstborn

Interactions Initiated by the Child

Child's Behavior

Frequency of overtures per 30 minutes (median): 2
Purposes of overtures (frequency):

To please	0	To annoy	0
To gain approval	0	To direct	0
To procure a service	0	To compete	0
To gain attention	1	To ease discomfort	0
To maintain social contact	0		

Adult's Response (percent frequency)

1. Timing and direction
   of adult's response:
   a. Immediately   100.0
   b. Delayed   0.0
      Length of delay (seconds)   0.0
   c. No response   0.0
   d. Rejects   0.0

2. Perceptions of child's need:
   a. Accurately   100.0
   b. Partially   0.0
   c. Not at all   0.0

3. Level of difficulty of words:
   a. Appropriate   30.0
   b. Too complex   0.0
   c. Too simple   0.0
   d. Babytalk   0.0
   e. None   0.0

4. Provision of related ideas:
   a. Yes   40.0
   b. No   60.0

5. Complexity of language:
   a. Complex sentence, 3s   0.0
   b. Phrase/sentence, 3s   80.0
   c. One word   20.0
   d. None   0.0

6. Provision of encouragement,
   reinforcement of enthusiasm:
   a. Yes   80.0
   b. No   0.0
   c. Inappropriate   20.0

7. Teaching realistic limits:
   a. Yes   0.0
   b. No   0.0
   c. Inappropriate   70.0

8. Satisfaction of child's needs:
   a. Yes   100.0
   b. No   0.0
   c. Partial   0.0

Average duration of adult's response (seconds): 15.3.
Time spent by adult responding (percent): 1.7.

Adult Assessment Scales Data: 11 to 16 Months

Subject Number: 56   Group: Pediatric Firstborn

Interactions Initiated by the Adult

Frequency per 30 minutes (median):   15

Purposes of adult (percent duration):
    Stimulate child   30.3
    Contol positive   0.8
    Control negative   1.4
    Routine caretaking   10.6

Emotional tone (percent frequency):
    Positive   97.7
    Negative   1.0
    Neutral   1.3

Average duration of adult-initiated interactions (seconds): 51.7.
Time spent by adult in adult-initiated interactions (percent): 43.1.
Total time spent by the adult in interactions with the child (percent): 44.8.

Task Data (Percent of Total Time): 11 to 16 Months

Subject Number: 56   Group: Pediatric Control Group Firstborn

Social tasks:
All social tasks	11.4
To cooperate	6.1
To procure a service	0.4
To gain attention	1.7
To maintain social contact	2.8
To assert self	0.0

Nonsocial tasks:
To eat	2.7
To gain information (visual)	8.8
To gain information (visual and auditory)	7.8
Live language	6.0
Overheard language	0.0
Mechanical language	1.6
Nontask	20.4
To pass time	0.0
To procure an object	5.3
To gain pleasure	0.0
To ease discomfort	0.0
To explore	10.4
Mastery	12.7
Gross motor	9.6
Fine motor	5.0

Test Data

Subject Number: 56   Group: Pediatric Control Group Firstborn

Test	Age (months)	Score	Group Median
Bayley Scales	4½	100	104
of Infant Development	12	81	102
Mental Index	24	85	109
Stanford-Binet	36	88	111.5
Preschool Project	12	14	16
Receptive Language Test	14½	18	18
(score in months)	24	18	30
	36	33	46.5
Preschool Project	12	1	2
Abstract Abilities Test	14½	3	3
(score in levels)	24	5	7
Preschool Project	12	2	2
Dissonance Test	14½	3.5	4
(score in levels)	24	7	7

Group PC₁

Subject Number:	57
SES:	III
Sex:	Male
Mother's Education:	High School
Mother's Quick Word Test:	88
Father's Education:	High School, plus
Father's Occupation:	Salesman

Adult Assessment Scales Data: 11 to 16 Months

Subject Number: 57   Group: Pediatric Firstborn

Interactions Initiated by the Child

Child's Behavior

Frequency of overtures per 30 minutes (median): 8
Purposes of overtures (frequency):

To please	0	To annoy	0
To gain approval	0	To direct	0
To procure a service	2	To compete	0
To gain attention	0	To ease discomfort	0.5
To maintain social contact	2.5		

Adult's Response (percent frequency)

1. Timing and direction
   of adult's response:
   a. Immediately   87.1
   b. Delayed   6.5
      Length of delay (seconds)   79.2
   c. No response   6.5
   d. Rejects   0.0

2. Perceptions of child's need:
   a. Accurately   100.0
   b. Partially   0.0
   c. Not at all   0.0

3. Level of difficulty of words:
   a. Appropriate   51.7
   b. Too complex   0.0
   c. Too simple   34.5
   d. Babytalk   0.0
   e. None   13.8

4. Provision of related ideas:
   a. Yes   31.0
   b. No   69.0

5. Complexity of language:
   a. Complex sentence, 3s   34.5
   b. Phrase/sentence, 3s   48.3
   c. One word   3.4
   d. None   13.8

6. Provision of encouragement,
   reinforcement of enthusiasm:
   a. Yes   69.0
   b. No   0.0
   c. Inappropriate   31.0

7. Teaching realistic limits:
   a. Yes   13.8
   b. No   10.3
   c. Inappropriate   75.9

8. Satisfaction of child's needs:
   a. Yes   57.1
   b. No   7.1
   c. Partial   35.7

Average duration of adult's response (seconds): 42.7.
Time spent by adult responding (percent): 19.0.

Adult Assessment Scales Data: 11 to 16 Months

Subject Number: 57   Group: Pediatric Firstborn

Interactions Initiated by the Adult

Frequency per 30 minutes (median):   10

Purposes of adult (percent duration):
  Stimulate child   10.2
  Contol positive   3.7
  Control negative   1.0
  Routine caretaking   3.2

Emotional tone (percent frequency):
  Positive   78.6
  Negative   3.8
  Neutral   17.6

Average duration of adult-initiated interactions (seconds): 32.8.
Time spent by adult in adult-initiated interactions (percent): 18.2.
Total time spent by the adult in interactions with the child (percent): 37.2.

Task Data (Percent of Total Time): 11 to 16 Months

Subject Number: 57   Group: Pediatric Control Group Firstborn

Social tasks:
All social tasks	17.3
To cooperate	0.4
To procure a service	0.0
To gain attention	0.3
To maintain social contact	12.2
To assert self	0.0

Nonsocial tasks:
To eat	13.3
To gain information (visual)	16.4
To gain information (visual and auditory)	8.6
Live language	1.8
Overheard language	0.0
Mechanical language	4.3
Nontask	4.7
To pass time	3.0
To procure an object	0.0
To gain pleasure	0.0
To ease discomfort	6.2
To explore	10.9
Mastery	9.7
Gross motor	1.4
Fine motor	8.4

Test Data

Subject Number: 57   Group: Pediatric Control Group Firstborn

Test	Age (months)	Score	Group Median
Bayley Scales	4½	128	104
of Infant Development	12	102	102
Mental Index	24	106	109
Stanford-Binet	36	117	111.5
Preschool Project	12	16	16
Receptive Language Test	14½	18	18
(score in months)	24	27	30
	36	48	46.5
Preschool Project	12	4	2
Abstract Abilities Test	14½	4	3
(score in levels)	24	7	7
Preschool Project	12	3.5	2
Dissonance Test	14½	4	4
(score in levels)	24	7	7

Group PC₁

Subject Number:	58
SES:	III
Sex:	Female
Mother's Education:	High School
Mother's Quick Word Test:	86
Father's Education:	High School
Father's Occupation:	Post Office Clerk

Adult Assessment Scales Data: 11 to 16 Months

Subject Number: 58   Group: Pediatric Firstborn

Interactions Initiated by the Child

Child's Behavior

Frequency of overtures per 30 minutes (median): 10
Purposes of overtures (frequency):

To please	0	To annoy	0
To gain approval	0	To direct	0
To procure a service	3	To compete	0
To gain attention	5	To ease discomfort	0
To maintain social contact	1		

Adult's Response (percent frequency)

1. Timing and direction
   of adult's response:
   a. Immediately   94.9
   b. Delayed   2.6
      Length of delay (seconds) 50.4
   c. No response   2.6
   d. Rejects   0.0

2. Perceptions of child's need:
   a. Accurately   92.1
   b. Partially   5.3
   c. Not at all   2.6

3. Level of difficulty of words:
   a. Appropriate   13.2
   b. Too complex   0.0
   c. Too simple   60.5
   d. Babytalk   5.3
   e. None   21.1

4. Provision of related ideas:
   a. Yes   0.0
   b. No   100.0

5. Complexity of language:
   a. Complex sentence, 3s   0.0
   b. Phrase/sentence, 3s   73.7
   c. One word   5.3
   d. None   21.1

6. Provision of encouragement,
   reinforcement of enthusiasm:
   a. Yes   91.9
   b. No   5.4
   c. Inappropriate   2.7

7. Teaching realistic limits:
   a. Yes   10.8
   b. No   0.0
   c. Inappropriate   89.2

8. Satisfaction of child's needs:
   a. Yes   97.3
   b. No   0.0
   c. Partial   2.7

Average duration of adult's response (seconds): 24.7.
Time spent by adult responding (percent): 13.7.

Adult Assessment Scales Data: 11 to 16 Months

Subject Number: 58   Group: Pediatric Firstborn

Interactions Initiated by the Adult

Frequency per 30 minutes (median):   9

Purposes of adult (percent duration):
  Stimulate child   2.8
  Contol positive   3.5
  Control negative   0.4
  Routine caretaking   0.1

Emotional tone (percent frequency):
  Positive   91.9
  Negative   4.0
  Neutral   4.0

Average duration of adult-initiated interactions (seconds): 13.8.
Time spent by adult in adult-initiated interactions (percent): 6.9.
Total time spent by the adult in interactions with the child (percent): 20.6.

Task Data (Percent of Total Time): 11 to 16 Months

Subject Number: 58   Group: Pediatric Control Group Firstborn

Social tasks:

All social tasks	20.4
To cooperate	1.7
To procure a service	1.5
To gain attention	2.9
To maintain social contact	10.6
To assert self	0.0

Nonsocial tasks:

To eat	2.0
To gain information (visual)	24.1
To gain information (visual and auditory)	1.9
Live language	1.9
Overheard language	0.0
Mechanical language	0.0
Nontask	27.2
To pass time	0.0
To procure an object	1.9
To gain pleasure	0.3
To ease discomfort	1.7
To explore	5.4
Mastery	7.4
Gross motor	4.2
Fine motor	3.8

Test Data

Subject Number: 58   Group: Pediatric Control Group Firstborn

Test	Age (months)	Score	Group Median
Bayley Scales	4½	89	104
of Infant Development	12	91	102
Mental Index	24	104	109
Stanford-Binet	36	a	111.5
Preschool Project	12	12	16
Receptive Language Test	14½	b	18
(score in months)	24	24	30
	36	a	46.5
Preschool Project	12	1	2
Abstract Abilities Test	14½	3	3
(score in levels)	24	6	7
Preschool Project	12	4	2
Dissonance Test	14½	6	4
(score in levels)	24	6	7

[a]Not tested.
[b]No valid score.

Group PC$_1$

Subject Number:	59
SES:	II
Sex:	Male
Mother's Education:	High School, plus
Mother's Quick Word Test:	85
Father's Education:	Graduate Training
Father's Occupation:	Teacher

Adult Assessment Scales Data: 11 to 16 Months

Subject Number: 59   Group: Pediatric Firstborn

Interactions Initiated by the Child

Child's Behavior

Frequency of overtures per 30 minutes (median): 7.5
Purposes of overtures (frequency):

To please	0	To annoy	0
To gain approval	0	To direct	0
To procure a service	3	To compete	0
To gain attention	1.5	To ease discomfort	0.5
To maintain social contact	1		

Adult's Response (percent frequency)

1. Timing and direction
   of adult's response:
   a. Immediately   90.0
   b. Delayed   6.7
      Length of delay (seconds) 36.0
   c. No response   3.3
   d. Rejects   0.0

2. Perceptions of child's need:
   a. Accurately   96.6
   b. Partially   3.4
   c. Not at all   0.0

3. Level of difficulty of words:
   a. Appropriate   58.6
   b. Too complex   0.0
   c. Too simple   34.5
   d. Babytalk   0.0
   e. None   6.9

4. Provision of related ideas:
   a. Yes   17.2
   b. No   82.8

5. Complexity of language:
   a. Complex sentence, 3s   10.3
   b. Phrase/sentence, 3s   82.8
   c. One word   0.0
   d. None   6.9

6. Provision of encouragement,
   reinforcement of enthusiasm:
   a. Yes   60.7
   b. No   10.7
   c. Inappropriate   28.6

7. Teaching realistic limits:
   a. Yes   24.1
   b. No   0.0
   c. Inappropriate   75.9

8. Satisfaction of child's needs:
   a. Yes   89.7
   b. No   0.0
   c. Partial   10.3

Average duration of adult's response (seconds): 34.8.
Time spent by adult responding (percent): 14.5.

Adult Assessment Scales Data: 11 to 16 Months

Subject Number: 59   Group: Pediatric Firstborn

Interactions Initiated by the Adult

Frequency per 30 minutes (median):   8.5

Purposes of adult (percent duration):
    Stimulate child   14.2
    Contol positive   2.1
    Control negative   0.2
    Routine caretaking   4.1

Emotional tone (percent frequency):
    Positive   98.3
    Negative   1.0
    Neutral   0.7

Average duration of adult-initiated interactions (seconds): 43.6.
Time spent by adult in adult-initiated interactions (percent): 20.6.
Total time spent by the adult in interactions with the child (percent): 35.1.

Task Data (Percent of Total Time): 11 to 16 Months

Subject Number: 59   Group: Pediatric Control Group Firstborn

Social tasks:
All social tasks	a
To cooperate	0.9
To procure a service	0.0
To gain attention	3.3
To maintain social contact	11.4
To assert self	0.2

Nonsocial tasks:
To eat	10.3
To gain information (visual)	11.5
To gain information (visual and auditory)	3.2
Live language	3.2
Overheard language	0.0
Mechanical language	0.0
Nontask	13.8
To pass time	2.2
To procure an object	1.1
To gain pleasure	0.0
To ease discomfort	0.3
To explore	14.8
Mastery	8.5
Gross motor	3.7
Fine motor	2.5

a Data not available.

Test Data

Subject Number: 59   Group: Pediatric Control Group Firstborn

Test	Age (months)	Score	Group Median
Bayley Scales	4½	104	104
of Infant Development	12	100	102
Mental Index	24	116	109
Stanford-Binet	36	118	111.5
Preschool Project	12	14	16
Receptive Language Test	14½	18	18
(score in months)	24	24	30
	36	39	46.5
Preschool Project	12	2	2
Abstract Abilities Test	14½	2	3
(score in levels)	24	7	7
Preschool Project	12	1	2
Dissonance Test	14½	4	4
(score in levels)	24	7	7

References

Anderson, S., and Messick, S. Social competence in young children. *Dev. Psych.* 10 (1974):282-293.

Barker, R.C. *The Stream of Behavior.* New York: Appleton-Century-Crofts, 1963.

Bayley, N. Mental growth in young children. *Yearb. Nat. Soc. Stud. Educ.* 39 (1940):11-47 [21-22, 314].

Bernstein, B. Language and social class. *Brit. J. Sociol.* 11 (1960):271-276.

Bloom, B. *Stability and Change in Human Characteristics.* New York: Wiley, 1965.

Bowlby, J. Maternal care and mental health. Monograph 2. Geneva: World Health Organization, 1951.

Brazelton, T.B. *Infants and Mothers.* New York: Dell, 1969.

Bronfenbrenner, U. Is Early Intervention Effective? Vol. II, DHEW Publication No. (OHD)74-25, 1974.

Brown, R.E., and Halpern, F. The variable pattern of rural black children. *Clin. Pediatrics* 10 (1971).

Caldwell, B. A new "approach" to behavioral ecology. In J.P. Hill (ed.), *Minnesota Symposia on Child Psychology* 2, Univ. of Minnesota Press, 1968, pp. 74-109.

Caldwell, B.M., Wright, C., Honig, A., and Tannenbaum, J. Infant day care and attachment. *Amer. J. of Orthopsychiat.* 40 (1970):397-412.

Church, J. *Three Babies.* New York: Random House, 1966.

Clarke-Stewart, A.K. Interaction between mothers and their young children: Characteristics and consequences. *Monographs of the Society for Research in Child Development* 38, Serial No. 153, Nos. 6-7. Chicago, Ill.: Univ. of Chicago Press, 1973.

Dodson, F. *How to Parent.* New York: Signet, 1971.

Fox, N. Attachment of Kibbutz infants to mother and metapelet. *Child Development* 48 (1977):1228-1239.

Gordon, I., and Lally, J.R. *Intellectual Stimulation for Infants and Toddlers.* Institute for the Development of Human Resources, University of Florida, 1967.

Heber, R., Garber, H., Harrington, S., Hoffman, C., and Falender, C. Rehabilitation of families at risk for mental retardation. Progress Report, Rehabilitation Center and Training Center in Mental Retardation, University of Wisconsin, Madison, Wisconsin, 1972.

Hess, R.D., and Shipman, V. Early blocks to children's learning. *Children* 12 (1965):189-194.

Hess, R.D., and Shipman, V. Early experience and the socialization of cognitive modes in children. *Child Development* 36 (1965):869-886.

Honzig, M.P., Macfarlane, J.W., and Allen, L. The stability of mental test performance between two and 18 years. *J. Exp. Educ.* 4 (1948):309-324 [21-24, 31].

Jacobs, B.A., and Moss, H.A. Birth order and sex of sibling as determinants of mother-infant interaction. *Child Development* 47 (1976):315-322.

Kilbride, H.W., Johnson, D.L., and Streissguth, A.P. Social class, birth order and new born. *Child Development* 48 (1977):1686-1688.

Leiderman, P.H., Leifer, A., Seashore, M., Barnett, C., and Grobstein, R. Mother-infant interaction: Effects of early deprivation, prior experience and sex of infant. *Early Development* 51 (1973):154-175.

Lewin, K. *Field Theory in Social Science.* New York: Harper and Row, 1951.

Madden, J., Levenstein, P., and Levenstein, S. Longitudinal IQ outcomes of the mother-child home program. *Child Development* 47 (1976):1015-1025.

McCarthy, D. Language development in children. In L. Carmichael (ed.), *Manual of Child Psychology*, 2d ed. New York: Wiley, 1960.

Meyerhoff, M.K. Social competence from birth to three years of age: A critical review of the literature. Cambridge, Mass.: Harvard Univ. Special Qualifying paper, 1977.

Passamanick, B., Knobloch, H., and Lilienfeld, A.M. Socioeconomic status and some precursors of neuropsychiatric disorder. *Amer. J. Orthopsychiat.* 26 (1966):594-601 [335].

Piaget, J. *The Origins of Intelligence in Children*, 2d ed. New York: International University Press, 1952.

Schaefer, E. Infant Education Research Project, Washington, D.C. A report by the U.S. Department of Health, Education and Welfare, 1969.

Schaefer, E. Intellectual stimulation of culturally deprived infants. Excerpted from Mental Health Grant Proposal No. MH-09 224-01. Laboratory of Psychology, National Institute of Mental Health, 1968.

Schoggen, M., and Schoggen, P. Environmental forces in the home lives of three-year-old children in three population sub groups. *DARCEE Papers and Report* 5, No. 2, 1971.

Sears, R.R., Maccoby, E., and Levin, H. *Patterns of Child Rearing.* Evanston, Ill.: Row, Peterson, 1957.

Siegel, A.E. Editorial. *Child Development* 38 (1967):901-907.

Skeels, H.M. Adult status of children with contrasting early life experience. *Monographs of the Society for Research in Child Development* 31 Serial No. 105, No. 3. Chicago, Ill.: Univ. of Chicago Press, 1966.

Spock, B. *Baby and Child Care.* New York: Pocket Books, 1968 (paperback); New York: Meredith, 1968 (hardback).

Thomas, A., Chess, S., Birch, H.G., Hertzig, M.W., and Korn, S. *Behavioral Individuality.* New York: New York University Press, 1964.

United Nations Educational Scientific and Cultural Organization. Meeting on Preschool Education on the First Phase of Life-Long Education. Final Report. Paris, France, January 1976.

Uzgiris, I.C., and Hunt, J. McV. *Assessment in Infancy—Ordinal Scales of Psychological Development.* Chicago, Ill.: Univ. of Illinois Press, 1975.

Walker, D. *Socioemotional Measures for Preschool and Kindergarten Children.* San Francisco: Jossey-Bass, 1973.

Weikart, D.P. A comparative study of three preschool curricula. Paper presented at the biennial meeting of the Society for Research in Child Development, Santa Monica, California, March 1969.

Wenar, C. Executive competence in toddlers: A prospective observational study. *Genetic Psychology Monographs* 93 (1976):189-285.

White, B.L. Love is not enough. *The UNESCO Courier* (Paris, France), May 1978.

White, B.L. Reassessing our educational priorities. An edited transcript of an oral presentation to the Education Commission of the States Early Childhood Education Symposium, held in Boston, August 1974, and published in *COMPACT Magazine*, the bimonthly magazine of the Education Commission of the States, 1975.

White, B.L. *Human Infants: Experience and Psychological Development.* Englewood Cliffs, N.J.: Prentice-Hall, 1971.

White, B.L. An experimental approach to the effects of experience on early human behavior. In J.P. Hill (ed.), *Minnesota Symposium on Child Psychology* 1, Univ. of Minnesota Press, 1967, pp. 201-226.

White, B.L., Castle, P., and Held, R. Observations on the development of visually-directed reaching. *Child Development* 35 (1964):349-364.

White, B.L., Kaban, B., and Attanucci, J. Competence and experience. In Ina C. Uzgiris and F. Weizmann (eds.), *The Structuring of Experience.* New York: Plenum, 1977.

White, B.L., Kaban, B., Attanucci, J., and Shapiro, B. *Experience and Environment: Major Influences on the Development of the Young Child*, Vol. 2. Englewood Cliffs, N.J.: Prentice-Hall, 1978.

White, B.L., Kaban, B., Attanucci, J., Shapiro, B., and Comita, M. Childrearing Practices and the Development of Competence. The Harvard Preschool Project Final Report, Grant No. OCD-CB-193, U.S. Office of Child Development, December 1974.

White, B.L., Watts, J.C., Barnett, I., Kaban, B.T., Marmor, J.R., and Shapiro, B.B. *Experience and Environment: Major Influences on the Development of the Young Child*, Vol. 1. Englewood Cliffs, N.J.: Prentice-Hall, 1973.

Wright, H.F. Observational child study. In P. Mussen (ed.), *Handbook of Research and Child Development.* New York: McGraw-Hill, 1960.

Yarrow, L.J., Rubenstein, J.L., and Pedersen, F.A. *Infant and Environment: Early Cognitive and Motivational Development.* New York: Wiley, 1975.

Index

Index

About the Authors

Burton L. White founded and directed the Harvard Preschool Project for thirteen years. He is now director of the Center for Parent Education in Newton, Massachusetts, which was established to improve the quality of childrearing and family life. White received the B.A. in mechanical engineering from Tufts University, the B.S. in philosophy and the M.A. in psychology from Boston University, and the Ph.D. in psychology from Brandeis University. For twenty years he has taught and done research in early childhood development at Brandeis, Tufts, MIT, and Harvard. He has contributed many articles to scholarly journals and has written a number of textbooks as well as a popular book for parents, *The First Three Years of Life,* dealing with the role of experience in the development of abilities in young children.

Barbara T. Kaban was assistant director of the Harvard Preschool Project. She has written extensively on the family's role in early education, and, along with Jane S. Attanucci, collaborated with Dr. White on several of his books.

Jane S. Attanucci has been closely involved in the implementation and analysis of the Harvard Preschool Project and has taught in parent-education workshops.